How Psyche(
Can Help Save the World

"A stirring and timely call for humanity to co-creatively unite in altruistic service and give birth to a regenerative whole-systems planetary culture—a shared experience of reverence and respect for all our relations, human and nonhuman, seen and unseen. I predict this remarkable book will quickly become required reading in the hands of all entheogen-honoring servants of the Great Work—HIGHLY RECOMMENDED!"

OSCAR MIRO-QUESADA, AUTHOR, KAMASQUA CURANDERO, AND FOUNDER OF THE HEART OF THE HEALER

"The contributors write passionately on what each of us can do to restore the natural harmony so the full diversity of species can flourish. No easy answers but an amazing amount of wisdom, especially from Indigenous traditions who have incorporated psychedelic visions and insights into their cultural matrix for hundreds of years. Reading this book will leave you sobered, inspired, and determined to do what you can. Truth telling is often uncomfortable, but nothing moves us forward more forcefully."

JAMES FADIMAN, PH.D., AUTHOR OF
THE PSYCHEDELIC EXPLORER'S GUIDE

"The breadth of perspectives offered by each of the contributors helps balance the daunting and inescapable challenges of our planetary crisis."

SELMA HOLDEN, M.D., INTEGRATIVE PHYSICIAN
AT GOOD MEDICINE COLLECTIVE

"This book is an extraordinary overview of the promise psychedelics have for opening our hearts, seeing our self-imposed, culturally reinforced spiritual blindness, and waking us to the creative possibilities for our collective future."

ALEX GREY, AUTHOR OF SACRED MIRRORS

"Comprehensive perspectives on the current evolution of human consciousness, now increasingly catalyzed by the competent, respectful use of psychedelic substances. Not only do these visionary essays educate and enlighten the reader, but they also somehow dampen our cynicism and invite courage to affirm life with courage and hope."

WILLIAM A. RICHARDS, PH.D., AUTHOR OF SACRED KNOWLEDGE

"Ever since the 1960s, psychedelic enthusiasts have claimed that if you turn on the world, the world will change for the better. Now that plant medicines and magic molecules are hitting the global mainstream, this flowering is arguably closer than ever before. But we need more than high hopes to bring on the bloom. The voices in this stellar collection—young Turks, old heads, First Peoples, doctors of science and Spirit—fan the flames of possibility with the courage, vision, and canny wisdom demanded by the task."

ERIK DAVIS, AUTHOR OF *HIGH WEIRDNESS*

"Gray has once again assembled a truly inspired group of top thinkers in the psychedelic renaissance to contribute to this timely and important work. As psychedelics become more mainstream and corporate interests, venture capitalists, and ignorant 'influencers' attempt to sink their fangs into a culture they know nothing about, books like this one serve as an important counterweight to amplify the voices of those who truly love, respect, and understand the dynamics of plant and fungal medicines."

THOMAS HATSIS, AUTHOR OF *LSD—THE WONDER CHILD*

"Often—but not solely—informed by their skillful use of psychedelic sacraments, these twenty-five brilliant contributors show how we can awaken our hearts and minds and work toward creating a world we and our descendants can embrace and rejoice in."

DAVID BRONNER, CEO OF DR. BRONNER'S MAGIC SOAPS
AND PSYCHEDELIC PHILANTHROPIST

"This book is a call to action. Gray has put together a much-needed collection of hopeful essays, images, poetry, and prayers to inspire us to forge through our suffering into an awakening of the conscious and unconscious collective."

DOMINIQUE MORISANO, PH.D., C.PSYCH.,
ADJUNCT PROFESSOR AT THE UNIVERSITY OF TORONTO

"An authentic, heartfelt, and spiritually inspired work! Stephen Gray has put together an eloquent collection of writings by those who are deeply connected to the spirit of nature in all her glory. Each contributor shares marvelous insights into what it means to be human in our age of potential accelerated psycho-spiritual evolution. Will we meet the challenge? This book is one more step on that path. The time is now. Tune in, energize, evolve, and engage."

KEITH LOWENSTEIN, M.D., AUTHOR OF
KRIYA YOGA FOR SELF-DISCOVERY

How Psychedelics Can Help Save the World

Visionary and Indigenous Voices Speak Out

Edited by Stephen Gray

Park Street Press

Rochester, Vermont

Park Street Press
One Park Street
Rochester, Vermont 05767
www.ParkStPress.com

Text stock is SFI certified

Park Street Press is a division of Inner Traditions International

Note to the Reader: *This book is intended as an informational guide and should
not be a substitute for professional medical care or treatment. Neither the author nor
the publisher assumes any responsibility for physical, psychological, legal, or social
consequences resulting from the ingestion of psychedelic substances or their derivatives.*

Cataloging-in-Publication Data for this title is available from the Library of Congress

ISBN 978-1-64411-490-2 (print)
ISBN 978-1-64411-491-9 (ebook)

Printed and bound in the United States by Lake Book Manufacturing, Inc.
The text stock is SFI certified. The Sustainable Forestry Initiative® program
promotes sustainable forest management.

10 9 8 7 6 5 4 3 2 1

Text design and layout by Virginia Scott Bowman
This book was typeset in Garamond Premier Pro and Legacy Sans with Gandi Serif
and Frutiger used as display typefaces

To send correspondence to the editor of this book, mail a first-class letter to the
editor c/o Inner Traditions • Bear & Company, One Park Street, Rochester, VT
05767, and we will forward the communication, or contact the editor directly at
www.stephengrayvision.com.

Stephen Gray will donate 10 percent of the royalties from this book to
Indigenous and environmental causes and initiatives.

Contents

Foreword

Julie Holland, M.D.

What the world needs now, is love, sweet love; it's the only thing that there's just too little of.

BURT BACHARACH AND HAL DAVID,
"WHAT THE WORLD NEEDS NOW IS LOVE"

I'M JUST COMING OUT OF a five-hundred-day practice of making music with my husband, Jeremy, and our kids. Gathering the family to rehearse and record was occasionally easy and fun; at other times it seemed like a job I didn't feel like showing up for anymore. We reminded ourselves and each other that we had agreed to this daily ritual, and so we sacrificed ourselves onto that altar again and again. There were some sunny days when we were lucky enough to play music with friends, which is a high unto itself, I can assure you. I'm sorry to say, we never choose to play this schmaltzy song, "What the World Needs Now Is Love," about love—its dearth and necessity—but I'd like you to imagine hearing it right now all the same, perhaps even in harmony.

This song, and dare I say this book, are really about the same thing. The vision for a world in crisis is this: that we all learn to embrace love; that we insist on loving one another and treating each other with the compassion we would want for ourselves and our loved ones.

❧

So how do we learn this compassion? And how do we open our hearts?

We can sit in stillness, focus on our breath, and appreciate that even this is a struggle. If we can experience the challenge of simply trying to pay attention, surely we can develop sympathy for others and their hardships. And if we can learn to feel tenderness toward others who are struggling, then perhaps over time we can turn that tenderheartedness back toward ourselves.

The perennial lesson that psychedelics teach us, that spirituality teaches us, that even immersion in nature can teach us, is that separation is an illusion. We are all in this together. It is easier to see this when we travel into the solar system and send back an image of the whole Earth. And it is easier to experience for ourselves when we travel outside our normal waking consciousness. It is in these altered states that we can truly appreciate the interconnectedness of all things, and the ineffability of our everyday experiences. To have a mystical experience is to bathe in the waters of unity and connection. In a mystical state, the obvious answers are all around us—love, oneness, and the universal latticework of light and energy that connects us all.

The scientific device to objectively measure altered states of consciousness has a dimension of scoring called "oceanic boundlessness." The idea here is to try to quantify where you draw the line, where you end and the rest of the universe begins. We know that many psychedelics, including cannabis, can help us to access this sensation of boundarylessness.

The renowned Hungarian Canadian physician Gabor Maté says that we either experience love, or we experience what's in the way of it. Psychedelics allow us to experience love, that most renewable of resources. When I feel its full force, I am overpowered and break down in tears. That this happens again and again, throughout my decades here on Earth, is a miracle.

In my book *Good Chemistry* I explained the neural and pharmacological underpinnings of the premise that the opposite of love is fear. Our brains toggle back and forth between these open and shut states.

Closed down by our sympathetic nervous system, the "fight-or-flight" response, we are stressed-out, paranoid, and narrow-minded. If we spend more time in the parasympathetic mode, where we can rest, digest, and repair our bodies and our relationships, we can be more open to connection, to being cared for and loved. In truth, oneness should be our default position. We are wired for connection, and our survival depends on our ability to cooperate just as much as it depends on our ability to attack or escape.

We learn to be comfortable in an open or a closed position, depending on our life lessons and traumas. Some of us along the way hardened as we grew up. Every wound leaves a scar; every scar tells a story; every story yields a belief. Within that belief lies a limitation. As soon as we're sure of one thing, we've shut ourself off from a thousand other explanations. Stuck in our ways, in our beliefs, in our limitations, we grow inflexible; our circle narrows and closes down. We are not open to new people, new experiences, or new perspectives.

When we're caught in our ruts, in our rigid beliefs, in our small social circles, we are closed off to other ways of being in the world. In the psychiatric world, we see addictions, obsessions, compulsions, and delusions all coming down to this issue of cognitive rigidity. Given their ability to loosen cognitive strictures, this is where psychedelics can really shine. These transformative medicines can help us to break out of our destructive patterns and out of our fear-based behaviors.

By experiencing oneness, interdependence, and connection firsthand we know there is another way of being. We abandon "rock logic" for "water logic" as we move from rigidity to fluidity. Things are often in process, and not yet fully formed. By staying fluid we remain resilient, responsive, and adaptable.

And this is where neuroplasticity comes in. The brain has an innate ability to reorganize its connections, whether in response to stress, injury, or learning. In a sense, the brain can rewire itself. Certain states optimize this: awe, pregnancy, falling in love, and many psychedelic states. This is why psychedelics are under consideration to treat traumatic brain injury and stroke.

Let me overstate this: Plasticity in the brain and in behavior is the key to our salvation. Learning to grow and change, to adapt, is what allows us to pass on our genes.

A newly proposed name for medicines that induce neuroplasticity is *plasticogens*. I have no idea whether this term will catch on, but I do know that psychological flexibility is an important concept. Studies of racial trauma conducted by therapist and author Monnica Williams (and others) found that psychedelics confer potential benefits in decreasing symptoms of racial trauma among BIPOC research volunteers, and that psychological flexibility may be an important mediator of these effects.*

What enables neuroplasticity? The hormone and neurotransmitter oxytocin, for one. What enables oxytocin to flow? We know that MDMA and LSD can enhance oxytocin levels, but so can hugging, kissing, extended eye contact, hand-holding, cuddling . . . also known as love. Being in this relaxed, cared-for state, the body can put down its defensive armor and get to the business of connection.

James Taylor sings that the purpose of living is to love and be loved, again and again. I'd like to remind you that connecting with ourselves, our loved ones, and the very planet we inhabit is what's needed for our salvation. My vision for our world in crisis is for us all to embrace awe, to volunteer ourselves into the world of wonder, to have the curiosity of a child with a "don't know" mind. Rather than being afraid or even just being certain, we must simply be *open*.

Let us all compare what we know about love, connection, and oneness with how we act in our day-to-day reality, when we deal with people we don't know, or with whom we disagree. Don't forget that we are all traumatized, and we all would benefit from some compassion. Altruism is a natural survival skill. Acts of service are anti-inflammatory.

Open your heart, open your mind, heal yourself, heal your community, heal the planet.

---

*BIPOC: black, indigenous, people of color. Other terms and words that may be unfamiliar to the reader have, like this one, been added to a glossary at the end of the book. —Ed.

DR. JULIE HOLLAND is a psychiatrist and psychopharmacologist, and the author of several popular books including *Weekends at Bellevue,* and, as editor, two nonprofit books: *Ecstasy: The Complete Guide* and *The Pot Book.* While now a medical advisor to the Multidisciplinary Association for Psychedelic Studies (MAPS), she was a medical monitor for several clinical studies examining the efficacy of using MDMA-assisted psychotherapy or cannabis in the treatment of PTSD. Her newest book is *Good Chemistry: The Science of Connection, From Soul to Psychedelics.*

Acknowledgments
and Expressions
of Gratitude

MY FIRST EXPRESSION OF GRATITUDE is for the twenty-five contributors to this book. I don't believe I'm being naïve in saying that every single one of them participated because they care deeply about the fate of the world and all its inhabitants. They grok who we really are and what we're capable of, underneath all the confusion and turmoil.

A special thank-you to Chris Bache, one of the book's contributors and the author of the remarkable *LSD and the Mind of the Universe: Diamonds from Heaven*. Chris has been unwavering kind and supportive in all of my dealings with him, going back to 2018 when we brought him to Vancouver to speak at the Spirit Plant Medicine Conference.

When I told Chris I was feeling the pull to put this book together but wasn't completely sure how, or perhaps even *if* I should proceed, he immediately said he would contribute to it. This was the trigger that set the wheels firmly in forward motion with no reverse gear, headed toward what you have in front of you. In the same way, the brilliant Kathleen Harrison's promise to contribute to *Cannabis and Spirituality* transformed that vision from a maybe to a definite commitment back in 2012.

I also want to make special mention of the important role of Zoe Helene in this project and the remarkable work she is doing through her Cosmic Sister initiative to bring more women into the forefront of psychedelic work. Zoe has contributed her own powerful chapter to this book and, through Cosmic Sister, has brought many of these marvelous female contributors into my world. They include The Dank Duchess, Minelli Eustàcio-Costa, Rachel Kann, Solana Booth, Laurel Sugden, and Martina Hoffmann, all of whom have received Cosmic Sister grants and awards.

Another big thank-you goes to my dear friend and colleague Sofia Reis. She has been incredibly supportive throughout the half dozen or so years of our friendship and collaborations. Sofia spent many hours guiding me painstakingly through every word of the translation from the Portuguese of the chapters by Grandmother Maria Alice Campos Freire and Ailton Krenak. Despite my protestations, she adamantly refused compensation for this hard labor of love, (forcing me to surreptitiously send occasional restaurant gift certificates and such).

This is the second book I have put together for Inner Traditions • Bear & Company. Everyone I've dealt with there has been great. In particular (since they're the ones I've mostly dealt directly with), I want to thank acquisitions editor Jon Graham for immediately understanding that this message is important, just as he did in 2015 with the previous book on cannabis as a spiritual ally; assistant to the editor in chief Patricia Rydle for patiently stewarding me through the various technical challenges of getting a manuscript like this—with so many varied parts—ready; and publicist Manzanita Carpenter Sanz who, once before with me and now again, steps up with diligence to make sure the message reaches the eyes and ears of all those who can benefit from it.

Finally, and as the old cliché goes, by no means "least," I am deeply grateful for the continuing love, support, and solid, sane presence (and occasionally, tolerance) of my kindhearted wife of more than thirty years, Diane.

Embracing an Essential Vision

Stephen Gray

THE POTENT ADJECTIVE *extraordinary* barely rises to the task of describing the unprecedented and almost overwhelming challenges facing humanity at this time. Visionaries—including contributors to this book—have sensed that hundreds of thousands of years of collective and individual history, struggle, and karma are coalescing right now. Cynics may dismiss this recognition as magical thinking—a "my-generation" delusion. Others may downplay the urgency of the moment. Still others turn away in denial and cling to chimeras and false, even dangerous, promises and premises. But the signs are clear for those willing to look and to listen.

Mystics, explorers of deep psychonautic realms, intuitives, the long-held prophecies of multiple Indigenous/traditional tribes and societies around the planet, and the clearly evident and observable developments of increasingly rapid climate change, madcap materialism, and gross economic and social inequality and imbalance all point to an inescapable truth: the longstanding dominant mindset of spiritual disconnect that has cast its shadow over the human enterprise has run its course and is no longer viable or sustainable. The flatland days of continuing as we have been are all but over.

Until very recently we've had wiggle room. This endlessly generous planet has been giving us everything that keeps us alive second by second, year after year, and generation upon generation. She has allowed the great majority of us to grievously misunderstand our true nature as interwoven, interdependent participants in a vast, living, creatively evolving web of energy and intelligence. She has allowed our species to plunder her bounty, taking far more than we give back, not grasping the core truth that, in the words of legendary Chief Seattle (1790–1866), "Whatever we do to the web, we do to ourselves. All things are bound together. All things connect."[1]

But now the jig is up. The naked apes have overrun the planet. The ominous facts of our predicament speak for themselves. The scientific consensus on runaway climate change is beyond debate. Piecemeal stabs at incremental change not founded in a deep transformation of understanding—however well-intentioned and innovative they may be—will not save us, much less bring back comforting old certainties and business as usual. As the great prophetic bard of song and poetry Leonard Cohen put it in his song "The Future": "The blizzard of the world has crossed the threshold and it's overturned the order of the soul."

But while all that may sound distressingly disheartening and bleak—even hopeless—it's far from the whole story. It's not even *the* story of the indescribable magnificence and brilliance of life altogether. And that's where this book comes in. Many are seeing and feeling a death and rebirth process underway that is drawing the whole species in. The great teachings, the great teachers, and all the rest of us who have at least briefly landed on "what is," recognize that there is an unconditioned, eternal reality. It's far beyond words, and even our proximate symbols can only hope to carry a modicum of meaning if they're sourced in experience. Then maybe we could call it Divine Light, Love, Holy Spirit, Creator, Eternal Source Consciousness, the Synchronous Field, the Noosphere (coined by famed philosopher Teilhard de Chardin), or any of a number of considered or even inspired attempts at symbolic reference. The intention and prayer of the participants in *How Psychedelics Can Help Save the World* is to share insights and visions to help us embrace the message and rise to what we are capable of as a custodial species of awakening and awakened beings.

The call now is for us humans to humbly and courageously face our situation without turning away; engage unequivocally with the inner and outer work that must be done to build a sane and sustainable future for the generations to come; and learn what it will take to collectively embrace and apply our best visions. *If* we can turn in that direction, we may be able to give birth to a "mature planetary civilization" as Duane Elgin has called it.

A grand chorus of voices is coming forward to call out from the depths of the heart that the time has come—right now. No matter how dark the horizon looks there is simply no other functional attitude to take. We have to believe in what Archbishop Desmond Tutu of South Africa called "the possibility of possibility." That is the true understanding of prayer by those who have seen it at work: the power of shared intention to manifest real change in the material world. And that understanding is central to the vision at hand, which several of the book's contributors explore.

Let's be clear from the outset that none of the contributors to this book are naïve, picturing or promising a golden age of peace and harmony around the next bend. All of us understand that we are moving into an extremely difficult period that may last decades or longer, and that the successful fruition of this period of Great Transition is far from certain.

But the participants in *How Psychedelics Can Help Save the World*, along with a great many other individuals past and present, do have some understanding of what this remarkable species is capable of. Ancient spiritual teachings remind us that underneath all the turmoil of the confused samsaric mind we are all awake by nature. And at this juncture, the old proverb "Necessity is the mother of invention" has never been more true or more applicable.

So then what is the nature of this *invention* we're being so urgently called and invited into? And what might a healed humanity look like? Questions like this are at the center of this book.

There's a feeling in the air that the time is ripe for this message to be heard. Another—now well-known—Leonard Cohen line, in his song "Anthem," hits the mark beautifully. "There is a crack, a crack in everything, that's how the light gets in." In a similar vein, a few years ago I had a close relationship with revered Native American elder and Native American Church roadman Kanucas Littlefish. Kanucas shared a vision with me that he and some of his associates had been receiving: that there will come a point when the crack has opened far enough and the existing system has lost sufficient viability to make room for a new vision.

As that potentially paradigm-shattering reality dawns on more people, the deep intuition is that the new story *will* be heard and it *will* be understood. Nineteenth-century French writer Victor Hugo famously declared that "Nothing is more powerful than an idea whose time has come." When the great, unimpeachable idea whose time has finally and truly arrived has taken hold and becomes more compelling than the increasingly less functional and sustainable worldview now dominating the conduct of human affairs, many of us envision widespread outbreaks of recognition, relief, and liberation, as if looking back on a painful relationship that we are now so gratefully free from.

The role of psychedelics (a.k.a. entheogens and sacred plant medicines) in the journey of individual and collective transformation requires some context here. They're not magic bullets, and they're susceptible to misappropriation and to misuse that can sometimes be damaging. Although the contributors to this book have a deep understanding of the capabilities of these sacramental medicines—and they *do* play an essential role in the book—they're not always the lead actors. The overarching mission is this urgent need for widespread awakening and redirection.

However, when the patient is in an advanced state of illness, strong medicines are often required. Abundant evidence has shown that when used in optimal circumstances in the right hands with skill and appropriate intention, and when the openings and insights are brought back into the daily walk as components of ongoing spiritual work and compassionate action, psychedelic medicines are the most potent tools at our disposal. Though most definitely not for everyone, the record shows that they can uncover and help heal suppressed wounds. They can help open the doors of perception to what Buddhist teachings call an unconditional reality, which wisdom carriers have described as more real than the versions of reality most of us experience every day.

So as an old saying goes, "Let us take heart." No matter how isolated and divided we may feel, we are all being pulled into the same story. A collective vibration is gradually awakening. The energetic imprint of each one of us has at least some impact on the field. What humans think, feel, and do matters more than ever. Great teachings throughout history remind us that we *can* awaken. Now it appears that a great number of us *have to* awaken. And that is a prayer and a vision worth holding and feeding.

There's so much more to say, but you have stumbled upon a treasure trove of inspiration here, so I'll leave that to the twenty-five brilliant and caring contributors you are about to encounter. For the moment, I'll end this introduction with some challenging and inspiring words from the remarkable writer and shaman Martín Prechtel. "We live in a kind of dark age, craftily lit with synthetic light, so that no one can tell how dark it has really gotten. But our exiled spirits can tell. Deep in our bones resides an ancient, singing couple who just won't give up making their beautiful, wild noise. The world won't end if we can find them."[2]

The Birth of
the Future Human

Christopher M. Bache, Ph.D.

CHRISTOPHER BACHE is professor emeritus in the Department of Philosophy and Religious Studies at Youngstown State University in Youngstown, Ohio; adjunct faculty at the California Institute of Integral Studies; emeritus fellow at the Institute of Noetic Sciences; and on the advisory council of Grof Legacy Training. He is also the author of four books, including his most recent, *LSD and the Mind of the Universe: Diamonds from Heaven*. His website is https://chrisbache.com.

◆ ◆ ◆

I AM NOT WRITING THIS ESSAY for you but for your children and your children's children for uncounted years. They are the ones who will bear the burden of what is coming, who will cry out to understand the events that have overtaken them, and who will have the power to change humanity forever if they act with courage and insight.

With every scientific report released on climate, it becomes clearer that we have driven our planet into a state of such overload that humanity is coming to the edge of an abyss. Given the escalating severity of the destabilization of our climate, the twenty-first century will see a cascading spiral of crises: melting ice caps, unstoppable coastal flooding, record-breaking hurricanes and severe weather events, possible interruption of the oceanic conveyor belt, devastating forest fires and longer fire seasons, severe droughts, collapsing water tables, empty reservoirs, life-claiming heat waves, accelerated soil erosion, collapsing agricultural production, and fished-out oceans. The list could be doubled or tripled. These crises will take place in the context of an expanding world population, shrinking nonrenewable resources, unchecked industrial pollution, extreme wealth disparity, massive refugee migrations, and state weapons of terrifying power. Many serious observers believe that the converging forces are so severe that humanity is facing either extinction or a shattering that will throw us into a new dark ages.

In the context of this grim forecast, I want to share a series of visions of humanity's future that I received inside a twenty-year psychedelic odyssey that I undertook between 1979 and 1999. When I was a young professor of religious studies and quite naïve about ecological matters, I did seventy-three carefully planned, therapeutically structured LSD sessions following a protocol developed by Stanislav Grof.[1] I worked at the 500–600 mcg. dose level. I mention the dose only to signal that the visions I'm reporting here came from extremely deep states of consciousness in which the limits of space and time were being transcended on a regular basis. Over the years I was repeatedly taken into "Deep Time," where I experienced the broad contours of humanity's evolutionary trajectory, not as an individual looking on from the outside but dissolved into the species-mind itself. The complete story of this journey is told in *LSD and the Mind of the Universe*. I know it sounds arrogant to speak like this and I apologize, but I have no choice if I am to describe the visions that repeatedly came through my sessions during these years.

Ego death destroys the existential isolation and constant self-referencing that organizes our ordinary experience of the world. When the partitions of our personal consciousness are surrendered, our experience spontaneously opens to the larger rhythms of life that we are part of. One portion of these rhythms is the collective psyche of our species. At the subtle level of consciousness we can dissolve into the human species-mind so deeply that the beginnings and endings of our personal lives become insignificant. When the "small self" opens to the "species self" this completely, it is only natural that insights into humanity's larger developmental trajectory sometimes emerge in our awareness. We would be surprised if this did *not* happen. When we open still further we can dissolve into the Creative Intelligence of the universe itself, experiencing all evolution as the self-emergence of its creative genius.

Sharing one's visionary experiences is a tricky business. However meaningful my psychedelic experiences are to me, they are naturally less meaningful to others. I hope my experiences will speak to you, but whether they do or not will largely depend on two things: whether you trust the potential of psychedelic states to yield true insights into our universe, and whether my experiences are mirrored in the experience of other psychedelic explorers. In these matters it is always the collective witness of the community that matters most. I offer the following experiences in this spirit and with an open hand.

THE VISIONS OF AWAKENING

While the threat of a global crisis has grown steadily worse decade by decade, the vision of our future that has repeatedly come through my sessions is that humanity is rapidly approaching a breakthrough of evolutionary proportions. Despite the fact that we have repeatedly failed to heed the ecological warnings, and rein in our rapacious greed and Earth-damaging policies, the message I've received has been one of promise and hope—more than hope, a message of emerging greatness.

Between 1991 and 1994, I received six visionary initiations into what appeared to be an evolutionary pivot that humanity is entering. These were not things I "saw" but historical processes I entered experientially. In earlier sessions I had been shown that reincarnation is a natural fact of life. It is the higher octave of evolution, the driver of humanity's perpetual growth as we pulse back and forth across the membrane of space-time.

The six visions I experienced then built on this to show me where reincarnation is taking humanity. Boiled down to their essential components, here are the key insights conveyed in these visions.*

1. *Divine Love:* Creation is an act of Cosmic Love, and the suffering we experience in life takes place *inside* this love. Because we have each voluntarily chosen to participate in this difficult cosmic process, our suffering is noble beyond words. No matter how intense the pain becomes in future years, we are not being punished or abandoned. Rather, we are cooperating with a transformational fire that is re-creating humanity.

2. *All Humanity:* It is difficult to describe the enormity of what is being birthed in history. The Creative Intelligence of our universe is working to awaken not just some individuals, but all of humanity. What is emerging is a consciousness of unprecedented proportions—the entire human family integrated in a unified field of awareness: the species reconnected with its Fundamental Nature and our thoughts tuned to Source Consciousness.

3. *Guiding Intelligence:* After millions of years of struggle and ascent, we are poised on the brink of a sunrise that will forever change the conditions of life on this planet. Though we do not know the deep future at a personal level, there is a more encompassing level of consciousness that can see it clearly. There is an intelligence in nature and in our species that is preparing us for this transition and working to bring it about.

4. *Our Species as a Single Being:* The evolution of our species is the systematic growth of a single organism. Nothing in our theological or philosophical systems does justice to the grandeur of this being, to the subtlety and brilliance of the interplay of its many parts and the whole. This unified being is moving decisively to become more aware of itself; it is waking itself up from within.

---

*The complete versions are presented in *LSD and the Mind of the Universe,* chapter 9, and *Dark Night, Early Dawn,* chapter 8.

5. *Collective Purification:* To awaken to this higher self-awareness, we must let go of everything that has kept us small. I saw that the generations born in our period of history were being deliberately configured to precipitate an intense cycle of collective purification. This century is a watershed into which the karmic streams of history are flowing. The poisons of humanity's past are being systematically brought to the surface in us. By transforming these poisons in our individual lives, we are making it possible for divine awareness to enter more deeply into future generations. As this purifying process comes to fruition, the future condition of our species will be beyond anything we might project from our current state of fragmentation.

6. *The Future Human:* At one point, I was carried deep into the future and allowed to experience the abiding state of humanity at that time. What magnificent beings we humans had turned into. Just touching the Future Human filled me with rapture, calm, and awe. It felt clear, warm, and whole. There was an abiding sense of being truly One beneath the diversity of life. It had such expansiveness; such breadth of being! It was fully embodied spiritual realization, the tantric awakening of our entire species—Spirit and Matter in perfect balance.

THE DEATH AND REBIRTH OF HUMANITY

As inspiring and clarifying as these visions were, nowhere in them was I shown *how* this collective transformation would actually take place. What would it take for humanity to make this evolutionary jump? This critical piece of the puzzle was missing. Then, in December of 1995, a particularly powerful session dissolved me into the species-mind and, in this form, took me into the heart of humanity's coming death and rebirth. It was as though all the expansions and purifications I had undergone in my previous sessions had been exercises preparing me for this seminal visionary download. This session was so intense it took me more than a year to recover from it.

The collective convulsions I describe below appeared to be driven by a global ecological crisis, but I was not given any details about how or when this crisis would take place. Instead, this session showed me the *fact* of a global crisis; it took me inside the *collective psyche's experience* of this crisis; and it showed me some of the *mechanisms of collective awakening* that will be activated by this crisis. Following is the "core scenario" revealed to me in Session 55.

In a field of relative calm, a small anxiety began to grow. Slowly, people were looking up and becoming alarmed. Like people living on an island who gradually become aware that a hurricane is overtaking them, humanity was gradually waking up in alarm to events that had overtaken them. Conditions got worse and worse. People became more and more frightened as the danger increased, forcing them to let go of their assumptions at deeper levels. There was less and less for people to hold on to, fewer givens that they could assume—how they would live, where they would live, what they would do for a living, how society was organized, what could be possessed. The world as they knew it was falling apart.

Decades were compressed into minutes, and I felt the people's fear deepen as they lost more and more of what they considered the normal and necessary structures of their world. The events that had overtaken Earth were of such scope that no one could insulate themselves from them. The level of alarm grew in the species field until eventually everyone was forced into the melting pot of mere survival. We were all in this together. Families were torn apart— parents from their children and children from each other. Life as we had known it was shattered at the core. We were reduced to simply trying to survive.

For a time it looked as though we would all be killed, but just when the storm was at its peak, the worst of it passed and the danger slowly subsided. Though many had died, many were still alive. As the survivors began to find each other, new social units began to form. Parents and children from different families joined to form new types of families. Everywhere new social institutions sprang into being that reflected our new reality—new ways of thinking, new values that we had discovered within ourselves during the crisis. Every aspect of our lives was marked by new priorities, new perceptions of the good, new truths. These new social forms reflected new states of awareness that seemed to spread through the survivors like a positive contagion. These new social forms then fed back into the system to elicit still newer states of awareness in people, and the cycle of creativity between the individual and the group spiraled.

The whole system was becoming alive at new levels, and this aliveness was expressing itself in previously impossible ways. It was as if the eco-crisis had triggered the myelination of nerve cells in our species-brain, allowing new and deeper levels of self-awareness to spring into being. Repeatedly, there was the message: "These things will happen faster than anyone can anticipate because of the hyperarousal of the species-mind." Thousands of fractal images drove this lesson home again and again. Faster than anyone can anticipate. *The pace of the past was irrelevant to the pace of the future . . .*

History is intensifying. Feedback loops are accelerating. Time is becoming concentrated. Developments are unfolding exponentially. The past is rapidly catching up with us; debts put off for generations are coming due; a new beginning approaches. The ecological crisis will precipitate a death-rebirth confrontation that will shatter our psychospiritual isolation, both individually and societally, and bring forward an awakening of common ground within us.

I saw that once we made this painful transition, we would discover that all was gain. Nothing essential had been lost. We will look with amazement at the depth of ignorance that had set us on this course of self-decimation, and we will not long for that past at all. All is gain, all is gain.[2]

This session showed me that humanity's transformation will come about through terrible suffering. This suffering will be driven by a global systems crisis triggered by a series of ecological crises. Our species will change when our collective pain simply becomes unbearable. In this, Session 55 echoes the conclusion reached by Duane Elgin in *Awakening Earth* where he wrote: "It is the immense suffering of millions—even billions—of precious human beings coupled with the widespread destruction of many other life-forms that will burn through our complacency and isolation. Needless suffering is the psychological and psychic fire that can awaken our compassion and fuse individuals, communities, and nations into a cohesive and consciously organized global civilization."[3]

While the suffering that is coming will be terrible to endure, this session showed me that humanity will come through this crisis, not intact but changed for the better. In the context of the earlier visions of awakening it affirmed that, through this ordeal, we are giving birth not just to a new period of history but to a new form of human being.

As the years have passed and I have watched the shadows of history deepen, I find that this promise means more and more to me. Without a vision of where nature is taking us, without understanding the higher good that our collective suffering is bringing forward in history, we might drown in the sorrow that lies ahead, and we must not drown. Too much is at stake.

THE NONLINEAR DYNAMICS OF AWAKENING

In order to comprehend how our species can make such an enormous transition in a short period of time, it is important to understand the mechanisms of our collective awakening and the role that the collective psyche will play in it. Space restrictions allow me to make only a few quick points.*

The key insight is that the suffering that is coming will be so severe that it will impact not only our personal psyches but the ground of the collective unconscious itself. As we spiral into this global crisis the

---

*For a more detailed discussion of the nonlinear dynamics of awakening, see *Dark Night, Early Dawn*, 233–45.

collective psyche will be put under enormous pressure from billions of human beings across the planet experiencing the collapse of industrial civilization. These experiences will be so traumatic and so widespread that they will drive the field of the collective psyche into a hyperaroused *far-from-equilibrium* or *nonlinear* state. Science and chaos theory have shown us that *physical* systems are capable of doing extraordinary things when they are driven into nonlinear conditions. This session showed me that the same is true for *psychological* systems. The following excerpt is from *Dark Night, Early Dawn:*

> If the species-mind were driven into something analogous to a far-from-equilibrium state, it too might show increasingly nonlinear characteristics. Nonlocal psychological effects might become more prominent; something like psychological phase-locking might take place. Under these extreme conditions, systems that were previously isolated might spontaneously begin to interact with each other to form new connecting patterns . . . If this were to happen, it would feel as though the human psyche were becoming alive at new levels, causing the human family to experience itself in new and previously impossible ways. Interconnections between people that had previously been too subtle to detect could start to become obvious. As our sense of psychological isolation began to break down, compassion for the now less distant "other" would increase. And because these developments were being generated within a far-from-equilibrium system, they would occur much faster than anyone might have predicted on the basis of linear behavior alone.[4]

Ordinarily we might think that the forces generating this crisis are so deeply entrenched in our behavior and social institutions that there is little that we can do to change the outcome. But the highly charged state of the species-mind in the future will translate into conditions that are dangerous but filled with opportunity for humanity. When a system goes sufficiently into the far-from-equilibrium state, it comes to a fork in its destiny known as a bifurcation point. At this point a flux occurs in which many possible futures exist. Chaos theory tells us that at this critical juncture, systems become extremely sensitive to influence. Small changes can be disproportionately amplified by the hypersensitivity of the system. The severity of the global systems crisis, therefore, may be lowering the threshold of influence and *amplifying the impact that individuals can have* on shaping the outcome of this crisis.

> In the highly unstable, supercharged morphic field of tomorrow, those persons who have already made the transition individually that humanity is trying to make collectively, who have begun to think and act as ecologically responsible global citizens, who have truly lifted from their hearts the divisions of race, religion, class, gender, nation, and so on, may function as *seed crystals* . . . to catalyze new patterns in human awareness. In this setting, each of our individual efforts to bring spiritual, social, political, and ecological sanity into our lives may have far-reaching consequences.[5]

THE DIAMOND SOUL

I want to close this essay by asking a question. If history or nature or the Creative Intelligence of the universe is giving birth to a new form of human consciousness through the global systems crisis, what form will this consciousness take? What will our future self look like? I believe that we can see the form of the Future Human if we look deeply into the dynamics of reincarnation.

The understanding of reincarnation that emerged in my sessions is different from the classical Eastern view. In the Asian religions, reincarnation is seen as a long developmental process that culminates in a spiritual awakening that frees us from physical existence. When we realize our divine essence beneath the many layers of earthly "illusion," physical existence has served its purpose and we can move on. In Hinduism, for example, this awakening is called moksha (escape), for through it one escapes samsara (cyclic existence) and returns to Brahman. In Buddhism, nirvana (enlightenment with a body) is followed at death by the higher state of *parinirvana* (final enlightenment without a body). Even the bodhisattvas who return to Earth after their enlightenment are ultimately seeking to liberate all sentient beings into parinirvana and thus empty the planet.

While I understand the noble intent of this view and value the methods it has given us to realize our essential nature, I believe it is an incomplete and inadequate understanding of existence. It fails to grasp the true nature and purpose of physical reality, and it therefore misconceives what the goal of reincarnation is.

Our contemplative spiritual traditions tell us that we are made of the stuff of God, that Atman is Brahman, and my sessions affirm this truth. But something special happens to this Atman-essence inside the incubator of the physical universe beyond just waking up to itself. In repeatedly entering and leaving physical reality, in the constant folding and refolding of human experience, something new is being forged—not simply adding new layers one by one but eventually *fusing all these layers into a new form of life.* Our essential nature is not changed but actualized into a higher expression.

I believe that the goal of reincarnation is not simply to awaken spiritually and then leave the physical universe behind. The goal is to awaken and actualize our full divine potential within the physical universe. Just as "young souls" become "old souls," old souls eventually become "complete souls." When our former lives are integrated and fused into a single consciousness, an explosion in our self-awareness takes place. The shell of the ego pops, and we no longer experience ourselves as simply hundred-year-old beings, but as hundred-thousand-year-old beings. When we look out on the world, we feel our connection with countless people formed over countless lifetimes. We see the Earth as our home for a thousand incarnations. In short, we know ourselves to be incarnating souls, and with this knowledge comes a greater capacity to create the life we want in physical reality.

I did not come to these conclusions on the basis of theoretical reflection, but through experience. At an important juncture in my psychedelic work, I was taken into a state of awareness in which all my former lives began to come back into me, each filled with the learning it had gathered across the centuries. It was like winding kite string around a spool. As I rewound the threads of my existence, I rose to quieter and quieter levels of awareness and into deeper intimacy with what appeared to be the Source of our universe. Against a vast temporal landscape, I became step-by-step what I had been before I had incarnated in space-time. At the same time I also focused and clarified what had been accomplished by entering space-time. So there was both the sense of return, with a profound resonance of homecoming, and also the sense of realization of accomplishment, of seeing clearly what had been the purpose of the entire exercise. It had not been about what had happened in any individual lifetime. It had been about learning to control the powers of creativity that were my innate nature. We were, in effect, learning how to be gods, learning how to create inside space-time.

With this discovery, a brilliant diamond light suddenly exploded from my chest, fusing all the strands into one and giving birth to what I came to call the "Diamond Soul." It was both me and more than I had ever been. Composed of many lifetimes, it was more than the sum of all their years. In coming together, a burst of energy was generated that fused all these centuries of experience into a single being. I was an individual but an individual beyond any frame of reference I had previously known. I was a point of infinitely dense, infinitely transparent diamond light.

I now understand why it is called Diamond Consciousness . . . It had the characteristics of brilliant light, of sparkling luminosity, but also perfectly aligned density. It was extremely concentrated, like a laser, yet at the same time completely transparent. It was perfectly focused power. I suddenly knew that all my experiences in space-time over all these centuries served the cultivation of this Diamond Energy. This is what I am here for, what we are all here for, to learn how to consciously control this extraordinary power.[6]

I believe that what I experienced in this session was a foretaste of what humanity is becoming. Through all the centuries that we have been taking on the human form and growing its extraordinary capacities, nature has been bringing us toward this evolutionary crescendo. The powers that terra-formed this planet, that initially brought forth life here, and then self-aware life, are now taking us across a new threshold. The emergence of the Diamond Soul in history, the shift in our identity from ego to soul, is the natural and inevitable consequence of the relentless cycle of rebirth as we integrate more and more experience into the vessel of our precious human body.

Gestation is long and slow, but birth is sudden and quick. We have been growing the Future Human inside us for thousands of lifetimes. Our planet is going into labor and will soon give us no choice but to deliver our deeper self into history. The problems that are coming at us now are too large to be solved by egoic awareness, even well-intentioned, collectively organized egoic awareness. There is a structural relationship between the self-centered and shortsighted thinking that created this crisis, and the nature of the ego itself. The ego of the private self built our divided world and is being consumed by the fires that are consuming this world.

In order to truly resolve this crisis, we will need to grow up as a species, to shift from what Duane Elgin calls "our adolescent self" to our adult self. From a reincarnational perspective, "growing up" means owning and integrating the larger being that has been gestating within us for thousands of years—opening to it, seeing the world through its eyes, and letting its accumulated wisdom shape our choices. The form of our future self is implicit in our past. The Future Human *is* the Diamond Soul.

With this transition, all things begin anew.

The Great Medicines

A Primer (Mostly)

Stephen Gray and Contributors

IT WILL BE OBVIOUS by now that psychedelic, sacramental medicines are playing a major, though definitely not exclusive role in the mission/vision of this book. If you read the powerful chapter by Chris Bache that precedes this one, you've already got a strong taste of what is all but certain to come. For those perhaps less familiar with some of the major psychedelic plants, fungi, and related substances, what follows is a brief informational survey of a handful of those most implicated in the work of consciousness transformation and most likely to play significant roles as the planetary transformational journey intensifies. (Those already familiar with these medicines will also find a few gems here.)

There are certainly many more "great medicines," psychedelic or not, than you'll see here. In the words of the herbalist and healer Eliot Cowan for example, "There is nothing exotic about this. Don't be misled by talk about the Amazon. If you want to meet the most powerful healing plants in the world, just open your door and step outside."[1] As Cowan and many others have said, what makes something medicine is one's relationship with it, with the spirit of it you might say. And the implications and potential of that learned relationship can extend well beyond working with plants and fungi exclusively.

AYAHUASCA:
VINE OF THE SOUL

Twenty years or so ago, most people in mainstream society had never heard of ayahuasca. Now almost everyone has at least encountered the word somewhere (even if they can't quite spell or pronounce it). The natural habitat of this psychoactive medicine is northern and western South America, and includes parts of Brazil, Bolivia, Peru, Colombia, Ecuador, and Venezuela. A key difference between ayahuasca and other entheogenic plants and fungi is that two complementary plants brewed together are required to activate its power—a climbing vine called *Banisteriopsis caapi,* and a shrub known as *Psychotria viridis,* or *chacruna.** Other DMT-containing plants are sometimes substituted for the chacruna, and other medicinal plants are occasionally added to the mixture.

The nature of the interaction between the two plants and the uncanny story of the independent discovery of the combination in far-flung regions of Amazonia has been told in a number of other places and doesn't need retelling here. Suffice it to say that properly prepared and administered, the foul-tasting purgative brew is a powerful visionary and healing medicine. Those experienced with ayahuasca know that it can assist in healing deep emotional wounds, open up vast alternative worlds often described as more real than this reality, show supplicants a path forward, and connect them to divine reality.

As testament to the power of ayahuasca, here is part of a hymn from the Brazilian syncretic religion known as Santo Daime, which utilizes ayahuasca in its practice. In English, the medicine called Daime means "give me." It's said that these hymns are received from the spirit of that medicine.

---

*The *Banisteriopsis caapi* vine by itself also has its own distinct power. In his excellent book *Plant Teachers* Jeremy Narby quotes Gayle Highpine saying that the vine without the DMT admixture is "the teacher, the healer, the guide."

I live in the forest, I have my teachings.
I don't call myself Daime, I am a Divine Being.
I am a Divine Being, I came here to teach you.
The more you ask of me, the more I have to give you.

Little is known about the ancient history of ayahuasca. Spanish missionaries encountered it in the western Amazon in the sixteenth century. But like other sacred plant medicines, it has likely been in use far longer. Regardless, from its Amazonian origins the ayahuasca medicine has now spread around much of the world. *Ayahuasqueros,* properly trained and ethically trustworthy or not (an important concern going forward), are leading ceremonies everywhere—from forest malocas (large, rudimentary communal houses) to urban apartments. Churches that use ayahuasca, such as the Santo Daime, which is a legal church in Brazil, are popping up, expanding, and gaining legal recognition in multiple countries.

Some say this is no accident of history as humanity enters a period of extended crises. In fact, many now sense that however the story is framed, ayahuasca and other similar medicines are rapidly spreading at this time precisely because of our dire planetary situation. It's as if Spirit, Gaia, the Creator(s), or whatever name (or none) you wish to put on "It," is saying, "You clever monkeys are digging your own graves right now. No god, goddess, or guardian angel can do your work for you, but we can at least make you aware of powerful ways to shock yourselves out of ignorance and reconnect to who you really are as divine sparks of love and brilliant intelligence in an eternal, creative cosmos."

I'll close this brief introduction to ayahuasca with a personal anecdote. I was in a maloca outside of Iquitos, Peru, in ceremony with about a dozen others, being guided by two experienced ayahuasqueros. It was the strongest and most long-lasting ayahuasca encounter I'd had of the three or four dozen such encounters I'd experienced over a couple of decades. Deep in the medicine space, I felt the presence of beings. I asked, "Who are you?"

The answer came back, "We offer love. It is unlimited. The only choice you have to make is how much of it to accept."

PEYOTE: THE HEART OF THE GREAT SPIRIT

"Peyote" (from the Nahuatl *peyōtl*) is the Spanish name for this small, spineless cactus whose primary psychoactive alkaloid is mescaline. Its natural habitat ranges from the Chihuahuan desert and mountain scrublands of northern Mexico into southwestern Texas in the United States. Researchers have found specimens carbon dated to roughly 3700 BCE (nearly six thousand years ago).[2] However, a plausible guess would put the beginnings of peyote's presence among human communities much earlier, since most if not all ancient peoples didn't miss anything of use in their environments.

Peyote's historical and current use has mostly been with traditional peoples of Mexico, most famously among the Huichol (perhaps more respectfully known as the Wixáritari), and among many Native American tribes. Scant record exists of the truly ancient use of peyote in the present-day United States. The late Kanucas Littlefish, a widely respected elder and roadman in the Native American Church, told me that peyote found its way up to the northern states long before any records existed. Considering that precontact Native Americans traded widely around the continent, it stands to reason that a powerful healing and visionary medicine like peyote would have found its way into many communities.

Ironically, you might say, it was American government policies that provoked a massive expansion of the religious use of peyote. In the nineteenth century many tribes that had previously not been in close contact with each other were forced together onto reservations in Oklahoma. Peyote use spread rapidly. Comanche chief Quanah Parker (circa 1845–1911) and others figured out that the way to skirt endless suppression of their spiritual use of peyote was to incorporate it as a religion. Hence the birth of the Native American Church (NAC) in the late nineteenth century.

There are now many chapters of the NAC, primarily in the western half of the United States, along with some in Canada and Mexico. Estimates of the current number of church members range from two hundred fifty thousand to over four hundred thousand. There are strong commonalities as well as variations in the practice rituals. The typical ceremony (or meeting) takes place in a tipi overnight, with a central fire and an altar constructed on the ground for that meeting. Much of the night is carried by the prayer songs that people in the circle take turns leading.

There is a strong case to be made that the situation with peyote is unique among the major entheogenic plant medicines and needs to be protected in ways not necessarily applicable to contemporary use of those related medicines. Peyote has been described as a "cultural keystone species": "those plant and animal species whose existence and symbolic value are essential to the stability of a culture over time."[3] Native Americans have been subjected to a centuries-long, brutal assault on every aspect of their lives and worldview. They have had to fight (and pray) hard to keep their practices strong and uncorrupted. Adding to that, peyote grows very slowly, taking years to mature, and its habitats are endangered.

I've been around the spiritual/psychedelic block so to speak and been a part of a range of ritual environments. Among them was a twelve-year period of frequent participation in Native-run NAC peyote prayer ceremonies. In my experience, the power of that container is unparalleled. The simple rules that these ceremonies are bound by exist solely for the purpose of keeping the healing channels open and clear between spirit and human. This way of life has saved countless lives. And as members say, it *is* a way of life. It's not something to be trifled with, watered down, or commodified in the psychedelic marketplace.

Without directly imitating or in any other way co-opting the principles and practices of the NAC, its ways may be able to serve as role models for the renaissance of effective ceremonial practices that will play an essential role in the birthing of the "Future Human" and the regeneration of sane and sustainable societies. The container created is highly protective; the structure of the church is nonhierarchical; the teachings are absorbed through direct contact with Spirit in the embrace of Grandfather Peyote; the fireplace and other elements of the ritual practice are recognized as living spirit energies; prayer is understood to be shared intention that can powerfully influence "the field of probability," and in my experience, while the donation hat is often passed around in the morning, there is never an actual charge for the meetings.

After the long night of hard spiritual healing work in the tipi, the dawn brings a time for participants to express themselves from the heart. At one meeting I attended there were five or six first-time participants. In the morning, Kanucas looked around at them and said, "You new people might wonder what happened last night. It will take time for you to discover this for yourselves. For now I'll tell you that what you experienced was *reality*."

SAN PEDRO: SACRED CACTUS OF THE ANDES

Laurel Sugden

[Laurel fleshes out this succinct introduction to San Pedro cactus and its key role in planetary consciousness transformation in much greater detail in chapter 16. —Ed.]

◆ ◆ ◆

San Pedro cacti are native to the mid-elevation Andes of Peru and Ecuador, where they thrive in rocky, moist river valleys. Often called "Huachuma" in its homeland, the plants are known to botanists as *Echinopsis pachanoi* and related species. Like their much smaller peyote cousins, San Pedro produces mescaline, among other phenethylamine and isoquinoline alkaloids—some of which chemically resemble MDMA (Ecstasy). Traditional preparations involve simmering chopped plants for several hours and straining out the fiber to produce a well-brewed "tea."

As a master plant, San Pedro teaches with joy, happiness, and sensory delight. The medicine opens drinkers to connection with the elements, with other people, and with our more-than-human kin of the living Earth. Drinking San Pedro often induces physical purging, and its concentrated effects last between ten and twelve hours.

Modern San Pedro shamanism is centered in north coastal Peru, where the medicine's renowned mestizo carriers treat patients and pilgrims from throughout South America. The plant has been an ally of humans for at least four thousand years in a relationship that was fundamental to the stunning artwork and peaceful cooperation of early Andean civilization.

TEONANÁCATL: THE SACRED MUSHROOM OF IMMORTALITY

The future of planetary sustainability may depend on the convergence of human consciousness with mycelial intelligence.

PAUL STAMETS, *FANTASTIC FUNGI*

Psilocybin mushrooms grow in most regions of the world and have been deeply intertwined with humanity's journey longer than anyone knows, almost certainly stretching far back into prehistory. Mushroom stones, cave paintings, mosaics from ancient church ruins, and other evidence suggest that known human experience with the mind-expanding mushrooms may date back to at least 9000 BCE and as far back as 15,000 BCE.[4]

While almost completely unknown to contemporary mainstream societies until well into the twentieth century, the sacred mushrooms were thrust dramatically back into the big world when a New York bank executive and mycophile by the name of R. Gordon Wasson was permitted to participate in a Mazatecan mushroom *velada* (ceremony/ ritual) in the Mexican state of Oaxaca. He subsequently published a prominent article, with photos, in the iconic, widely read magazine *Life* in May of 1957. Most observers would agree that something major was unleashed from that one event. It reverberated resoundingly in Western society, at least among curious and adventurous would-be explorers of altered states, of whom it turns out there were many, especially given the countercultural explosion of the 1960s and early 1970s.

Fast forward to today and we're seeing a remarkable renaissance of the uses of these ancient healing and awakening allies. As the dark shadow of heavy-handed prohibition lightens in the twenty-first century, the mushrooms are being used to great beneficial effect in a variety of ways and contexts. As a prime example and but one of numerous initiatives undertaken in the first two decades of the twenty-first century, the Center for Psychedelic and Consciousness Research at Johns Hopkins University in Baltimore, Maryland, has been conducting carefully designed and administered studies showing remarkable benefits and/or great promise treating such conditions as cancer-related anxiety, depression, tobacco and alcohol addiction, and Alzheimer's disease.

Meanwhile, research is beginning to blossom again after that long freeze, regulatory approvals are being granted anew, degrees of legalization are occurring in multiple jurisdictions, and "unsanctioned" therapeutic and ceremonial work is taking off like crazy. In parallel with these exciting developments, a multitude of home growers and small, under-the-table entrepreneurs are making psilocybin mushrooms available to almost anyone who makes a little bit of an effort to seek them out.

Many are sensing that these mushrooms are on the verge of taking on a far larger space in society. Along with their aforementioned medical and psychiatric benefits, in optimal conditions of skill and safety the mushrooms have ushered psychonauts into mystical realms that can be permanently life changing. Because of their ready accessibility and the expanding recognition and legal approval of them, they may in fact be poised to play an essential role in the urgently needed consciousness transformation work.

A key component of the value of a much greater role for the mushrooms is their potential for a sea change in attitudes about medicine and health altogether. We may be in the early stages of a revolution of understanding regarding natural plants and fungi and our capacities for self-healing holistically—body, mind, and spirit together. Among other important benefits of such a shift in understanding is the clear implication of a dramatically diminishing dependence on pharmaceutical drugs and the powerful corporations that control them.

On a final cautionary note, the almost cartoonish term *magic mushrooms* may give people a misleading impression of the numinous power of psilocybin mushrooms. Especially in higher doses—"heroic" or "committed" doses as Terence McKenna called them—the "little saints" can function as potent ego dissolvers. This can be shocking and frightening. Encountering the mushrooms casually, recreationally, with no attention to set and setting, can easily be, as Terence's brother Dennis McKenna put it, "a dangerous mistake."

CANNABIS: SACRAMENT OF PEACE

While not technically a psychedelic by a narrow biochemical definition in that it doesn't act on the 5-HT2A receptor, by a real-world definition, when understood and used skillfully, cannabis deserves the label.* The word *psychedelic* translates as "mind-manifesting" or "soul-manifesting." Cannabis can do that, potentially manifesting both mind and Mind. A synonym for *psychedelic* is *entheogen,* from the Greek "becoming or generating the Divine within." Cannabis can help with that too.

That's the still not widely understood open secret about cannabis. With the right intention, setting, and perhaps cultivar, dosage, and method of intake, cannabis has a unique "style" and capability that is both powerful and gentle at the same time. In other words, she has the power to shock the monkey (ego), but when you surrender to that power, she can invite you into a state of peace, and evoke a sense of the holy.

---

*Like the so-called major psychedelics, cannabis may be thought of as a nonspecific amplifier. She will graciously nudge you farther along whatever direction you're already heading. It's well-known that that can be and *is* problematic for a lot of people who feel the need to put a gloss on things and avoid reality, with all its jarring bumps and grinds. Hence the necessary admonition to approach our ancient ally with respect, intention, and skill.

Embodiment is a significant aspect of the consciousness transformation necessary to shift the direction of human affairs. Tibetan Buddhist master Chögyam Trungpa called it "synchronizing mind and body." Most of us in the large civilizations are not fully embodied in that sense. When you can calm the heart and mind and get out of your own way, cannabis can relax and open the mind and body in tandem.

In fact, as medicines go, cannabis just might be our best medicine for this necessary embodiment, for becoming more connected to body and earth, more energetically aligned with the vast, enveloping nonhuman world—as in slower and more spacious—that to a great degree is painfully lacking in the culture at this time.

Because of this unique style of gentle power, its easy accessibility, and its safety and nontoxicity, cannabis has been called "the Sacrament of Peace." It's not for everyone of course, but if enough people understand and work with cannabis in these skillful ways, it would be unwise to undervalue its potential to nudge the species closer to our true nature.

LSD: ALBERT HOFMANN'S "PROBLEM CHILD"

What a long, strange trip it's been.
THE GRATEFUL DEAD, "TRUCKIN"

If there is one substance on this short list of "great medicines" whose story has been the strangest, wildest, and most controversial, it is without a doubt LSD. First, a clarifier. People often think of LSD as a synthetic "drug," and for that reason some in the world of psychedelics/entheogens reject it as not "natural." But it is more accurately labeled "semi-synthetic" since lysergic acid is a naturally occurring compound found in rye seeds. As well, its uncanny entry into the world bears the signs of something meant to be, and its potential for cracking open the doors of perception is indisputable.

Lysergic acid diethylamide, or LSD-25, was the twenty-fifth in a series of ergot derivatives synthesized in 1938 by Dr. Albert Hofmann, a Swiss chemist working for Sandoz laboratories. Hofmann's story with

LSD is in itself strange and wonderful (and has been well told elsewhere). The really short version is that the 1938 lab experiments proved fruitless and the medicine was kept around on a near-forgotten back shelf for the next five years—a highly unusual practice at Sandoz. In 1943 Hofmann had a "strange feeling"—call it an intuition—that he should look into this drug again. He accidentally got a tiny amount on his fingertips, which found its way into his mouth and resulted in some very odd alterations of consciousness. A second, deliberate encounter with what the good doctor still thought was a miniscule dose (250 micrograms, or millionths of a gram) produced a stunningly powerful alteration that set into motion the "long, strange trip" that brings us to today.

Along the way, LSD has been used and misused in numerous ways: extensive and extremely promising (and legal) psychotherapeutic work (think *Stanislav* Grof); bizarre and even cruel medical and military experiments (think Project MKULTRA, etc.); and the explosive culture-shifting but often careless and even dangerous use of "acid" among the "hippies" of the counterculture era of the 1960s and early 1970s.*

Bear in mind that until 1968, LSD was legal in the United States. But the expansiveness and chaos of the 1960s produced a huge backlash among controllers and conservatives, which resulted in LSD being unceremoniously dumped into the U.S. Controlled Substances Act as a Schedule 1 drug.†

So while the "illicit" use of acid and underground therapy continued (think The Secret Chief‡), legitimate research came to a screeching halt almost overnight. But again, like its relatives in the psychedelic pantheon, the fog of ignorance is lifting and the wheels of research are

---

*Terence McKenna once wrote that he thought the sixties were in some ways "misplaced," since most people were relieved to have gotten through a psychedelic trip without an ego-death experience—wherein lay their most life-changing potential.

†Schedule 1: A drug with a "high potential for abuse" and "no currently accepted medical use"—the same absurd category in which our largely benign, ancient ally and friend cannabis continues to languish.

‡The Secret Chief was an influential pioneer of the underground psychedelic therapy movement in the United States.

again turning. It's not a stretch to surmise that within a few years LSD will settle into its rightful place and use in psychotherapy and beyond.

5-MEO-DMT: "THE GOD MOLECULE"

chad charles

[This discussion by chad charles is elaborated on in chapter 20. —Ed.]

◆ ◆ ◆

5-MeO-DMT is very versatile. This molecule has been detected in a number of plants, many of which have been used/ingested in various forms over human history in arguably most of the six habitable continents. In 1965 it was detected in the secretion of one animal: a toad endemic to North America (*Incilius alvarius:* the Sonoran Desert toad or Colorado River toad—often referred to as *toad, sapo,* or *bufo*). The pure/isolated molecule (often referred to as *jaguar,* the *God molecule,* or *five*) was first synthesized in 1936 in Japan.[5]

Although it's a DMT, this molecule apparently functions in a way that's different from other DMT variations/derivatives/analogues. This is observed experientially as well as scientifically. The nature of the mystical experience induced by the ingestion of 5-MeO-DMT is extremely difficult to explicate, mostly due to the absence of a visionary component (which often characterizes psychedelics in general). Neurologically, the depth and breadth of its interaction with our receptors is thus far unparalleled among many tested.[6] It is characteristically dissociative, allowing for a complete disengagement with memory.

Inhalation is the only way that *toad* may be ingested. With the pure molecule, administration may happen via a variety of routes: rectal absorption, insufflation, inhalation, and/or IM and IV injection. This considerable variation results in different durations of time between onset (which is typically extremely fast, ranging from a few seconds to a couple of minutes) and a return to baseline consciousness.

Despite this versatility, my chapter 20 of this book will focus on the known contemporary application and usage: the ingestion of the vapor/smoke of *toad* as well as *jaguar*. The chapter will not distinguish between psycholytic, psychedelic, or any other orientations/ methodologies, as there are many approaches to applying the substance. Instead, chapter 20 will speculate mostly on why its mere presence is current and why its presence may deserve acclaim and importance.

IBOGA: THE HEALING ROOT OF AFRICA

Iboga (*Tabernanthe iboga*) is an unassuming perennial shrub native to equatorial West Africa. While it has only become known in the West in the past few decades, it has an ancient history in West Africa, particularly in Gabon, Cameroon, Angola, and the Republic of Congo. Traditional use of iboga is perhaps most associated with Bwiti, an animist, syncretic religion primarily based in Gabon. It is typically used in elaborate initiation ceremonies to bring adolescents into adulthood and the community of "real" people. Bwiti is legal in Gabon, where it has been declared a national treasure.

Ibogaine, the primary psychoactive alkaloid derived from the root bark of the iboga shrub, was isolated in 1889. In the past several decades—along with some variations of the alkaloid and the iboga root itself in combination—it has gained considerable traction as a promising treatment for addiction. This medicine has some remarkable and highly unusual properties. Some have said that it can effectively pull down a mental movie screen and show addicts scenes from their childhood where trauma forced them to, in essence, turn away from themselves and bury the pain. In combination with that, people have reported that ibogaine can temporarily knock out drug cravings for up to a few weeks. This is said to provide the addict with a precious window of opportunity to make lifesaving changes.

In the West, iboga is sometimes used for psycho-spiritual insight and growth in ceremonial contexts. Ibogaine and other variations are much more commonly used in residential addiction-treatment environments. While unsurprisingly, iboga and ibogaine are currently in Schedule 1 of the Controlled Substances Act in the United States, it is either legal or unregulated in many other jurisdictions around the world. Numerous centers can be found for those individuals wanting to pursue that treatment option.

It's important to be aware that ibogaine is extremely powerful and on rare occasions has proved fatal. And of course, since these treatment facilities typically function in gray areas of legality, they are generally unregulated. Caveat emptor (let the buyer beware) applies. It's also important to note that as iboga and ibogaine have spread around the world, the shrub has become endangered in its natural habitats. Gabon has made its exportation illegal.

MDMA: A GENTLE INVITATION TO INSIGHT

MDMA (*3,4-methylenedioxy-methamphetamine*), also known as Ecstasy or Molly, isn't per se a *psychedelic* or *hallucinogen* (a dubious term).* Common labels for MDMA are *empathogen* (generating empathy) and *entactogen* (to produce a touching within). Psychiatrist Lester Grinspoon, M.D., describes MDMA as "a gentle invitation to insight." And while it is of course not a plant or fungus, MDMA isn't as synthetic as one might think. It has chemical similarities to several naturally occurring plants such as dill, parsley, and sassafras root, which produces safrole, "the major natural precursor in the synthesis of MDMA."[7]

MDMA was synthesized prior to 1912 by the German pharmaceutical company Merck, but basically languished until the chemist Sasha Shulgin rediscovered it in 1976 and introduced it to friends and colleagues in California. Here it became popular in (legal) therapeutic use, with remarkable results. Unfortunately, as is so common with promising medicines like those discussed in this chapter, the Drug Enforcement Administration (DEA) observed that MDMA (Ecstasy) had escaped into the world of uncontrolled recreational use. As a result, in 1985 the

---

*It's often said by experienced psychedelic journeyers that the visuals seen under the influence of psychedelics are visions and not hallucinations. Visions can be as real as or more real than "waking" perceptions. The term *hallucination* can suggest a reductionist pathologizing of such visions as "unreal."

DEA dumped it into the reviled Schedule 1 category of the Controlled Substances Act.

Labels, categories, careless use, impure facsimiles, and poorly considered crackdowns aside, there is no doubt that MDMA deserves to be granted a seat at the head table of honored healing medicines. As a therapeutic adjunct to therapy for PTSD, it has several remarkable characteristics: knocking out or significantly diminishing the fear factor, opening up compassion, and keeping the mind clear for communication and recall. If you're not familiar with the excellent work of the Multidisciplinary Association for Psychedelic Studies (MAPS), you may be surprised at how far along their legally approved clinical trials with MDMA in several countries have come.

There should be no doubt that when it's pure (which is a challenge) and used in the right context with healing intention, MDMA is a beautifully effective medicine. As Dr. Julie Holland put it in her introduction to *Ecstasy: The Complete Guide,* "The judicious, supervised, and infrequent use of single oral doses of MDMA as a psychiatric medicine may be a revolutionary tool to assist the fields of psychology and psychiatry."[8]

KETAMINE: IN A CLASS OF ITS OWN?

Dr. Rae St. Arnault (naturopathic physician), **Helen Loshny** (counsellor), and **Madison Nobbs** (nurse) have been working toward the legal recognition and safe use of ketamine for therapeutic purposes.

◆ ◆ ◆

Ketamine has a long history of use, and extensive long-term data supports its safety. It is considered an essential drug by the World Health Organization and is carried by military field personnel and by paramedics. Ketamine was first synthesized in 1962 by Parke-Davis organic chemist Calvin Stevens through efforts to produce a compound that was a safer and more predictable anesthetic agent than prior attempts, one of which was phencyclidine (PCP). In 1964, ketamine was administered to the first human test subjects, and its hallucinogenic properties were discovered. The psychological effects have often been described as "dreamlike."

Although ketamine is proving to be an effective antidepressant, it also comes with a reputation partly shaped by its use in "underground" and unregulated settings. John Lilly was a famous neuroscientist, psychiatrist, and "psychonaut" who for a period of his life used ketamine in high and frequent doses. He documented his experiences, some of which became sensationalized.

Ketamine given in a certain dose range produces a disconnection or a dissociation from one's body. The recipient becomes what has been described as "a conscious observer." They are still themselves but a version of themselves that is removed from the ordinary states of mind, separated from external inputs, given space from the normal difficulties of having a human mind, and transported somewhere else for a temporary (forty-five minutes to one hour) out-of-body journey.

Ketamine is unique in that it is considerably shorter-acting than other psychedelics. This lends well to therapy because a ketamine-assisted therapy session can be completed and the client can be safe to go home within a three-hour period.

Ketamine is used to effectively treat chronic pain, depression, and other mental health conditions that have not been amenable to treatment with conventional remedies. Depending on the treatment setting, the psychedelic effects of ketamine can be seen either as a powerful adjunct to therapy or an undesirable side effect. For example, in surgical or other medical settings the psychedelic effects of ketamine are considered undesirable and may be intentionally reduced or prevented with benzodiazepines. Most ketamine research focuses on intravenous administration at a dose range that is below the threshold of a full psychedelic experience.

Ketamine is the only current, fully legal psychedelic medicine, although its use is restricted to medical prescription only (i.e., it's not been decriminalized or been approved for use in recreational or psycho-spiritual settings). Ketamine has a versatile range of administration methods, including intranasal and lozenge that are effective in psy-cholytic psychotherapy, as well as intramuscular administration. Higher doses administered in this way generate the classic psychedelic proper-ties that offer transformative healing in themselves and are amplified when combined with trauma-informed and somatic therapies in a holis-tic, interdisciplinary, and community-based service model.

HONORABLE MENTION

There are many plants, fungi, and semi-synthetic and synthetic sub-stances with mind-altering, mind-manifesting (psychedelic), and heal-ing properties. There are far too many to list here. Some of the naturally occurring ones are little known to most of the world and the general public in particular. How many people in the public sphere, for example, are familiar with the climbing vine known by the Nahuatl (Mexican) name ololiúqui? It's a species of morning glory, the seeds of which con-tain an ergoline alkaloid similar in structure to LSD, and it likely has a long history of use among Native peoples.

One plant that deserves a nod at least is *Salvia divinorum*. Most people who experiment with this unique member of the mint family are quickly turned off by the strangeness of its effects. But researchers and advocates such as Christopher Solomon in California are convinced that in the right context with the proper dose and method of adminis-tration, *Salvia* has significant therapeutic and spiritual potential. One current advantage it has over some of the other mind-manifesting medi-cines is that in many jurisdictions it is legal (so far).

We'll see. Knowledgeable and responsible advocates are needed on behalf of this plant.

Creatrix
By Martina Hoffmann

Psychedelic Feminism

When My Heart Hurts

Zoe Helene

Zoe Helene, M.F.A., advocates for women, wildlife and wilderness, and the right to journey with sacred psychoactive and psychedelic plants and fungi— our coevolutionary allies. She founded Cosmic Sister, an environmental feminist collective and creative studio, and originated Psychedelic Feminism to support women of the Psychedelic Renaissance. Zoe identifies as Indigenous in diaspora in honor of ancestors who developed nature-based, female-led, entheogen-elevated mystery traditions dating to the Neolithic era. She grew up exploring primary rainforest and teeming tidepools in Aotearoa (New Zealand) and was mentored by the legendary theatrical Patricia Zipprodt. An artist and educator, her work has been covered by top-tier media outlets. She is happily married to ethnobotanist Chris Kilham.

◆ ◆ ◆

WITHOUT A TRUE BALANCE of power across the gender spectrum— globally—humans (and non-humans) will not survive. Thousands of years of patriarchy (a euphemism for male supremacy) have warped the way we evolved as a species and brought us to where we are today: a narcissistic, invasive species on the fast track to global annihilation. Violent misogyny is on the rise, and we're witnessing the human-caused Age of Extinction.

If we don't see a collective paradigm shift, we will render Earth uninhabitable for ourselves and all the other living beings we share her with. We need rapid evolution. Rapid evolution is when a species evolves much faster than normal to survive drastic environmental change that will likely lead to its extinction. Male-dominated science emphasizes *physical* change, typical patriarchal reductionism that misses the issue at hand. Humans don't need rapid physical evolution; our *bodies* are not the problem. Whatever big threat to the planet you look at, human *behavior* is the problem. We need rapid *cultural* evolution. Psychedelic Feminism promotes rapid *cultural* evolution from within, starting with women.

WE ARE NATURE

The idea of "reconnecting with nature" is a human-supremacist construct. We *are* nature. We are nothing but nature. We are embodied psyches living in vulnerable flesh-blood-and-bones vessels. We're born, we live, we die, we decompose. We're animals—wildlife indigenous to Earth. And like other wild species, without freedom we fall apart. We are able to habituate to codes of conduct and the urban matrix so we can maintain a degree of control (an illusion), but our psyches are untamable.

Like all other species, we have inherent traits we can't change— "human nature"—and adopted or learned behaviors we *can* change. For instance, forming social groups is inherent to human nature. Just as wolves form packs, lions form prides, and orcas form pods, humans form communities—tribes, clans, subcultures, and so forth— led by an alpha. There's nothing we can do to change this. It's how we roll.

Male-dominated cultures value females *first and foremost* based on a superficial, cookie-cutter concept of beauty, then discard us when we're no longer useful for decoration, commercialization, entertainment, sexual service, or breeding. This is an example of *adopted or learned behavior.* We can change this behavior—and we must.

WALKING WOUNDED

Anyone raised female in this male-dominated culture is a survivor of insidious, omnipresent, multifaceted oppression. This does *not* mean we are stuck in victim consciousness. Quite the opposite. We've been victimized, yes. We've been traumatized, yes. We're disappointed, yes—and sometimes downright disenchanted. Yet we remain fiercely loyal to the dream of a better way. After all, humans *are* capable of greatness.

Women are the walking wounded. We've endured constant cultural abuse from an early age. Patriarchal constructs have permeated almost every facet of "civilization." Male-conceived, male-owned, male-led entities glorify an obscene hoarding disorder. Conforming is rewarded, creativity commodified, and personal and collective liberty monitored and controlled. Hardcore "chew 'em up, spit 'em out" models are socio-economically acceptable. Males still hold the majority of monetary resources and decision-making seats of power, with most females in supportive positions, influencing as best they can.

Misogynists, masquerading as spiritual leaders, force-feed monotheistic father/son dogma with evil messages of female inferiority, designed to repress sensuality and undermine self-esteem, clip wings, nip Spirit in the bud, and burden psyches with guilt, shame, and fear. Girls are subjected to indoctrination and are expected to be compliant, to either accept subservience or risk being shamed, shunned, even stoned in some countries. *His*tory, served up through a heavily filtered male-supremacist lens as "evidence" and "fact," includes little or no female representation, even though we represent half of the human population.

We're trained to smile through it—it's uncanny how convincing we can be, *even to ourselves*—but this is a serious human rights violation, and we're ready for real and lasting change.

PSYCHEDELIC FEMINISM IS FOR EVERYONE

We can't change the past, and no one alive today is responsible for what happened hundreds or thousands of years ago. Not you, not me, not anyone. We're here now, though, *in a reality that requires immediate attention,* and we're responsible for our own actions and reactions. Patriarchy is systemic. Everyone is harmed by male-supremacist constructs and the Age of Patriarchy. The more I do this work, the more I feel for males (and anyone alive, really), who suffer from their own screwed-up gender socialization, whether they know it or not.

This is about balance. I don't believe matriarchy is any better than patriarchy. If women had been in charge for thousands of years, it's pretty likely we, too, would have made a mess, because "power-over" corrupts. Whatever new leadership strategies we embrace must represent the full divine spectrum—working together and coexisting in exquisite diversity.

Psychedelics show us how interconnected everything is. They help us understand and empathize with each other's humanity and see how unequal positioning detrimentally affects everyone. Almost universally, these medicines show us Oneness—and this isn't just poetic. Humans actually do share ancestry with all life on Earth—and beyond—interconnected through the stars. Over billions of years, the elements in our bodies, the atoms in our DNA—and in all other living beings on Earth—were formed from stars that died in the endless, sacred cycle of death and rebirth.

Oneness is real, but patriarchy has infected it like a global pandemic. Until patriarchy is nothing but a nightmarish cautionary tale, we must focus on *women.* We're celebrating a new type of male hero. If you identify as male and you're willing to explore your patriarchal cultural conditioning, please join us. We welcome you in our sacred sanctuaries. This is an "all hands on deck" emergency, and there's a lot of work to do.

WOMEN ARE EXTRAORDINARY

Sacred psychedelic medicines have the power to help our psyches rapidly evolve so we, as a species, can be better citizens of Earth, starting with hundreds, then thousands, then millions, then billions of individual revolutions within. The journey starts with ourselves, then moves ever outward.

These medicines are calling to people all over the world. For many, this work is about shifting perspectives, breaking through deep social programming and self-destructive patterns, and opening to expansion. For those of us who identify as female, it's also about healing traumas and symptoms of internalized oppression directly caused by the lunacy of male supremacy, including rage—even if it's righteous or "sacred" rage, which anyone who is paying any attention carries.

I *love* being a woman. Women are extraordinary, and the world needs the full scope of our magic. After working with women in pre-psychedelic preparation, immersive journeying, and postpsychedelic integration for many years, I've come to recognize some universal themes in what women bring to the medicine space. Here are but a few.

Women want to heal from sexual discrimination, objectification, harassment, coercion, and violent assault and move beyond "guilt and shame" programing, people-pleaser mode, imposter syndrome, and a host of other self-deprecating narratives. They're dealing with savage and ubiquitous beauty ideals, body image dysmorphia, life-threatening eating disorders, hyper-competitiveness, and paralyzing perfectionism. They suffer from low self-esteem, self-hate, anxiety, depression, substance abuse, addictions. They want to exorcise gender-based ancestral trauma; discover and celebrate *her*story; reclaim prepatriarchal heritage; and abolish sexism, racism, ageism, ableism, classism, and bigotry in all their ugly, interconnected forms. They want to develop and hold healthy standards and boundaries, strengthen emotional shielding, and prioritize self-care, creativity, and play.

Motherhood and reproductive rights also come up again and again. Mothers must figure out how to navigate careers. Women coping with infertility face stigmatization and abandonment, and women who choose not to have children are vilified as selfish, even though the human population is at eight billion. Some women are heartbroken by miscarriages; others carry inner turmoil in response to abortions. Some mothers have postnatal PTSD from life-threatening pregnancies or births; some struggle with postpartum depression. These women are pressured to meet impossible ideals of the "perfect" mother with little or no societal support—especially single moms.

As women, we want to mourn without being consumed by sorrow and channel righteous rage constructively. We want to be heard, find and free authentic voice, be credited and compensated for our contributions. We want to learn how to laugh again, cry again, try again, trust again, love again.

Many of us have become masters of emotional alchemy by necessity, but the micro-aggressions keep on coming, as do the micro-informants—subtle and not-so-subtle reminders that our culture values males more than females—a steady barrage of indignities accumulating in the catacombs of the psyche. As women, we also deal with economic inequities and an overall imbalance of opportunities, as well as gaslighting, mansplaining, censorship, silencing, and *so much more.* The gag effect—sometimes to the point of feeling invisible—is a key driver in Psychedelic Feminism. We're taught to deal with it, so we do. Sort of. Not really. Because it's in there, pushed down and back, doing damage.

To address burdens this enigmatic and debilitating, I have never seen anything work as effectively as intentional journeying with sacred psychedelic plants and fungi. These medicines are truth serums that can bring clarity, perspective, and freedom from insatiable sorrow, emotional scars, self-doubt, and even self-hatred. In the medicine space, women can explore the inculcations that stunt and silence. We can make sense of them, learn to live with them differently, or purge them altogether.

This transformation is *experiential,* rather than academic or theoretical, and it requires courage, commitment, humility, and sometimes very hard work. Some people believe "faith" is necessary for this work, but I've grown wary of belief systems. As a spiritual agnostic, I'm comfortable *not knowing.* I've settled on *intentional,* temporary suspension of disbelief, a conscious willingness to travel outside the norms of what I consider "real" or "logical" for the sake of full immersion into the mysteries. I do this with hope, because without hope there is only despair.

WILDERNESS WITHIN

All sacred psychedelic plants and fungi have personalities that help me tune into different aspects of myself. Cannabis can be a potent psychedelic for journeying, a trusted ambassador in transcendent spaces, a versatile master plant that elevates, enlivens, and enlightens. Peyote ("the sacrament") is alert, attentive, and immediate, surrounding me with twinkling, kaleidoscopic *aha!* messages and curious, exuberant life spirits that illuminate the way of heart—fluid, fractal watercolor lights invite this mortal fool to dance—a reunion, an initiation. Ayahuasca is a tempestuous shape-shifter who wants me to thrive and shine—she wants everyone to thrive and shine. She teaches through extreme experiential storytelling, and she's always loving, even if it's tough jungle love. Shrooms taught me that however insignificant I am, I still play a part in Gaia's vibrant, complex miracle of an ecosystem. They're all nature spirits—as am I, as are you, as are we all.

I have had the honor and privilege of journeying with ayahuasca and peyote in mesmerizing Indigenous-led ceremonies. The unchartered, otherworldly wilderness within *feels like home*. I'm a seasoned journeyer, yet I know these medicines will continue to surprise me. Over time, I've learned to flow-surf surreal visionary states by navigating and surrendering all at the same time. Life-enhancing messages come in abstract, symbolic, and universal poetic languages. Many people encounter non-human animals and plant spirits that encourage, console, challenge, devour, scan, and deep clean us. Sometimes they become us; sometimes we become them. Sometimes we merge and become One.

I've been engulfed in spectacular, surging kinetic visuals that were frightening and nauseating until I learned how to cocreate with the tempest. Some visions come in fantastical surrealist narratives, some as divine archetypes—human and non-human, flora and fauna, feminine, masculine, nonbinary, elemental, cosmic. Calling, coaxing: "Reset. Rebirth. Remember. Reclaim." Often a voice of wisdom from my heart of hearts, or perhaps even through it from beyond, gives me messages and clues to follow, or challenging tasks to prioritize "in real life." My marching orders are always recognizable as actions that lead to growth.

We coevolved with psychedelic sacred plants and fungi, and their medicine can help us discover and remove obstacles to health and wellness, setting the stage for peace, inspiration, revelation, and even full-on metamorphosis. The illusion that we are somehow separate from (and better than) nature dissolves, morphing into visions of interconnectivity and universal kinship. Psychedelics can also help us forgive ourselves and others, enabling us to move forward more freely and productively in the work we do for a brighter future.

These medicines have helped me find a center of strength and serenity where I can remain open and receptive to women's intense, sometimes horrific stories while maintaining balance. I've learned to hold space for their vulnerability without feeling overwhelmed by their suffering and to focus on their secret hopes and dreams. I'm touched by their willingness to trust. Primal medicine work can be turbulent, but *it's a myth that you need to suffer to heal.*

Like many others, I am working for the sacred plants and fungi, helping spread the word about them to a global audience—particularly kind, creative, courageous women who honor sacred reciprocity—because if you help this type of woman to heal, empower, and liberate herself, she will, in turn, help others.

I see this as a catalyst for rapid evolution.

BEYOND DIVIDE AND CONQUER

To survive and succeed in a system that is stacked against us, women have had to occasionally engage in behaviors that are beneath us. It is past time we stop tearing each other down. We make it far too convenient for the powers that be when we do their work for them—and that's the point. Over thousands of years, we've been expertly manipulated by "divide and conquer" tactics because colonizers, dictators, tyrants, and crusaders for dominator religions understand that one of the most efficient, effective ways to conquer and control people is to pit one group against another. For real progress to take place, more women need to join forces—but that takes *trust,* and trust is often a very real obstacle.

If oppression and self-sabotage had a monster child, her name would be Internalized Misogyny—a wretched, devious beast that hides in broken places, striking when least expected with a venom that weakens all parties (including herself). Stereotypes like "mean girls" and "catfights" are not inherent to our nature. They're bad seeds, planted by entities and energies that thrive on exploitation. Perceived scarcity of power amplifies the dynamic, fueled further by trauma responses. Even the best and brightest grow weary, disillusioned, and despondent, disheartened by the infighting, which makes them (us) easier to coerce and subjugate.

The "divide, conquer, and rule" tactic has been especially successful in poisoning cross-generational female friendship and collaboration. Why? Because we're threatening when we're powerful, and we're powerful when we trust one another.

A core part of my work is to encourage intergenerational groups of women to share ceremony. We journey together with gifted Indigenous ancestral healers who graciously open their malocas to *pasajeras* (passengers) from foreign lands. Women from all times of life and all walks of life, representing a wide variety of ancestral lineages, have healed, grown, and bonded together, gaining invaluable insight from one another. When this works, it is profound.

Good men—good *people*—are also welcome. Wherever we are in the world, I cherish the presence of my psychonaut sweetheart, Chris, tripping beside me.

WHEN MY HEART HURTS

This work is about relationship—with sacred medicines, self, loved ones, community, humanity, and the miracle of life on Earth. None of our healing, empowerment, and self-liberation matters if we cannot be in high relationship with this most exquisite and extraordinary home planet—and all the other precious living beings we share her with. That is the ultimate and essential goal.

Chris and I are fortunate to live in a "treehouse" in Western Massachusetts, surrounded by diverse, mostly indigenous, green habitat supporting mostly indigenous wildlife. We steward and share this little sanctuary with a delightful menagerie of wild neighbors—almost every species native to the region.

These are my kin and teachers; they bring me joy and give me sustenance. I *adore* them. It pains me when the pollinators' wildflowers are mowed down in spring so we can have this strange ecological disaster called a "lawn," or when an entire species is branded "pest" or "vermin." The gunshots ringing out in the woods during hunting season are excruciating. Killing for sport or profit and culling wildlife is a patriarchal perversion of the highest degree.

The way I see it, declarations of ownership of and dominion over anything that lives (or sustains life) isn't just delusional—its criminally insane. When a culture chooses to believe anything that is not human can be property—a "resource" to burn, bulldoze, bastardize, pimp, torture, enslave, exterminate—this leads to the aggressive destruction of entire ecosystems, including old-growth forests, grasslands, wetlands, deserts, waterways, and other essential habitat. This destruction is speeding up, not slowing down, and is a direct and major cause of extinction—including our own if we don't stop the madness.

For me and for many others, these are hate crimes. It's a kind of a rape, but rape culture teaches us to shut up and take it. I once endured a long, haunting ayahuasca vision that forced me to face and *feel fully* a collection of atrocities toward nonhuman beings that I'd saved in a folder in the archives of my digitalized monkey-mind. Another vision led me to a stockpile of pain packed up into tidy, glowing grief packages, pulsating in subterranean soul cages.

Some days—most days, recently—I *feel* the swell of grieving in the collective psyche, and I wonder, *if I surrender to healthy mourning, will I be sucked into a black hole of despair?* When I'm feeling helpless and hopeless about what has been lost, what might be lost, what will be lost if we continue on this path, the sacred medicines—in vivid technicolor—remind me of what I already know: love is the essence of life, a massive, unstoppable source of power channeling through all living beings, including myself. I grieve because I allow myself to love fully.

I get that I need to continue to take a stand, resolutely and with grace, along with billions of loving others. I get that our numbers are growing exponentially around an awakening world. I get that this is a last-chance effort, the odds next to impossible. I shudder, breathe in, breathe out, center myself, stoke the soulfire, sit silent, filling up, preparing to push beyond my natural introversion for another round of ambivert mode so I can be of better service.

Being on environmental feminist front lines means bearing witness to the best and worst of what we're capable of as a species. When my heart hurts, communing with sacred medicines and meditating on the miracle of life leaves me renewed, refreshed, and inspired to keep up the fight.

It's not too late. We *can* shift our self-centered and ultimately cannibalistic ways—but we need to act now. We've hit the nick of time.

*We are now moving through a collective rite of passage,
toward our early adulthood as a human community.*
DUANE ELGIN

Our Story Is Our Future!

*Four Stories of Our Planetary Journey
That Serve the Well-Being of All Life*

Duane Elgin, Ph.D.

DUANE ELGIN is an internationally recognized author, speaker, educator, and citizen-voice activist. Among his many involvements and accomplishments over a long career, he has worked as a senior staff member of the Presidential Commission on the American Future, been a media activist founding three nonprofit organizations, and given over three hundred and fifty keynote presentations to a wide range of audiences. He is the author of five books, most recently the powerful and visionary *Choosing Earth: Humanity's Journey of Initiation Through Breakdown and Collapse to Mature Planetary Community,* from which this chapter is excerpted. His personal website is DuaneElgin.com and his project website is ChoosingEarth.org.

◆ ◆ ◆

WITHOUT A STORY or vision of a promising future, we are lost and will create a ruinous future for ourselves. For example, the "American Dream" that pulled the United States and a good portion of the world forward for generations has become the world's nightmare as the excesses of consumerism produce climate disruption, species extinction, and enormous disparities of wealth. Instead of a different "dream," people need wide-awake visions of a purposeful and sustainable future, told in ways that are believable and compelling. To be effective, we require a narrative that speaks to the entire human family and to do that it must be:

1. Simple: able to be told in just a few words;
2. Universal: understood by everyone on the planet;
3. Emotionally powerful: people feel and care about it, and;
4. Evocative of our higher human potentials: a story that calls forth our gifts and explains how we are on a purposeful journey as a species.

We are just beginning to discover this story and to recognize core elements in our personal lives. In this rare moment in human history we are beginning to develop, for the very first time, the "story of, by, and for all of us." To illustrate, here are four widely recognized narratives we can use to portray the human adventure.

HUMANITY IS GROWING UP

Over tens of thousands of years, the human species has been learning and maturing. We have moved from our childhood as awakening hunter-gatherers to our late adolescence as a species that is on the edge of a planetary civilization. We are now moving through a collective rite of passage, toward our early adulthood as a human community. In shifting from our species adolescence to early maturity, we are building a new relationship with the Earth, one another, and the universe. This story is such an important one, offering deep insights for our time of Great Transition.

THE GLOBAL BRAIN IS WAKING UP

Our ability to communicate enabled humans to slowly progress from nomadic bands of gatherers and hunters to the edge of a planetary civilization. Now, within the space of a single lifetime, the human family has moved from the separation of geography and culture to nearly instantaneous global communication and connection. With stunning speed, we have developed tools of local to global communication that are transforming our collective communication and consciousness as a species.

The "global brain" is a metaphor for the worldwide network formed by people coming together with communication technologies that connect us into an organic whole. As the internet becomes faster, more intelligent, more ubiquitous, and more encompassing, it increasingly ties us together in a single communications web that functions like a "brain" for planet Earth.

Because we are in the midst of an unprecedented revolution in the scope, depth, and richness of global communications, the impact of this revolution on our shared consciousness is equally unprecedented. No longer isolated and cut off from one another, we are collectively witnessing our world in profound transition. Awakenings and innovations happening on one side of the planet are being communicated instantly around the world, enabling us to wake up together. With astonishing speed, we are rousing from our slumber to know ourselves as a single species, united by an extraordinary network of planetary communication.

THE PLANET IS GIVING BIRTH

Storytellers from around the world have long used the birthing metaphor to give meaning to suffering and transformation: the pain is worth enduring for the sake of what is being born. A powerful description of birth is taken from Dr. Betsy MacGregor's book, *In Awe of Being Human: Stories from the Edge of Life and Death.*

> Bringing a new human being into this world is not an easy matter. The ordeal that must be endured is huge, and it can take a significant toll. The life of either mother or child, and sometimes both, may be lost if all does not go well. . . . Tremendous forces must be

set in motion in order to expel the infant from the comfort of the womb, and the going can get extremely rough. Powerful maternal muscles create rhythmic waves of contraction that force the baby along, while the youngster's head leads the way, stretching apart tight maternal tissues and pushing past rock-hard bone, bearing the brunt of the work. The amount of pressure exerted on the infant's head is so great that the soft bones of its skull are squeezed hard against each other and made to overlap, only slowly regaining their normal position days after birth. Collections of blood may form in the infant's scalp from the battering as well. For hours upon hours the formidable process goes on, testing the limits of endurance for both mother and child. It's enough to make an observer exclaim, "Good Lord! Why has nature made it so hard for us to enter this world?"[1]

We may cry out with similar exclamations regarding the birth of our species-civilization. "Why is it so hard for us to wake up together and enter this world as a whole species?" A precious miracle is hidden within the pain of our time of Great Transition—a whole new life is being born. When we know a new life is emerging on the other side of the pain and unstoppable push for the birth, we are able to move ahead with less fear and with loving anticipation. Jacques Verduin, founder of the GRIP Program (Guiding Rage into Power), offers deep insight into how we can bear the suffering of this new world being born.*

> Amor means love. Fati means fate. Amor fati is a Latin expression that means loving your fate, including suffering and loss. The key to achieving Amor Fati is an attitude of deep acceptance of the events that take place in your life. It is the practice of embracing what happens, particularly the painful things. You don't have to like what is

---

*GRIP is a deeply transformative program for prisoners with life sentences (https://insight-out.org). *Amor fati* (love of fate) is a Latin phrase that may be used to describe an attitude in which one sees everything that happens in one's life, including suffering and loss, as good or, at the very least, necessary (https://en.wikipedia.org/wiki/Amor_fati).

going on and you don't have to agree with what's going on for you to be able to accept it. The fact that a situation is presenting itself simply means you get to have the opportunity to show up for it and accept that this situation is happening. . . There is an art to learning how to bear one's suffering. The word origins of the verb "to bear" relate to the verbs "to endure" and "to give birth." Perhaps bearing our suffering refers to enduring and sustaining pain in such a way that, ultimately, through our labor, it gives birth to a new and vital realization, a new state of consciousness that offers strong guidance on how to live.[2]

THE SACRED FEMININE IS REEMERGING

From at least fifty thousand years ago until roughly six thousand years ago, an "Earth Goddess" perspective provided the primary understanding of the relationship of humans with the larger world.* The feminine archetype recognized and honored the vitality and regenerative powers of nature and the fertility of life. Then, roughly six thousand years ago, with the rise of city-states, more differentiated classes (priests, warriors, merchants), and more complex cultures, a masculine mindset and a "Sky God" spirituality became dominant and supported the development of human society organized into larger-scale structures and institutions.

A masculine, patriarchal mindset has grown and developed over thousands of years and has encouraged the growing individuation, differentiation, and empowerment of people. It has also supported humanity's growing separation from and exploitation of nature that has led to our current time of crisis and need for transition. Perhaps the last vestiges of this mindset are being expressed in hypermasculine leaders who are seeking to retreat into isolationism, nationalism, and a renewed emphasis on materialism and authoritarianism. Nonetheless, a new mindset is now emerging with the reawakening of a feminine

---

*The evolution from an "Earth Goddess" perspective to a "Sky God" perspective to the rise of the "Cosmic Goddess" is explored in my book, *Awakening Earth*.

perspective that regards the Earth—and the universe—as a unified, supportive, and regenerative organism.*

Bringing these four narratives together, we can already begin to tell a compelling story that gives new meaning to our time of transition.

Humanity is growing up and moving toward early adulthood. The global brain and human consciousness are waking up, and a species-civilization is being born that embodies the relational and nurturing perspective of the deep feminine.

With these narratives we can begin to visualize a meaningful journey ahead. In turn, if we can imagine a common journey into a purposeful future, we can build it. With a common story, we can see our supporting roles. Our lives become more meaningful, and change is less overwhelming. In this vulnerable time, it is vital for the stories we tell to be worthy of our time of Great Transition. If we are without a compelling story and feel lost, then it is easy to be frightened and to focus on threats to our security and survival. New energy policies, for example, do not begin to go deep enough to change our species-mind and overall sense of direction. However, a powerful story of the human journey can provide the social glue to pull us together in a common effort, and take us in a regenerative direction.

Although the breakdown and unraveling of the current world system seems inevitable, it need not represent the end of our journey, but rather a stage of fierce transition. From this larger perspective, humanity seems midway along an infinitely larger journey than we'd previously imagined. At the same time, there is ample reason to think we are headed for a climate catastrophe within this century that, without a larger story to guide us, could produce a largely uninhabitable Earth.

These are challenging times for all of humanity, whether impoverished and oppressed or wealthy and privileged. Although the specific

---

*The soul of the universe from the perspective of a feminine archetype has been developed by Anne Baring. See her magnificent book, *The Dream of the Cosmos.*

challenges we each face may vary greatly, the overarching challenge of this planetary moment is shared among us all.

It is abundantly clear that the more privileged people of the Earth must rapidly transform nearly every aspect of their lives if some form of viable species-civilization is to emerge: the energy we use, the levels and patterns of consumption we choose, the work we do and skills we develop, the homes and communities in which we live, the food we eat, the transportation we use, the education we acquire, and the way we treat people who are of different races, genders, cultural and sexual orientations, generations, and more.

The wealthy and powerful may shield themselves temporarily, but not permanently. Eventually the privileged minority will inevitably be forced to address the fact that we cannot continue our current ways of living and still hope to have a habitable planet.

If we do not step up to meet both the material and social challenges of our times, then we are sure to follow the example of more than twenty great civilizations that have collapsed down through time, including Roman, Egyptian, Vedic, Tibetan, Minoan, classical Greek, Olmec, Mayan, Aztec, and a number of others. Our vulnerability is made starkly evident as we recognize the breakdown and disintegration of these great civilizations of the past. However, the current situation is unique in one key respect—human civilization has reached a global scale and encircles the Earth as an interdependent system. The circle has closed. Now the simultaneous downfall of all the intertwined civilizations on Earth is threatened. How can we even contemplate this devastating prospect?

An extraordinary push and unprecedented pull are at work in these transitional times. Looking only at the push and ignoring the pull places our journey in great peril. To visualize this process, imagine pushing on a length of string. Pushing ahead, the string will bunch up in front of us and create a tangle of knots. Then imagine simultaneously pulling on the string—it no longer bunches up in a jumble but can move forward in a line of progression. In the same way, if we understand and respect both the pushes and pulls of our times, we can move ahead without getting completely entangled in the process.

If we take into account only the unyielding push of the climate crisis combined with other adversarial trends, then our efforts will produce complex knots and we can easily become mired in confusion and despair. However, if we deepen our vision to include the pull already present, we have the potential to move ahead swiftly on a remarkable journey as a species.

The pull of opportunity does not eliminate the enormous tests we face. Instead it balances our approach by helping us see beyond immediate challenges to a larger vision of possibility. By recognizing and working with both the powerful push of necessity and the remarkable pull of opportunity we can find the courage, compassion, and creativity to work through the difficulties of transition.

5

The Turning of the Soil

Belinda Eriacho

BELINDA ERIACHO is from the lineages of the Diné (Navajo) and A:shiwi (Pueblo of Zuni). Her maternal clan is One-Who-Walks-Around, and she was born of the Zuni Pueblo people. She is the wisdom carrier, healer, and founder of Kaalogii LLC—which is focused on cultural and traditional teaching and inner healing—and an international speaker on various topics impacting Native American communities in the United States. Additionally, she is one of the founding members and a member of the board of directors of the Church of the Eagle and the Condor. She has also appeared on many podcasts on the topics of intergenerational trauma, cultural appropriation and cultural appreciation, and healing with sacred plant medicines. Belinda is the author of numerous articles available on charuna.net. More information can be found on her website: https://kaalogii.com.

◆ ◆ ◆

This chapter is dedicated to my dear mother, Irene. I was blessed to be a part of her life's journey and to know her unconditional love.

YÁʼÁTʼÉÉH SHIKʼÈÍ dóó shidineʼè (Hello my relatives and people).

This chapter provides a basic *innerstanding* of the Prophecy of the Eagle and the Condor and this time of great change that humanity is experiencing.[1] To innerstand is to have absolute, heart-centered knowledge from the core of one's inner being or Source, and is the zero-point to knowledge and being.[2]

This is a time of reawakening to ourselves, and a time of the reemergence of the ancient wisdoms of Indigenous peoples across the globe. Currently we are at the intersection between these ancient wisdoms and the psychedelic renaissance. Much of what I share in this chapter has been shared by many elders, both in the past and today.[3] Are we listening and trying to incorporate this knowledge, or is it seen as mere myth and folklore?

PROPHECY OF THE EAGLE AND THE CONDOR

We are in a time that many of our Native American and Indigenous ancestors prophesied about. These times of change were foretold by Indigenous and Native American people around the globe. It is a time of great change and awakening. As we look around us, we see the changes in our healthcare system, the dismantling of political systems across the globe, and the awakening to the truth that many of the institutions we believed were here to help us, are not. Let's not forget to go within and acknowledge the changes we are experiencing. Many of us have had to look at and deal with our shadows and the inner healing of our souls. These shadows are aspects we don't want to acknowledge, to look at, to accept, to embrace. And yet these shadows contribute to the collective consciousness of humanity.

In North America, Thomas Banyacya, an elder of the Hopi, delivered a message for all people.[4] In 1948 an elder had shared with Thomas a message to warn humanity to change its ways. The Hopi prophecy tells of two stone tablets that contained the instructions from Creator on how to take care of the land, and the consequences of what would happen if the instructions were not followed. One set of tablets was given to the brown brother and the other to the white brother. The older white brother was told to take the tablet and go in the eastward direction to take care of things on the other side of the world. The white brother was given special permission to record things if he followed the sacred circle. Once done, he was to return to look for his younger brown brother. In the end, the white brother did not follow the original instruction, and instead brought with him a symbol of the cross and the subsequent destruction of Indigenous people in the Americas.

In the south, yet another version of this Prophecy of the Eagle and the Condor is told.[5] In the Andean traditions and as relayed by Don Oscar Miro Quesada, a Pachakuti Mesa Kamasqa curandero, Alto Misagyoq,*

> According to the Prophecy, the essential feature of this nascent age is the extraordinary planetary crisis and upheaval. Tied to the cumulative effects of alienation, separation, and deep amnesia, this crisis increasingly characterizes both humanity and the world. The defining moment of this age is the "re-encounter" of all elements having suffered separation during humanity's prior unfolding. It becomes a time of coming together of peoples, ancestry, and traditions, along with the restoration of harmony between humankind and Mother Nature. It culminates symbolically in the meeting of all races, and their "breaking bread" together at the table of the World Teacher. This event indicates the emergence of humanity from its illusion of separation.

As I learned of these prophecies, I was reminded of these words: "Those that fail to learn from history are doomed to repeat it."[6] I believe there is no such thing as coincidence, that these prophecies are being told once again for a reason, just as they were told by our elders and ancestors of the Americas. The retelling of these prophecies warns us of our past and present behaviors and how they might impact our future if we do not change. We are at the eleventh hour.[7] The decisions we make will affect the future of our children, grandchildren, great-grandchildren, and their children.

---

*A Quechuan term that means "High Ceremonial Priest."

In the Diné culture my ancestors offered prayers with *táádidíín* (corn pollen) or white corn meal to the Diyin Diné (the Holy Ones) for protection, longevity, love for their families, and thanksgiving for all that exists.[8] These are the same prayers I offer with white cornmeal or táádidíín to the same Diyin Diné as the sun peeks over the eastern horizon. In the Diné teachings of the cycle of life we become the ancestors for those grandchildren and great-grandchildren when we are called back to the spirit world.[9] As the five-fingered people of the Earth, we are blessed to be the beings making the connection between the heavens and the Earth.[10] How fortunate we are, and yet many do not truly know their place and purpose. You see, my sisters and brothers, we each have a choice to make the decision of right actions.[11]

It is time to make a choice. Do we continue down the road to repeat history, or do we stand up for the natural order of life? What type of legacy will you choose for the children, grandchildren, and great-grandchildren? I have made my choice. When it is time to make that choice, I would suggest that the decision you make comes from your heart and not from your mind.

THE AWAKENING TO THE SELF

I remember the times when I was a child and my siblings and I would spend parts of our summer break with our maternal grandparents. We herded sheep, rode horses, and found time to play in our makeshift swimming pools, made from the soil and the muddy water that had collected after a rainstorm. Looking back at those times now as an elder, I am saddened that these similar experiences will not be experienced by my grandchildren. Today the old ways of living have been forgotten and things have become modernized.

My childhood was a time of being with nature and learning from my grandparents about the old ways.[12] Shima sani (my maternal grandmother) always knew when to harvest the banana fruit from the yucca plants; she knew when the ewes were lambing, and when and where to harvest food and medicine from the plants in nature. These were times for contemplation with ourselves and with each other. During these times with our grandparents, we sat around the rectangular, retro metal table as the kerosene lamp flickered between us, listening to our grandparents' stories and explaining to Grandmother that the world is round.

In my Diné culture there is a word, *hózhó,* that in a general way, defines such a time in terms of the principles that guide it. Hózhó is a short term for Sa'ah Naagháí Bik'eh Hózhóón (SNBH). This set of philosophical concepts informs our lives as Diné people. As such, they are keys to help guide our moral and behavioral conduct to live a long, healthy life. In these concepts, great value is placed on the importance of maintaining relationships "by developing pride of one's body, mind, soul, spirit and honoring life."[13] Hózhó reflects the process, the path or journey by which an individual strives toward and attains a state of wellness.[14] As I reflect on this concept of hózhó I can't help but wonder why we in Western society don't have such principles to guide humanity's conduct in these modern times. Is this the reason for the chaos in our world today?

The medicine we receive in our lives includes all aspects of life. Just as many of us have begun our inner healing journey sitting with a therapist or counselor, I too found myself in such a situation. I was a young professional at the time, and honestly, I had no idea why I was even there. Looking back on that experience I know it was Creator's way of nudging me onto the path of healing and onto my medicine journey. I was ready to begin my own hero's journey of healing the past.[15] Ultimately I found the conversations with the therapist helpful, as she peeled back the layers of the past and helped me to innerstand why I was there.

My first awakening to myself was during my first journey with Shima saní azééd (grandmother plant medicine, or ayahuasca). I wrote in my journal after that initial experience, "The biggest battle we will face is with ourselves." In that first mystical journey I recalled memories of my childhood. Some of those memories were pleasant and others not so pleasant. From a place of inner knowing, I began to ask, "Who is witnessing these events?" Was this the inner child that so many spoke of?[16]

As Grandmother Aya worked on me, I was able to release the emotional connectedness to the painful memories, to forgive myself and others surrounding those experiences. My tears helped to erase the emotions from my consciousness and to find inner healing. This healing also included the healing of my ancestors and the intergenerational traumas experienced at the internment camps of Hwéeldi, or on the Long Walk to Bosque Redondo, as well as helping clear the path for future generations of my family. From my own experiences, I know these beautiful relatives are here to awaken us and heal our inner being.

WE ARE RELATED

From my perspective as a Native American woman, I have always been taught from an early age by my parents, grandparents, and relatives to respect all beings. I have been taught that I am part of everything that exists—from the elements of air, fire, water, Mother Earth, and the ethers, the stones, and the stars in the heavens.[17] This interconnectedness also applies to our plant relatives. If we use our personal relationship with a family member as an analogy, just as we would take great care of our elderly grandmother, with reverence, so too should we take care and have reverence for all plants, including the sacred plant medicines. This care and reverence should occur throughout the entire cycle of life, from cradle to cradle of the plant, and not just pertain to the consumption of it.[18] In my culture there are prayers and offerings that are made when we take the life of a plant for healing. We explain to the plant why we are taking its life, and for whom the plant medicine will be used. We then offer a token of táádidíín or corn meal, a prayer, and gratitude. Through this sacred exchange we are considered equals in the cycles of Creation and we follow natural law.

As I travel the world and speak on topics related to psychedelics, I find Western society has forgotten this interconnectedness—not only the interconnectedness between themselves and their external environment, but with their inner selves. Without this innerstanding we will continue to experience the overcommodification of these sacred plant medicines. I find there is a mindset in Western society that "because I am privileged, I am entitled." This is contrary to Native American and Indigenous cultural teachings. I bring this point forward in order that we begin the healing process first with these sacred plant relatives. Not being in right relationship from the start can compromise the healing process with those who consume the plant medicines. This right relationship also implies that we do not use these sacred plant medicines for recreational purposes. As the prophecies indicate, our future communities will not tolerate duality and will operate from a place of equality. There will be no hierarchical systems of control, and we women will have a stronger voice in the care of our families once again.

THE INTERSECTION OF ANCIENT WISDOM AND THE PSYCHEDELIC RENAISSANCE

As the prophecies tell us, we are at an intersection of cultures, between the ancient wisdom of Indigenous people, through our lived experiences, and the so-called, "psychedelic renaissance." Where do we go from here as a human society, as sisters and brothers? What are the answers?

First, we must not see ourselves as human beings separate from the universe and everything that exists around us. In the Andean tradition of the Q'eros people there is a spiritual principle, *ayni,* which translates into "sacred reciprocity." The belief is that we give and receive in equal measure, and that we cannot take more from nature than we give to nature.[19] In order for Western society to appreciate sacred plant medicine, everyone will need to come to this innerstanding.

The second point I'd like to make is that the field of psychedelic medicine will need to embrace the concept associated with spirituality and healing. We can no longer teach those in the helping professions about healing without a conversation and lessons about the interplay that spirituality has on human beings. It has been my personal experience in my travels that researchers, psychologists, therapists, and medical doctors are afraid to incorporate spirituality into their practices. Another point to be made is that many do not know how to embrace the concepts of spirituality, such as ritual and ceremony, into their practices. In my conversations with medical students I am saddened that many of these concepts are not taught in our institutions of higher learning. The best antidote I can offer is that as a practitioner one needs to come from the heart and not from the mind in the care of clients and patients. I am reminded of the wisdom a Takelma elder once shared, "The greatest distance in the work is the fourteen inches from our minds to our hearts."[20]

My third point is that much can be learned from Indigenous and Native American ways of healing. The wisdom of these rituals and ceremonies is based on the practical experiences of our ancestors over millennia. It is a true model of wholeness. In the Diné culture it is said that we have physical, mental, spiritual, and emotional bodies. If one of these bodies is not in sync with the other, an imbalance is created in our life and in our well-being. Unfortunately, there is often a reluctance by Western, science-based models to include aspects of this wholeness model. My suggestion is that Western practitioners incorporate these culturally based modalities into their practice when working with Native American individuals and communities. They should also innerstand that these practices are very real and not derived from folklore.

From a Native American perspective, there is a place for the Western medical model of healing. However, I believe this model misses the opportunity for healing at its core, which is comprised of the emotional and spiritual levels. As practitioners, if our focus is to be the catalyst for healing those who come to us, we need to open our hearts, open our under- and innerstanding as to what is possible to achieve, and meet our clients and patients where they are in order for true healing to occur.

As I look to the future and the world that my grandchildren, great-grandchildren, and the next seven generations will inherit, I see and know that the paradigm of healing is shifting.[21] I have seen this in my visions with the sacred plant medicines. This shift is partly due to a change in our understanding, to an innerstanding of who we are as human beings, and a return to natural law. Fundamental to healing is the concept of energy, and from energy is frequency.[22] The ancient teachings, prayers, chants, rituals, and ceremonies performed by my ancestors and with traditional healers today are fundamental to creating healing at an energetic level.

Another key point is that we are our own best healers. I know this from my own healing journey with systemic lupus. The ceremonies and prayers I experienced with traditional healers have helped me restore my health back into wholeness. At an energetic level, my belief in my healing transmits energy to my four bodies and restores my health, which the relatives of the plant kingdom were very much a part of. The insights I received from the sacred plant medicines also gave me the understanding of who I am as a wisdom carrier of the teaching of my ancestors, and principles for healing.

The prophecies are a great reminder to each of us of our role in the microcosm and macrocosm of the universe. There is much to be said for the phrase *we create our own reality.* For the longest time, I, like others, believed that my reality was created by external influences on me. I was wrong. Through our inner knowing as five-fingered people, we individually create the world that exists outside of ourselves. If we take this as the truth, then we have a choice in the future and the legacy we will leave our children and grandchildren. This is a time to replace our fears with compassion. It is a time to come from our hearts and not our minds.

In conclusion, I offer cedar to the sacred directions, and a prayer for the healing of humanity, for the healing of our ancestors, gratitude for Mother Earth, connection to our cosmic families, and a world of light and love for the next seven generations.

We can practice resurrection. We can dance each other home.

JAMIE WHEAL

6

The Cosmic Orphan and
the Wound of the World

Jamie Wheal

JAMIE WHEAL is the coauthor of the global bestseller *Stealing Fire: How Silicon Valley, the Navy SEALs, and Maverick Scientists Are Revolutionizing the Way We Live and Work,* and the founder of the Flow Genome Project, an organization dedicated to the research and training of human performance. His work and ideas are in great demand and have been covered in numerous leading publications. His latest book is *Recapture the Rapture: Rethinking God, Sex, and Death in a World That's Lost Its Mind.* Jamie lives in the United States, near the Colorado River, with his wife, Julie, their two kids, and a golden retriever named Aslan.

◆ ◆ ◆

> *I tell you this*
> *to break your heart,*
> *by which I mean only*
> *that it break open and never close again*
> *to the rest of the world.*
>
> MARY OLIVER, "LEAD"

A FEW MONTHS AGO someone called me out as a *cosmic orphan.* The phrase intrigued me, so I looked it up. Turns out that it's an expression of the German concept of *weltschmertz,* which roughly translates as "world weariness" or "the wound of the world." John Steinbeck wrote about it in *East of Eden,* Ralph Ellison, speaking of the African American experience, riffed on it in his *Invisible Man,* and Kurt Vonnegut name-checked it in *Player Piano.* One author called it "homesickness for a place you have never seen."[1] That's the cosmic orphan in a nutshell: a grieving for what is, coupled with a yearning for what could or should be.

WE'RE ALL COSMIC ORPHANS, REALLY

And in many ways, we're all cosmic orphans—thrust into this mixed-up, muddled-up, shook-up world, with barely a say in the matter. We're homesick for a place we've never seen, but still, somehow, *remember.* The Greek term for that feeling of deep remembrance is *anamnesis*—literally, the opposite of amnesia. It's the "forgetting of the forgetting," and it often shows up in ecstatic practices such as the ingestion of psychedelics. "There's something about [the profound psychedelic experience] that feels . . ." Ann Shulgin, therapist and partner to renegade chemist Sasha Shulgin, writes . . . "well, the only way that I can put it is that it's like coming home."[2]

Shulgin's words echo the Hebrew notion that our souls go through three phases of existence over our lifetimes—the pre-tragic, the tragic, and the post-tragic. And while not everyone makes it to the final stage, this three-step progression points out a way home for all of us.

In the pre-tragic phase, everything is safe, womb-like, peaceful. It's our #bestlife where everything works out, and our world is filled with endless possibilities. It's first felt in the buffered bliss of the amniotic sack, and maybe in the warmth that persists through a stable and loving childhood. But inevitably the pre-tragic phase—where we are safe, loved, and cared for—doesn't last. At some point, the contractions and pressures of the birth canal shunt us out into a hard, cold, loud reality. We run smack-dab into the wound of the world, and we feel it as pain, confusion, frustration, or resentment.

And now, welcome to the tragic phase. (If you've ever raised teenagers, this is where much of their angsty angst comes from. So too with many grievance-based social movements.) "We didn't ask for this, we didn't sign up for it!" we protest. All that happened to bring us into existence is that two random humans swapped genetic material. A brief flash of green light where sperm met egg and atoms of zinc exploded (as scientists at Northwestern University in Illinois discovered a few years ago).

Fiat lux. "Let there be light." And here we are.

But once we're wounded by the world and get swamped by the even bigger wound of the *whole* world, we often want out. There's an element of "f*ck this, didn't sign up for it, don't deserve it, don't want it!" So in the face of nearly overwhelming tragedy and injustice we attempt to crawl back into the womb (an awkward philosophical and gynecological prospect on the best of days). *We seek escape, transcendence, soothing.* It might be in binge-watching and digital distractions, in intoxication or psychedelic exploration, in acquiring the baubles of material status, in cultic groupthink and conspiracy theories, in esoteric spirituality and magical thinking where "everything happens for a reason."

No matter the mechanism, we seek to bypass the unsolvable train wreck of the human experience. We deny this life and devalue it because it hurts too much to embrace it fully. Lately it's only been getting more intense. We're all being dragged into the tragic experience of living through a world in crisis. Any and all of our pre-tragic notions, whether dreams of 2.2 kids, a picket fence, and a pension plan, or more idealized visions of spiritual enlightenment—or truly egalitarian civilization—are getting dashed on the rocks of brute reality.

This presents an existential threat to our very being. Because what we want, what we cosmic orphans often yearn for, is a return to the womb, where we're loved, safe, and secure, and everything is going to work out. But the obstacle, as the famous Roman emperor and Stoic philosopher Marcus Aurelius reminds us, *is* the way. What stands in the way becomes the Way. And the same is true for how we can move from cosmic orphans wrestling with the monkey puzzle of existence to humans who've found our way home.

ACCELERATE FORWARD TO THE END

Rather than trying to claw back our pre-tragic beginnings, we can accelerate forward to the *end*. We can face death, but on our own terms, and in our own time. *We can engage in the deliberate initiation of "death practice."* Lest that sound morbid or frightening, it's important to note that death practices are as old as human culture—ranging from Indigenous trials of shamanic dismemberment (and reassembly) to Lakota sun dances (where supplicants are suspended by their flesh) to the Eleusinian Mysteries of ancient Greece, which Plato attested "teach us not only how to die a better death, but to live a better life!" They've literally provided the *seedbed of most philosophy, art, culture, and belief for our entire species.*

All ecstatic practices—whether they involve psychedelics, meditation, sex, or extreme sports, are all in their way, death practices. We'd do well to reintegrate them into our lives and traditions.

Goethe perhaps said it best, "He who does not know the secret 'die and become' shall remain forever a stranger on this earth." Forever a stranger on this earth . . . sounds a lot like the cosmic orphanage.

So why all this waxing poetic about dying and becoming? What could possibly be so meaningful about becoming a "twice-born" human? Simply, choice.

THE POWER OF FREE WILL

Because remember, the first time we were born, we had little say in the matter. That lack of consent leads to much of our suffering, as well as our counterproductive efforts to escape or bypass the nitty and the gritty. But once we have experienced "dying and becoming" we, like Ebenezer Scrooge, or Jimmy Stewart in *It's a Wonderful Life,* or even Dorothy joyfully returning to Kansas, get to *choose this existence,* without qualification or compromise.

We were never given that choice the first time. But we can offer it to ourselves and each other a second time. We can do this by choosing to enact an initiatory death practice. Once we heed the call, once we say an unequivocal, full-bodied, openhearted "FUCK YES!" to the rest of our lives, *we are reborn into the post-tragic potency of being HomeGrown Humans.*

"Was Grace that taught my heart to fear, and grace my fears relieved," the old hymn goes, "how precious did that Grace appear, the hour I first believed!"

Our death right can become our (re)birthright. Once we step off the hamster wheel of seeking pleasure and avoiding pain, and embrace the full catastrophe of the human condition, we unlock a powerful force. Gandhi called it "satyagraha." Howard Thurman and Martin Luther King called it "soul force." It's the power that is unleashed when a human being sets aside their own references and preferences and takes a stand for Goodness, Truth, and Beauty. Twice-born. Anthropos. Once we've been born a second time, dying again won't seem so hard.

(And no one gets out of here alive.)

MECHANISMS OF ACTION BEHIND DEATH PRACTICES

What's so interesting and exciting is that, for the first time, the notion of death/rebirth rituals aren't philosophical or metaphysical anymore. There are actually straight-up *neuro-physiological protocols that reliably deliver the goods.* What transpires is:

- a deep reset of the brain stem
- a deceleration of brain waves into low delta frequencies (compounds such as nitrous oxide, ketamine, and 5-MeO-DMT all prompt this effect, as does electrical entrainment)
- a rise in heart rate variability and vagal tone
- a flushing of hormones and neurotransmitters

Code in those parameters and you will have a rich and ineffable experience of dying and becoming. Because we now know the mechanisms of action behind these experiences, we don't have to wrap them in esoteric or exclusionary belief systems—we can strip out the mythologies but keep the technologies.

Believe what you want to believe, just never lose the faith. 'Cause lord knows, we could all do with a bit more of it these days. We now have the tool kit for a DIY initiation into recapturing our rapture—our bliss, our belonging, our becoming—so that we can rise up, stand up, and lend our voices to how this all goes down.

Does it matter?

Will it work?

No idea. But it's a solid shot to nudge the scales at least a little bit in the right direction.

We don't have to remain cosmic orphans, isolated in our despair, alienated in our grief. We can learn to weep rather than whimper. We can find our brothers and sisters, who can hear the truth in what we say. And we can do it with creativity, courage, and conviction. If we lose our lives (for a moment) we get to fully *choose* our lives (forever after).

We can practice resurrection. We can dance each other home.

Within all of us there is this memory. Ancestral memory. It reconnects the thread of life; it can heal the pain of separation.

GRANDMOTHER MARIA ALICE CAMPOS FREIRE

Ancestral Memory

The Flowering of the Seed

Grandmother Maria Alice Campos Freire

MARIA ALICE CAMPOS FREIRE is a highly respected member of the International Council of Thirteen Indigenous Grandmothers. She is a healer with plant medicine, leader of Umbanda ceremonies, founder of Centro Medicina da Floresta, and cocreator of the Flower Essences of the Amazon. Grandmother Maria Alice has developed research and healing methods with plants of the Amazon, as well as educational programs for children that teach preservation of nature and sustainable development.

◆ ◆ ◆

DESPITE THE GREAT ATTACK and terrors inflicted on Mother Earth, she continues to show her beauty and generosity. In her infinite resilience, she draws from deep within herself the fresh water that comforts and quenches our thirst, the fruits that satisfy our hunger, and the forests that welcome our spirit and reconnect us to the universe and the stars. This beauty, this generosity, and this same resilience is also within us. Yes. Because we are her children. We are born from within her; we are part of her manifestation of life.

This chapter was translated from the Portuguese by Sofia Reis.

Many, however, are forgetful of themselves, sick in soul, lacking direction.

The first time I drank the sacred drink of the peoples of the Amazon, it lit up in me the light of this profound revelation—the revelation of this beauty, this abundance, this generosity, this light of love. Once again I received from Mother Earth, from the mysterious power of her plants, the gift of my divine memory.

When this happened, I was already committed to overcoming my own forgetfulness. After so much pain, the voice of the ancestors whispered in me. It wasn't in the mind, precisely because the mind had become forgetful of the inside. It was only a whisper that sang in my heart. It sang the song of the ancestors, the rituals of praise to nature, to divinity, to the elements, to all Creation. Where did that voice come from? It didn't come from the outside, it came from the inside, it was a memory. Great lesson. It taught me to pay attention to this breath of memory that manifests in the feeling of the heart.

Whenever I feel great anguish, I run to the waters. The waters speak to me from the beyond, from the mystery. They connect me to a safe place where there is peace. The memory of this peace is what led me on. This divine memory is enchanted within us. This is the big mystery—because we were born to carry out right here, on Mother Earth, the confirmation of this eternal lineage. And so even when our bodies go silent and become the compost of the Earth and our consciousness returns to the unity of the universe, we will always be Mother Earth's children.

Yes. Because she is the one who opens the door to our realization as humanity. When we are children, our universal memory is still fresh. We easily embrace the teaching of Mother Earth, we gladly surrender to her—to her beauty, to her waters, to the connection with all her kingdoms, and to her secrets.

I remember my childhood. My mother loved to grow flowers and I loved participating in her gardening. It was an intimate moment of interaction with her, with the land, and with the plants. I remember when I discovered that flowers were unique individuals with their own identities. Some liked the sun more, others the shade. They had preferences for socializing and it was possible to dialogue with them. That opened up a new world to my child soul. It was like an initiation. It propelled me toward the contemplation of nature. I discovered that the moon had an influence on plants, and that, for example, it was necessary to wait for the new moon to plant the flowers; they would bloom and grow with the movement of the moon. This was fantastic! A new portal opened with the contemplation of the moon, the sky, and the constellations. There were many families of stars and planets, as well as plant families, animal families, and people families. And they all formed one big family.

Between heaven and earth, there was an infinite world of experiences and discoveries, which naturally led me to understand myself as a very small part of a greater being. That time of the freedom of childhood, of natural discoveries, was a period of bliss in which my being grew along with all of life. Everything breathed in the same rhythm; there was harmony. Above all there was an underlying awareness of the existence of a higher unity that had to be revered and that was always present in the sky, on the earth, in the water, in the flower, in the bird, in the butterfly—outside us and within us. These experiences were seeds planted in my inner earth and would later germinate in my field of consciousness as a meaningful memory.

But then came the time of trauma, the denial of this freedom, the sowing of doubt and separation. It was the time for my insertion into society by way of school. And it coincided with a time of the military dictatorship. In that world, flowers didn't speak to us, and there was no room for experiments. There was no place for the presentation of knowledge born from the exercise of living and experimenting. It was another world. There was an incomprehensible hierarchy. Those who occupied the highest positions were not luminous; they did not resemble the sky, the moon, or the stars. They were stern and imperious. In this way, they did not help us to grow with joy or to cooperate.

That's why I shut up.

We were all supposed to be silent, and the main teaching was separation. Each one should reach for the top alone. Each one should strive to be the best, which would be the path of a successful human being in society. Therefore we remained silent. Talking was dangerous, as it might let slip some secret that could be the key to success. And where was that pulse of life that made us feel part of a whole—of a greater organism that was majestic, loving, and supreme? It wasn't there. There the supreme was something else altogether. There they spoke only of a grim and punishing god that we must fear.

So our questioning, our speech, became guarded, so well-guarded that it became hidden, and we even forgot about it. Yes, it was better to forget the question, as it might not be appropriate. You had to focus on the fear. That was the most important thing. Fear God, fear the authorities, and fear that our fellow men would get ahead of us.

When the speech decided to come out, it had already turned into a scream. And so the battle cry was born. The battle cry is difficult to unravel. It carries with it the extreme appeal of a life that doesn't want to die, that struggles to live. And in this sense, it is positive, it drives action. The challenge is to discover what that action is, which can be assertive in the sense of rescuing the thread of life, of joy, of the bliss of the soul. The battle cry is very strong. It can no longer be stopped.

The dangerous thing about it is that it always tries to hit an enemy, but it can't always identify which enemy this is. An enemy that hinders us, that is unjust, that is oppressive, that overshadows the grace of living. Who is it? Where is it? I found that going out in search of the culprit is a detour. The enemy is oblivion itself, and it is within us. Therefore it becomes important to consider our cry, because it springs from the life we want to live. It is the link to our own nature. It expresses the yearning for liberation.

With this cry caught in my throat, I went in search of release. And throughout this existence I've been overcoming mistakes, I've been counting blows, I've been breaking through clouds of illusion and opening horizons. With each new step, with each realization that it wasn't quite the right shot, I would find myself again with my battle cry. What war is this that I want to fight, if I don't want to hurt people, if I don't want to kill, if I don't want sadness or loneliness?

I had to go through the pain. I had to know prison, torture, persecution, exile, humiliation, always looking for a reencounter with the bliss of the soul. Always in search of beauty, equanimity, harmony—something, anything—that would soothe my soul, suffocated by a cry that was still looking for the right path.

It was when the voice of Spirit, of the ancestral root, whispered in my heart, that I was guided to the sacrament of the forest. Tired of the battle cry, I dove into the memory and into the true nature of my cry. Cry of Peace! Cry of Life! Cry of Freedom!

Within all of us there is this memory. Ancestral memory. It reconnects the thread of life; it can heal the pain of separation. What memory is this? Where is it? It is within us, in our suffocated scream, in our abandoned childhood. It's in the deep waters of our being where the cry of our pain lives, where the memory of our ancestry also lives. Hear the voice of the heart. It speaks to us, directs us to discover that we are not alone, that we are part of a whole, that we belong to a larger organism to which our life is directly linked, that feeds us, that quenches our thirst, that comforts us, that introduces us to beauty and harmony.

We often forget. Forgetting is part of the plunge into the dark that will clear up with the awakening of consciousness—the mysteries of Mother Earth. We came from the light, we were born from love, but we need to know pain and forgetfulness to reach knowledge, and to choose to be what we came here to be. It is like the seed, which was born from the flower, from the fruit, from the sunlight. It must dive into the dark of Mother Earth, know the cold, and lose its shape, to open the bud and restart the cycle of life.

So too the sacrament, the sacred drink, teaches us—ayahuasca, *camarambi, uni, daime,* Santo Daime—each name a secret. The sacred drink is born from the vine and the leaf, from the fire and the water. Each part does not reveal knowledge in itself. It must lose its form and surrender to the simmering of the preparation to be able to liberate the light of its true identity and destiny.

Everything in Nature's mirror reveals our own nature.

And so here are we—humanity, submerged in the dark. We have forgotten, we are inside out. But within us we can observe the germination of seeds, the blossoming of buds, the promise of flowers. And all of this experience can be transformed into living knowledge, capable of recovering the thread of life. We have the data, we can process it.

Live, yes. Kill, no more.
Unite, yes. Separate, no more.
Yell, yes.
Cry of Peace, yes.
Cry of War, no more.
Planting, yes.
Cultivating, yes.
Our divine memory.
Cooperate, yes. Compete, no more.
Change, always.
Learn, always.
Praise, always.
And forever—gratitude.

*Beyond the brilliant immersion into La Medicina in the
dark of the jungle night, our task is to carry that light . . .*
CHRIS KILHAM

8

Out Past
the Shipping Lanes

Chris Kilham

CHRIS KILHAM is a medicine hunter who has conducted medicinal plant exploration in more than forty-five countries. He has taught yoga and meditation since 1971, has appeared on over five hundred TV and two thousand radio programs worldwide, and is the author of fifteen books including *The Ayahuasca Test Pilots Handbook* and *The Lotus and the Bud*. He lives in Leverett, Massachusetts. His website is www.medicinehunter.com.

◆ ◆ ◆

FROM MY EARLIEST childhood to now I have enjoyed at least some of each summer along the Maine coast, swimming, bodysurfing, kayaking, and playing in bracing, cold Atlantic water. On a clear day you can look many miles out to sea and make out the outlines of cargo ships, fuel ships, and other large vessels working the coastal shipping lanes. Between the little bay where I enjoy summer and the shipping lanes is a great expanse of islands and miles of fishing waters. After that, it's the deep blue sea. When I have kayaked around the islands in greater Casco Bay, I've had a closer look at the monster vessels that ply the seas. Minke whales, fin whales, great white sharks, and other large creatures of the sea also hunt and play there. It's spooky. The water is deep, the currents unfamiliar, the winds stronger. Nobody kayaks out past the shipping lanes.

And yet right now I am way out past the shipping lanes, a spirit wind in my hair, the depths of the space around me unknown. I sense large and powerful entities around me, shifting and swirling tides. Insects chirp and crick, and disco music plays just audibly enough on scratchy speakers to annoy, miles away. In a small maloca outside of the Yarinacocha area of Pucallpa, Peru, I sit in the Amazon night with my friend Lord Nelson and two shamans, Rolando Tangoa and Cecilio Cauper. The maloca is at Rolando's center Noya Rao, named after a magical tree regarded highly by some of the Native people in Peru's Amazon. I know Rolando from ceremony years before. Back in the heady days of *Espiritu de Anaconda,* Rolando showed up sometime in 2008 and sang spellbinding *ícaros,* which are healing, shamanic songs. I liked him immediately. He is one of three extraordinary shamans, along with Ricardo Amaringo and Jorge Lopez, who apprenticed for many years with Guillermo Arevalo. These three are titanic, and their ceremonies are profound. Cecilio is new to me.

Rolando is big and stocky, while Cecilio is light and compact. Rolando wears shorts and a white T-shirt, while Cecilio wears black. Rolando sits in one spot, sings and smokes, while Cecilio stands and waves his arms while he sings. Yin and yang. The *mareacion,* the effects of the ayahuasca, come on slow and steady, and then just keep on coming. Rolando the immovable object and Cecilio the body in motion trade ícaros, sing together, smoke, laugh.

My body is dissolving in the warm night air, the boundaries of my physical form melting into the darkness. I am at times luminous ecto-plasm, pulsing with energy, from low-level photon emissions to electri-cal cardiac pulses, a million energized nerve channels and plexuses. The spirit world yawns open as it always does when I drink ayahuasca, and various diaphanous figures float about in the ceremonial space. A multi-tentacled form, electrical and undulating, hovers above me. From this form, energy pulses directly at me, each pulse a mystic breeze blowing me further out to sea. Over to the right in a corner a giant anaconda peers out through the blackness, looking at me from across the room. The snake stares dispassionately while a smoky mist radiates from its head. The anaconda almost always shows up, from my first ceremony ten years prior to now, an ally I did not ask for but gained at the onset of my journeys with La Medicina. On my first encounter, the anaconda pounded the center of my chest with energy until I was sure that my ribs would crack. At other times it slithered around the maloca. The anaconda and I have stared deeply into each other's eyes, into infinity, into the all and the everything. The anaconda embodies the medicine. It delivers and conveys energy and mystic awareness and a sense of gigantic nature—of the expansion of my being—so broadly and vividly, that there is at times very little left of me at all. Occasionally the anaconda has swallowed me whole, and I have returned the favor.

It is altogether weird.

Neuroscientists say the number of connections that can be made between the one hundred billion neurons in the human brain exceeds the number of atoms in the universe. And we know that while we all live by patterns that correlate to neuronal channels in the brain, we make new channels, perhaps many of hundreds of them, when we consume psychedelics. The sense of vastness we experience, and that I am experiencing as Rolando and Cecilio weave their spell of ícaros, has a lot to do with the suspension and dissolution of old neuronal channels. Instead of thinking, feeling, or reacting according to old grooves, we expand. This is a spacious experience, and the possibilities for new thoughts, feelings, and reactions are endless.

I encounter one entity after another, and recall wise advice from Hamilton Souther, founder of Blue Morpho. "Only let in the spirits that are kind, wise, and have your best interests at heart," he told me. Every ceremony I make the declaration that any entity that is kind and wise and has my best interests at heart can come close, and all others must stay away. I see many strange forms and entities move in, skim along the perimeter of an invisible fence of protection, and vaporize into darkness. There are robots with tomato-can heads, strange human-like creatures that move sideways and then skittle off into shadows, dark forms stained with death. Friendly spirits move in and brush up close, imparting feelings of goodness.

True healing puts into order the body, mind, and spirit with the past, present, and future. The medicine, and the talent of the shamans, conspire to establish that order. Rolando says that if you can't be the pencil that writes somebody's happiness, then be the eraser that takes away their pain. The strange visions that come and go are all part of a healing process that may seem utterly nonsensical yet results in an overall sense of profound refreshment of self, a renewal, a topped-off tank, and batteries fully charged. I have seen so many people arrive for ayahuasca ceremonies burdened one way or another by old wounds, and have witnessed equally many relieved of those burdens.

At one point the heads of a thousand souls rise in the air, all of them bearing curious resemblance to the figure in Edvard Munch's *The Scream*. Are they pretas, hungry ghosts? Are they wandering a netherworld dissatisfied and imprisoned there? I am curious, watching. I tell myself, *Remember to breathe. Allow everything to let go as much as possible. Relax the muscles I do not need. Allow the breath to move gently. Focus on the ícaros, the healing ayahuasca songs.*

Rolando sings and medicine pours out into the ceremonial space. The vast numbers of howling souls rise and are gone. Cecilio waves his arms, singing vigorously while standing in front of Lord Nelson. Cecilio is giving him the big treatment. Lord Nelson needs healing and is getting it.

Periodically Rolando asks amigo Chris, *"Como esta la ceremonia?"*

"Muy bien," I reply. *"Fuerte."* He and Cecilio like that and they chuckle. They are amused that we are ripped to the eyeballs. I bum a *mapacho* from Rolando, smoke part of it. "Elevator in the brain hotel" as Donovan sang in "Epistle to Dippy." According to some very fine, human clinical studies, the psychedelics modify gene expression, amplifying genes that enhance health, suppressing inflammation, boosting immune function, stimulating the production of neuroprotective factors. I watch a golden, blue, purple, and orange being working the vast and intricate wheels of time before me, even as I dissolve further until I am nothing much but a self-reflecting beam of energy. My genes are madly switching on and off, and I feel a magnifi-

cent power—not just raw energy but a holistic force that elevates and enhances everything.

Come back to the center. Stay focused, aware. Breathe. Close to fifty years of daily yoga and meditation aid me in navigating the spirit landscape. *Pay attention, form no attachments, ride the energy.* The Yoganusasanam, the great yogic sermon, says that a yogi does not bow to a gale, but rides upon its crest. I learned in my first ceremony to let go, to abandon resistance, to breathe and get into the center of the energy, to be swept away by the medicine while remaining alert, focused. It is the lotus and the vine, the navigational skills imparted by my daily integrative practice of yoga, and the spirit force of the ayahuasca. The maloca can be my MMA octagon with blood and pain and broken bones. Or it can be my temple, with the sweet and loving touch of spirit everywhere, wafting floral incense, flickering candles. I choose the temple.

I have a vision of my father, back when I was about thirteen, telling me something so hurtful no parent should ever say it. A string to pull, to follow to its resolution. I allow feelings of hurt, rage, incipient violence to rise unfettered, and then to stream upward into a fiery godhead of pure cosmic flame. Incineration of the pain. The shamans are singing, their ícaros penetrating the intercellular spaces of my entire being, bathing me in wise energy, washing away dirty soul residue. The yogis call these karmic accretions "samskaras," energetic impressions from our past. The ícaros, like meditation and yoga practice, cleanse and purify us. Like blowing dirt out of a clogged garden hose with pure water, the ícaros blow stuck energy out of our energetic channels, and then those channels beam and flow. I recall listening to holy songs in the Machendranath Temple in Katmandu, high on Nepalese temple ball hashish, immersed in Spirit like this.

I am very, very high now. Lord Nelson sighs audibly, and I call out to him. "You good?" He lets me know he's doing fine. "You need anything?" I ask.

"No, but thanks, amigo," he replies. I return my attention to the spirit sitting as me on my mat, to the rhythmic pattern of the ícaros, to the solar wind that blows me further out past the shipping lanes. Cecilio is on his feet waving his arms again, spectral and sinewy.

Rolando calls me up to him. I sit in front of him and he sings five ícaros for me, taking his time. The songs cleanse and beautify, illuminate and galvanize me. I am open like a V, expanded at the top, smooth energy flowing steadily upward. In the central channel of my spine, the energy intensifies and pulses upward, steady kundalini flow, the serpent power, the primordial force that animates us all and is the infinite wellspring from which the entire universe arises. A steady buzzing and ringing intensifies. It is the nada, the sound current, meditation upon which is the jewel in the crown of yogic practice. I merge into that current while the kundalini shakti intensifies from my coccyx to the crown of my head. In the corner of the maloca the anaconda stares, impassive, onyx eyes gleaming. *Go ahead,* I say to the anaconda. *Give me your best shot. I am unafraid.*

There is very little of me left to say "I." Very little thought. Instead there is the rushing energy of a vast current flowing—not just within me and not just in this maloca. It's a monumental force moving though all of human history and more. It's an aggregation of all the energy and all the life, all the molecular buzzing, frequencies of every kind—from radio waves to low-level photon emissions, the entire Big Wahoo of cosmic power. It has always been flowing. It will keep flowing.

The coastline from which I initially set sail on this journey is so far gone, it plays no part in this night. The vast and mysterious ocean beyond the shipping lanes sparkles with photoluminescence; splashes with energetic flares as big as the sun itself. It contains all the firmament, the northern lights, the Milky Way, the other billions of galaxies, the forty-nine dimensional realms of the Tibetan Buddhists, the *lokas* of the yogis.

My heart chakra bursts open. It feels as though the bones in the center of my chest have blown apart. A tractor beam of light blasts forth. The maloca lights up. I am connected to everything and everyone now. This is all grace. There is only one worthy thing in all existence, and that is love. I beam love and joy and gratitude and exaltation to my wife,

Zoe, my friends, my family, everyone I know, everyone I don't know.

After this reckoning with the infinite, after we return safely to shore, after the last mapacho has been smoked, the last ícaro has been sung, and the four of us in this wild ceremonial journey are snoozing into the earliest hours, we will need to carry this medicine forward into every aspect of our lives. It is not enough to sit mind blown and heart suffused in the maloca, diving into the luminous ocean of healing, realization, joy, gratitude, watching the wheels of time. It's a good start, essential in fact, the blowing open of interdimensional boundaries, the rising of enduring and all-conquering love, dissolution of any sense of self, the assuredness of the absolute indivisibility of the all and the everything.

Beyond the brilliant immersion into La Medicina in the dark of the jungle night, our task is to carry that light, that sense of connectedness, that obstinate compassion and determination to keep our hearts open. We cannot remain in that state of hyperintense, fully blown journeying. But we can carry what we glean; we can bring back treasures. The world with its tumult, chaos, despair, and myriad brands of suffering needs this medicine. We travel far and wide to return refreshed, invigorated to the core, ready to live as healing agents and allies of goodwill. This is the fulfillment of the medicine. May all beings be happy. May all beings find peace.

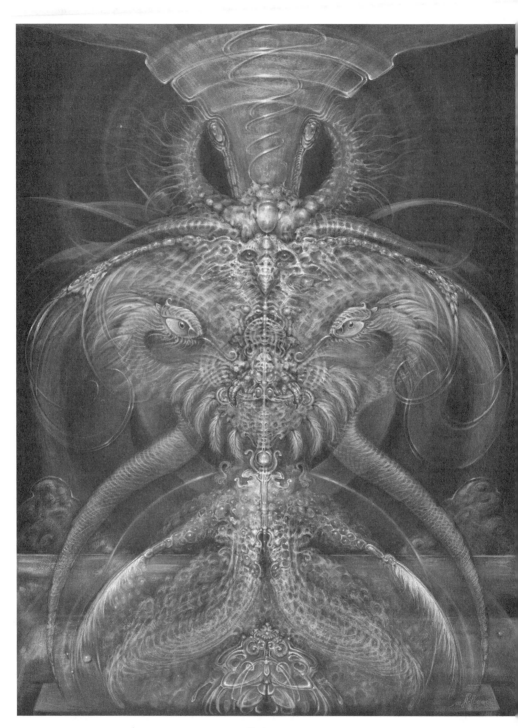

Totem
By Martina Hoffmann

9

The Role of Visionary Art in Elevating Global Consciousness

Martina Hoffmann

MARTINA HOFFMANN is one of the world's leading visionary artists. Her paintings are detailed views into her inner landscapes and portals into other realms—imagery that has been inspired by the dream state, meditation, and shamanic journeys in the Amazon rain forest. A world citizen since her childhood in West Africa, Martina lives and works in the United States and France. Much of her stunning artwork can be viewed on her website: www.martinahoffmann.com.

◆ ◆ ◆

AS AN ARTIST, I'm most passionate about the important role visionary art can play in raising awareness of the need for an elevated global consciousness in today's world. The general sense of anything stable or reliable has recently been seriously challenged and is beginning to topple in view of the changes in our environment and the way we live, work, maintain our health, and see the future. In taking into consideration the teachings of the age-old mystery schools as well as quantum physics, everything is, of course, always in motion and subject to change. And now it has become an increasingly delicate and difficult task *not* to manifest or worsen the challenging world situation by word, thought, action, or image.

We can't deny the apparent agents of change in action, and the need to make urgent adjustments in our behavior as a species. Given this, I believe that things can shift, stabilize, and come back to a healthy state of existence, assuming that humanity makes the appropriate changes in consciousness and in the material world—*tomorrow morning!*

For decades, devoted visionary specialists and thinkers the world over—including my honorable cocontributors to this book—have been offering obvious solutions. I too have been devoted to offering tools. Here I'd like to share what I feel are tremendous influences on me, which have created positive change in my personal life and evolution. The creative path of the artist offers a nonverbal mode of communicating ideas, concepts, symbols, and experiences with expanded states of consciousness and spontaneously encountered mystical experiences. Often this is accomplished with the help of powerful spirit-plant medicines used in Indigenous, shamanic settings in the Amazonian regions of South America. Such plant teachers are legal there and a part of the spiritual practice of healthy tribal communities. Those who have been guided to work with sacred plants have no doubt seen and recognized their great potential for shifting the field and opening the path toward wholeness and healing for the seeker.

None of these experiences are for everyone, and they need to be undertaken with proper care and preparation as well as with as the guidance of a spiritual elder, medicine person, or *shaman*. I'm using this term in the adapted sense of the original term *shaman*, referring to the spiritual teachers of Siberia—*shaman* being a Western word derived from northern Asia, its origins shrouded in lost oral traditions. The word *saman* comes from the Evanki tribe, a Tungus-speaking people of Siberian Russia. But the sense of the word is timeless, reaching back tens of thousands of years and spanning the globe in every language.

Generally speaking, in Indigenous culture, moments of challenge and crisis have forever been addressed by consulting the spirit world of the

Divine for guidance. Traditionally this is done through vision quests or shamanic journeys with spirit-plant medicines that bring about insights and healing information for the seekers as well for as their community.

In the Western world, exacerbated by the current world situation and everything attached to it, we are often left—individually as well as collectively—unprepared, unsupported, and now even more divided. Traditional Indigenous societies have offered and continue to offer solutions by way of preparing their communities and giving support for such difficult times through specifically arranged rituals, guided by trained spiritual leaders or shamans. These medicine people carry powerful knowledge to facilitate a state of balance within the tribe. In this they effect the healing of mental, emotional, spiritual, and physical ailments by way of accompanying their tribe members into such vision quests. The wise women and men are equipped with simple earth wisdom. They remind their communities that everyone is a part of the whole—a message that is also a very prominent feature in the visionary state. This essential, universal concept is equally valid in a village or urban setting, in short—globally.

Further, the visions received during such healing rituals allow the participants to receive intelligent solutions for themselves as well as for our larger community. To offer a careful suggestion: such supportive information, guidance, and ritual could also be very helpful during this time to aid humanity with feelings of disenchantment, frustration, and despair in light of the burning question of how to face these rapidly changing times with calmness, courage, resolve, and hope.

Additionally, in a healthy Indigenous setting, the collective community stands guard and accompanies the initiate with prayers and good intentions during their spiritual quest and times of challenge. This seemingly natural and obvious response has often become forgotten in contemporary societies, where competition and marching along the directed path as proposed by mainstream propaganda is the name of the game.

Looking at both the fundamental structures of earth-based and "modern" societies quickly exposes one of the greatest shortcomings of the current Western world model, where we see a pronounced disconnection from one another as well as from nature. This situation brings with it an unfortunate lack of a sense of true belonging and an ignorance of our interconnectivity and interdependence with all living things on this planet and with the universe at large. And so a key part of the solution is a deep process of reconnection, which can happen through various pathways.

As an artist who has created since early childhood, I'm deeply aware of the importance and great benefits that active participation in the creation of reality can have on our well-being. The creative process offers us responsible ownership of our reality and our world, puts us in touch with our deepest emotions, fears, aspirations, and paradigms. As well, it furthers self-reliance and offers extra perks such as joy, grounding, serenity, satisfaction, and the excitement of being part of the whole. In short, the creative process can be a spiritual practice, a deep meditation, and a shamanic journey into—as well as an expression of—our personal unconscious, subconscious, and collective unconscious.

But it goes deeper yet. Artists have always attempted to make sense of the human experience by creating images that describe all aspects of our existence as well as the realms beyond consensus reality; the archetypal mind and mystical experience itself. From the beginning it has been art—from early cave art to contemporary art: paintings, sculptures, and sacred architecture—that has charmed, inspired, and awed us. With art, we sense dimensions that go well beyond the limitations of the rational mind and what might be explicable by mainstream science. Mystics throughout the ages and in all cultures have spoken about this, and artists have given us the images that allow a direct, felt experience of and access to these mysteries without the need for words and the use of the left brain.

Direct access is the key term here for experiencing worlds beyond the visible that are too subtle to be seen and can only be felt. Images from caves dated to the Upper Paleolithic—such as the *Dancing Shaman* and *The Sorcerer* in Les Trois Frères cave in France—illustrate well the fundamental connection between so-called "visionary art" and the ritual use of plant medicines. Some have speculated that the artists and the shamans of antiquity may not have been one and the same. Regardless, as it still does today in some forms of artistic creation, this ancient art seems to reflect the artist's desire to illustrate the mysterious mystical experiences and processes that take place during non-ordinary states of consciousness, and our access to the superconsciousness.

Art with visionary content has been present throughout the ages and remains especially prominent in Indigenous cultures that have a sacred plant teacher at the center of their spiritual practices. This is the case with the Huichol Indians in Mexico, who use the peyote cactus, or the Amazonian Indians of South America who use ayahuasca, or yagé.

This is not the place for a deep dive into the vast history of visionary art. But to understand this long-standing artistic current, I feel it's important to point to its expressions in ancient sacred architecture and art of all cultures throughout time: medieval art, renaissance art, romantic art, symbolism, Pre-Raphaelite art, fantastic realism, aspects of surrealism, outside art, psychedelic art, shamanic art, and certainly in digital art for sci-fi movies, video games, and cartoon art. While the current of so-called "visionary art" has never been officially recognized as a solid school of art, it has been present since the beginning of humanity. As such, it has often been a part of and an expression of the mystery schools and the philosophers who sought to explain the sacred nonmaterial energy that makes all life possible.

It's only today, especially in the United States, that visionary art has become a household term, mainly for psychedelic art, while Europeans generally recognize visionary art as stemming from older traditions of previous centuries, if not millennia. To understand and identify the term *visionary art* properly, I feel it is helpful to consider the following: A visionary is someone who sees beyond the current moment and offers ideas that go beyond the temporal, anecdotal, and historical. All great civilizations and cultures have been accompanied, influenced, and in some cases even created by visionary thinkers, spiritual guides, and artists.

To understand the importance of art in creating reality we have to remember that what we see, and the concepts and philosophies we believe in, do imprint the mind and powerfully influence the way we experience the world. With that basic truth in mind, I think there is great value in freely expressing all aspects of our being, from dark to light, in words as well as images. But we can never be too careful in remembering that every emotion, thought, word, and action changes the entire web of life and re-creates reality at every instant. This has been an important guideline for me personally when creating art that shows the energy that keeps life flowing. It reveals the light that elevates us to an existence with the higher values of peace, health, mutual support, tolerance, and love toward each other.

Further, I use art and its visionary expression as my daily meditation practice. The long painting sessions, during which I enter a deep state of connection to the whole, allow me to become a channel for information, learning, and healing that is most pertinent to my current state of existence, as well as for my community at large. This is very much a state of expanded consciousness. As such, it is similar to the shamanic use of spirit-plant medicine and other forms of deep healing—while also calling on my everyday skills and capacities to create art.

Another suggestion: All paths of creating art as well as connecting with experiences of non-ordinary states of consciousness, however achieved, offer us invaluable tools for navigating the challenges of our inner and outer existence. And they're available to anyone.

My husband, the visionary master painter Robert Venosa, was diagnosed with cancer in 2003. When this happened we stepped up our creative/meditative practice. We also consulted the spirit world via the channels of powerful spirit-plant teachers during our extended travels to the Amazonian rain forest regions of South America. Today I'm persuaded that those practices helped Robert survive an initially projected three-month life expectancy by eight and a half years, as well as giving both of us yet a deeper spiritual foundation for our relationship. In short: all of these practices allowed us to navigate this very powerful time together with calm resolve, hope, and a sense of living fully in the moment.

When Robert's health shifted and his departure became imminent, the best way I knew how to cope and support him, as well as myself, during this profound passage was to create paintings of healing on all levels for him. These images offered Robert support for staying focused on his inner healing as well as his imminent "birth" into the next level of his existence, while also steadying my pace.

To fundamentally change our reality I believe it is now more necessary than ever to engage in a complete questioning and undoing of our preconceived ideas and paradigms—maybe even enduring a time of uncertainty in the process. In the words of renowned French author André Gide: "One does not discover new lands without consenting to lose sight of the shore for a very long time." For this the above-mentioned practices may become allies.

One can only speak from a place of personal experience. So in closing, I'd like to address my personal inner journey and the alchemical processes that have gracefully created continuous changes and provided me with an anchor. At the same time, they have set ongoing transmutations in motion, along with a deepening understanding of how art can be used as a tool for transformation. Having had experiences of a different order from the beginning of my life—such as lucid dreaming, migraine headaches that created auditory and visual hallucinations, and childhood trauma—I later dug deeper to understand and investigate these experiences and states as an artist and spiritual seeker, as well as to find healing.*

Since the beginning, my artistic work has been an attempt to portray the energy that animates all life. In my experience, this energy matrix is a unifying, universal force beyond the confines of religious and cultural differences. I feel that it arrives from a place beyond my individual self. Given this, I like to think that my most authentic

---

*I'm using the word *hallucinations* with some discomfort in this context and for lack of a better word, as during these highly expanded states of awareness my invaluable "inner guide" or "voice" was revealed to me for the first time.

inspirations and expressions come from that place and from a higher perspective of existence—a higher self perhaps, maybe the Divine itself.

Ultimately, in art as in the entheogenic experience, we become vessels for this divine information. The artist's body as well as an initiate's body literally seem to become the cauldron in which our base elements are being burned, until finally the body cauldron turns into the alembic that distills the cleansed components into an elevated form of themselves. This demands the greatest humility, preparation, care, intention, and gratitude.

Since the earliest days of prehistory, artists have been charting invisible territories of other worlds and creating maps of the inner landscapes.

Age-old mystical teachings tell us that it is the image we hold in our mind's eye that is the one that will come to pass. I feel that as artists, we hold a great responsibility for the content of our creations as we contribute to the changing of the world by imprinting others and the viewer with our visions. In my case I side with Johann Wolfgang Goethe's words: "In all things it is better to hope than to despair" by portraying images that uplift and show a way out.

The daily practice of creating art, along with undergoing experiences of non-ordinary states of consciousness, are incredible tools for navigating the challenges of our inner and outer existence and for opening unimaginable gateways to finding solutions, insight, and healing. Here we might find that by embracing our oneness as a global human family, the interdependence of all life, and our universal interconnectedness, we have a chance to heal and transform the planet's current state of woundedness as well as our own.

In this pursuit, art appears as a tool for transformation that might shift the way we perceive our daily lives. This is an invitation to collectively shift reality by creating images—whether they be mental or on canvas—of a shared reality. This shared reality will be as beautiful, healthy, and strong as our imaginations can see. And it turns out that visionary experience and the art created from it apply directly and powerfully to thinking about and planning the future with imagination and wisdom.

My hopes and prayers are for humanity to collectively begin birthing more light into our existence via the spirit-plant medicines, via art, via the creative process, and via meditations of various kinds. There are so many amazing tools at our disposal. May we choose them well! It is a good and tremendous journey. It's also our biggest journey—called life. So embrace it!

All my relations, so be it and so it is.

10

Becoming Divine Beings

G. William Barnard, Ph.D.

G. WILLIAM BARNARD is a professor of religious studies at Southern Methodist University in Dallas, Texas. He also facilitates transformative workshops called the Heart of Awakening, and is the author of three books on mysticism, philosophy, and entheogens, including most recently, *Liquid Light: Ayahuasca Visions and Embodying Divinity in the Santo Daime Religious Tradition*.

◆ ◆ ◆

FOR THE LAST DECADE or so I've been researching the Santo Daime—a relatively new religion that emerged out of the Amazon rain forest region of Brazil in the middle of the twentieth century, and which now has churches throughout the world. The Santo Daime is a "hybridic" religion that weaves folk Catholicism, West African religions, the spiritist tradition, neo-esoteric modes of discourse, and Indigenous/*vegetalista* practices and assumptions into its own utterly unique and inherently congruent tapestry of religious beliefs and rituals. This fascinating tradition is based on the sacramental use of ayahuasca (called "Daime" within the tradition), a psychedelic brew that *daimistas* (practitioners of the religion) only consume within a tightly structured liturgical format.

Not long ago, while immersed in writing *Liquid Light: Ayahuasca Visions and Embodying Divinity in the Santo Daime Religious Traditions,* I was rereading a series of interviews I'd conducted with two crucially important Santo Daime elders: Isabel Barsé and Padrinho Alex Polari.

I was intrigued to discover that both of these elders stressed that the main objective of the Santo Daime path is for each person to become increasingly aware of the higher self—that is, the I Am or Christic presence—within the force of the Daime. They both also emphasized that there are numerous other ways for a daimista to grow spiritually. Nonetheless, the highest goal of daimistas, according to these elders, is to awaken to their divine heritage as a daughter or son of God and the Divine Mother and then to increasingly embody that divine light and love and power within themselves, as much as possible, moment to moment, in their ordinary lives.

As I was pondering these ideas, both as an academic and as an initiate within the tradition for well over a decade, I realized that during Santo Daime "works" (ritual ceremonies), we are given the opportunity to repeatedly dive into a vortex of high-level, inherently sacred, and deeply transformative energies. We are given the grace of having structured times and spaces in which we can slowly, organically, learn how to resonate, in our cells, in our subtle bodies, with these vibratory frequencies of divinity. And then, with the grace of God and the Divine Mother, we can carry these energies out into the world, offering them in and through our own precious, unique individuality to the world in which we live.

And it struck me that this process of embodying various divine qualities is what key thinkers in early Christianity called *theosis* or divinization. The church fathers—the central, most important theologians of early Christianity—didn't mince words. For instance, Athanasius of Alexandria, in language that I've slightly updated for our modern gender sensibility, said that "God became a human being, so that human beings could become God." Drawing upon the biblical verse (Genesis 1:26, NABRE) that says, "Let us make human beings in our image, after our likeness," these church fathers often claimed that the image of God shines within as the basic structure of each person's humanity.

According to these theologians, the image of God is always present within, but we have forgotten this immanent presence due to the Fall. However, through the incarnation of the Word, and through experientially linking ourselves with the Son through baptism, we can gradually purify ourselves via the sacraments, as well as through the spiritual life more generally. This permits us to more and more accurately reflect the *image* of God within, ultimately leading to the restoration of the *likeness* with God that was lost during the Fall. These church fathers did not think that human beings could ever become one with God's transcendent and ultimately unknowable essence. Nonetheless, they insisted that through grace we *could* increasingly learn how to "participate" in the divine qualities or energies of God, in a process that ultimately leads to theosis, or divinization. For these theologians, divinization was not only possible, it was actually the completion of our humanity. It was the restoration of what was natural to human beings, and it was the accomplishment of God's plan for us.

I would suggest that divinization within the context of the Santo Daime is, if anything, even more radical than the early Christian understandings of divinization. To my mind it relies upon the innate divinity of the human soul/self. This is unlike the more orthodox Christian emphasis on the necessity of the ontological death of the old self/rebirth of the new self, which takes place in and through Christ, in and through the sacrament of baptism. Within the Santo Daime, divinization implies the gradual spiritual transformation of our being—the ever-increasing incarnation of divine energies—in and through the paradoxical realization of who we already are and who we always have been under the surface of our day-to-day awareness.

As a way to express and invoke these energies of divinization, I would like to share a series of mediumistically received insights into divinization that poured into me about four months into the writing process of *Liquid Light*. These are insights that arrived in one highly compressed download—the words simply flowed into my consciousness and were typed by my fingers without any break or editing. Because this type of language is really not meant to be read silently, I would like to suggest that, if you feel inspired to do so, you see what it feels like to read the words out loud. Or again, if you are inspired to do so, you could also listen to me reciting them, at Liquidlightbook.com.

What is divinization? For myself, as it was for early Christian mystics, divinization is the ongoing and ever-deepening incarnation, within my body and mind, of the energies and qualities of divinity—a process made possible only by divine grace. Divinization means sinking ever deeper into a calm, ongoing, softly blooming awareness of my rootedness, below the surface, in a divine Source. It is a process during which I increasingly discover, within myself, that sacred touchstone, the resounding and transformative mystical knowledge: I AM THAT. Divinization means that, over and over again, I lean back into that vastness—consciously, intentionally, aligning myself, again and again, with that profound, silent spaciousness that surrounds and compassionately holds each thought, each memory, each feeling. Divinization means remembering God and the Goddess with each breath, linking up with the presence that permeates each moment, that divine Source that is my true nature, the divine Self that shines from within, illuminating everything. Divinization means affirming, consciously, intentionally, my divine Sonship; it is the heartfelt decision, freely reaffirmed at each moment, to step into my inheritance as a fully mature son (or daughter) of God and the Goddess.

I attempt (with the grace of God and the Goddess) to do all of this, even while (like Christ who is fully human and fully divine at the same time) at times I fumble, and fall, and pick myself up. Hopefully I learn from every mistake and gradually, over time, release any harsh self-condemnation and judgments. In their place, I hope to offer myself the same unconditional love and compassion that God and the Goddess offer to everyone, always.

Swept up in the process of divinization, I discover within myself the ever-increasing ability, made possible by the compassionate blessing of the Divine Mother, shining her love straight from her heart to mine, to open myself, within multiple layers of my experience, to the flux of conscious, living energy that permeates this universe, the throbbing pulsation of life itself. Divinization is, at least in part, the ongoing, ever-deepening responsiveness to the varying "levels" or "frequencies" of that cosmic flux. Divinization is the process of creating living links between various dimensions of who I am and the various dimensions of our multileveled universe—a universe of ceaselessly dynamic, ever-new creativity. Divinization is the recognition, renewed each moment, that right here, right now, is a perfect, ever-new manifestation of the bodying-forth of the Mother, of the divine matrix, that universal, unstoppable creativity that is ceaselessly giving birth to each moment of experience. It is manifesting in and as our own consciousness, in and as our own intimate, unrepeatable, incalculable, personal flow of experience, right here, right now.

Sitting in the very center of that effortless creativity, I AM THAT. I revel in the joyous unfolding of each unpredictable moment, feeling the divine bliss coursing through my being as the pulsations prompt my body, infused with life, to spontaneously move in joyous celebration of my freedom, of my capacity (given by divine grace and received with profound gratitude) to re-orient in each moment to that divine center— my God-given ability to rest in that divine heart.

Divinization is when we stumble, and occasionally fall, but we pick ourselves up, each time more and more gracefully. It is when we shake off the dust of the world, and we shift, we re-orient ourselves, we come back. Divinization is learning how to be both fully ordinary and fully extraordinary at the same time: so utterly natural, at ease in every moment, no false masks, simply being true, free, alive. And in and as this "normalness," we are manifesting our divinity, we are shining forth our Buddha nature. Divinization is the increasing ability to feel deeply; it is honoring and ecstatically affirming the bone-deep knowledge of divinity, shining in and through the particular textures of each ongoing, flowing, ever-changing moment. Divinization is returning again and again to my breath as it flows in and out; to my heart as it surges with love, and gratitude, and wonder; to my body as it sways in delight, responding to the waves of power and joy that ripple in and through my being—swaying and undulating to the rhythms of that subtle (but oh so visceral and impelling) current that ebbs and flows in my physicality— organic, spontaneous, inherently alive.

Divinization is learning how to respond to every new moment from a place of centered, grounded presence and heart. It is learning how to "Rule every kingdom that you enter": acknowledging and affirming each moment, especially those that are challenging, with poise, calm, and an open heart. Divinization is radiating our own majesty, our own inherent nobility, as daughters and sons of God and the Goddess.

Divinization is when (with God's grace) we embody, more and more fully in this world, varying divine qualities, or energies. Within the Santo Daime path we see this thrust toward divinization most clearly (or at least frequently!) expressed in the words of Padrinho Sebastião's hymn, "I Am Not God" (no. 12 in the *Oração,* and no. 152 in *O Justiceiro*).* "I am not God, but I have a hope. I am not God, but I am His likeness. God is fire, God is water, God is everything. I invite my brothers and sisters to begin our studies. I am not God, but I have a hope. I am not God, but I am His likeness. God in heaven, God on earth, God in the sea. I invite my brothers and sisters to remain in their place."

Like the early Christian mystics, I affirm that I am not God the Father. But I have a hope, because I am a son (or daughter) of God. And, as such, via the ongoing influx of divine grace, I seek to open myself to the ever-new discovery of how to embody that likeness, that kinship; how to unfurl that divine potentiality that is waiting to be awakened, to be enlivened, to be set afire. I AM that likeness, and in that affirmation itself, I deepen my likeness. My "I AM" is that One consciousness, that divinity that is taking the form of everything—each ever-shifting quality of experience—the fire, the water, the earth, the sea. That divine consciousness (who I also worship as the Divine Mother of all) is manifesting in and as the particularities of this ongoing moment.

Therefore, in the midst of my sisters and brothers, surrounded by the beloveds who are accompanying me in this journey of awakening,

---

*Sebastião Mota de Melo (1920–1990) is the revered head of the most prominent "line" of the Santo Daime. "Padrinho" is an honorific. *O Justiceiro* and *Oração* are "hinários" or collections of "received" hymns.

I offer the invitation: let's begin our studies, let's truly explore what it means to be daughters and sons of God and the Goddess. Let's be eager students delighting in what we are discovering, uncovering, releasing, integrating, and transforming. God is that transcendent Source, the Beyond the Beyond, *gate gate parasamgate bodhi svaha*!* But God is also completely immanent, fully here, and is discovered and manifested in and as the completely unique, extremely pure "vibratory frequencies" of love, power, freedom, presence, consciousness, and on and on and on— the ninety-nine most holy names of God, the sephirot that radiate out from the Tree of Life.†

Divinization is the process of learning how to remain firmly in our place, in our heart, in the present, in the presence, letting love, and freedom, and power, and beauty, and creativity—any and all of the divine qualities—manifest in and through us, more and more purely, more and more freely, in each ongoing moment. It is allowing ourselves to become increasingly translucent so that there is less and less complication, confusion, forgetfulness, and contraction, and there is more and more simplicity, clarity, remembrance, and expansion.

Divinization is seeking to manifest each of these divine qualities as fully as possible, celebrating the beauty of their diversity—those scintillating, qualitatively unique, interacting colors of the one light. Those colors of divinity are shining forth (and shifting, and flowing, and intermingling) in and as this moment . . . and this moment . . . and this moment. Therefore, the invitation is this: remain steady and firm my sisters and brothers, rest in your own highest and deepest self, remain centered in the heart of it all, celebrating God's transcendent heavenly presence and beauty (a transcendent presence and beauty that is discovered and revealed with more and more clarity in the *mirações*), *and* over and over again celebrating God's presence and beauty as it is also

---

*This Sanskrit mantra is found in the Heart Sūtra of Mahāyāna Buddhism, and more or less means "gone, gone, everyone gone to the other shore, awakening, offered up."

†In Islam, God is said to have ninety-nine names in the Qur'an. The sephirot, according to Kabbalah, a mystical stream of Judaism, are the emanations of the Infinite.

revealed, here and now, fully, in each and every moment of everyday experience, the whole that is within every part.*

And there are no parts. There is no separation, only interpenetration. There are no walls, only interconnection.

And each of us is fully unique. We are all an ongoing miracle. We are all sisters and brothers, we are all heirs, and by recognizing and affirming proudly our kinship with God and Goddess and with each other we are profoundly helping the process of divinization. We are unfurling the evolutionary thrust that is propelling the universe forward in time to a wondrous culmination (a culmination that never stops), the full unfolding of divinity, in all, as all.

In the deepening process of divinization, I seek to affirm the vow, made in the timeless past, by each one of us, "to recover all, to redeem the Fall." Each one of us, by consciously seeking to awaken, by consecrating the miracle of that liquid grace that is pouring into us as the nectar of each moment, are helping to catalyze that universal transformation. And so we do not "merely" seek to awaken within our own being. We also seek to be servants of that cosmic awakening—an awakening that is unfurling within everyone and all things—the universe itself awakening to what has always been. And each of us is hastening that cosmic awakening by awakening ourselves to what fully is, now. And the impact of that revelation is such that it propels us to a transformative glimpse of an unimaginable level of joy and freedom that is beckoning to us from the future (and from the deepest strata of the now), a full, ongoing, and ever-deepening cosmic awakening for all that is so supremely glorious that we cannot even begin to limit it with words, no matter how uplifting and profound.

I affirm and celebrate that paradoxical interplay between the already and the not yet: both intermingling, and both distinct, Shiva and Shakti, the erotic dance of the knower and the known, pure being and creative becoming, the one that is two—and far, far beyond any and all limitations or concepts.

---

*Mirações are the visionary/mystical experiences catalyzed by the Daime.

The process of divinization is fueled by the play of love. It manifests in the desire to be swept away by the beauty of the Divine Mother as the petals of the now unfurl. It manifests in the longing to give ourselves fully, without holding anything back; to offer ourselves to her, as we are, as fully as we know how, asking to be filled with her presence and her love. We give our hearts to her at each instance, over and over again, with love, with joy. Divinization is also feeling so, so relaxed; so, so at home; so, so at ease; resting back into the soft and loving lap of the Divine Mother, and resting as well in the nest of our own utterly unique physicality. This physicality has its ever-shifting patterning of soft flesh and solid bone; sinking ever deeper to the center of our intimately personal, unrepeatable, utterly miraculous universe of experience.

Divinization is learning how to let go—of expectations, of the demand for perfection. It is also, paradoxically, the affirmation of the perfection of each moment, as it is. Simultaneously it sees, with clarity and compassion, the wounds, the buried hurts, the suffering—all which cry out for healing and transformation. And it doesn't matter whose suffering it is: daughters and sons of God and the Goddess, empowered by the Daime, their hearts opened by an influx of divine grace. Over time these hearts increasingly begin to feel the call to offer themselves up to help, to be vehicles of healing and transformation in this world that so desperately needs it. Daughters and sons of God, over time, with divine assistance, make their lives a sacramental offering. They let that divine presence shine fully in and through them in order that the pain of the world can be illuminated. The pain of the world is thus met with compassion, with tenderness, with kindness, with calm, with love, as each daughter or son of God, each to their own degree, consciously and freely dissolves their separateness and affirms their union with divinity, as well as their solidarity with all of the suffering ones—intertwining, in every moment, the one and the many.

And, miraculously, there's no end to divinization. There's no final moment of enlightenment when we stop growing, when we stop learning. There's always more. There's always more. And that more is ever new. Ever deepening. Ceaselessly creative and fecund. Always surprising. Love is infinite, and to feel that love, more and more fully, is itself the greatest gift we can possibly receive. I thank God and the Goddess for their presence in my heart, in and as that love. I feel this love so powerfully. It flows into me, and out from me, a river of love, an ocean of love, into which I throw myself with delight, with tears of unspeakable joy and gratitude. My separateness dissolves into that light, that love, as again and again I emerge from those holy waters reborn, shining with love, in love, as love.

May any and all obstacles to this awakening dissolve in the transformative recognition that these obstacles are themselves the fuel that catalyzes our transformation; they are themselves shining icons of divinity. May all illusion, all suffering, be healed and transformed in the light of that recognition. May we all increasingly recognize our oneness with that love, with that light. May we all come to know the hidden divine depths of our own self, as we awaken, with wonder, with stunned and joyous gratitude, to the new facets of our divinity that are shining forth in every moment.

May it be so, now and forever, amen.

Psychedelics are useful inocula against scientific arrogance, because they consistently remind us of how little we actually know.

DENNIS MCKENNA

Beyond Measure

Reflections on Experienced Realities
in an Awakening Universe

Dennis McKenna, Ph.D.

DENNIS MCKENNA, brother of Terence McKenna, is a true psychedelic elder. Among his many engagements and accomplishments he has conducted research in ethnopharmacology for over forty years, is a founding board member of the Heffter Research Institute, and was a key investigator on the Hoasca Project, the first biomedical investigation of ayahuasca. Since 2020, he has been working with colleagues to manifest a long-term dream: the McKenna Academy of Natural Philosophy (https://mckenna.academy), dedicated to the study of plant medicines, consciousness, preservation of Indigenous knowledge, and a revisioning of humanity's relationship with nature. McKenna is author or coauthor of six books and over fifty scientific papers in peer-reviewed journals. He emigrated to Canada in the spring of 2019 together with his wife, Sheila, and now resides in Abbotsford, BC.

◆ ◆ ◆

RECENT ONLINE CONVERSATIONS on the relevance of mystical experience to the therapeutic benefits of psychedelic therapies raise some interesting questions. For instance, an interview on Vice.com with philosopher Chris Letheby titled "Do Psychedelics Just Provide

Comforting Delusions?" argues that the measured correlations between mystical experiences and positive therapeutic outcomes and the posited causal relationship risks the imposition of nonempirical, unscientific, and unverifiable belief systems on the therapeutic process.[1] This "creates a 'black box' mentality in which researchers are content to treat certain aspects of the psychedelic state as beyond the scope of scientific inquiry."[2] This imposition can limit the scope of psychedelic therapies and may alienate those who do not share the therapist's views on mysticism and spirituality.

Beyond this, the article goes on to state, "Are there ethical issues when providing substances to people that lead them to change their beliefs about the nature of reality and the universe (as mystical experiences are wont to do) if those newfound beliefs may be untrue? If it makes people feel better, does it matter?"

It also bears pointing out that fundamental changes in belief systems, worldview, and personal reference frames are often a desired outcome of psychedelic therapy, whether "true" or not, whether mystical or not. Insights about one's existential situation triggered by psychedelic therapy often result in desirable changes in behavior that may constitute a kind of personal truth, valid for the person but having nothing to do with their compatibility with a reductionist view of reality.

Often people who have psychedelic experiences, whether seeking therapeutic outcomes or simply interested in exploring the outer edges of consciousness, do return from their journeys with the perception that there is more to reality than mundane, day-to-day experience; that there are transcendent aspects of reality that are unavailable to ordinary consciousness and that may well include encounters with nonhuman entities, hyperdimensional realms, or even what we sometimes call "God." Such experiences are automatically dismissed by the so-called naturists as the "comforting delusions" criticized in the article. Naturism as described in the article is equivalent to scientific reductionism as far as I can tell, and postulates that "the natural world," the world studied by science, is the only world there is . . . that mental phenomena—mind, consciousness, and so forth—are not something fundamental in the universe, they are something that develops . . . you can contrast that materialist or physicalist worldview with other views like panpsychism, idealism, cosmopsychism, and panprotopsychism.

All these views are variations on the claim that mind, consciousness, or protomind is somehow ubiquitous and fundamental in the universe . . . people who consider themselves naturists typically deny that . . . Naturists also typically also deny the existence of non-natural entities; they deny that there's anything like a literal God, literal disembodied spirits, a spirit world, or anything like that. . . . But the problem arises simply from the fact that lots of people who take psychedelics and have overwhelming, transformative experiences afterward claim to have experienced aspects of reality that naturism denies. In some cases, they claim to have experienced directly the existence of some kind of spirit world, divine universal consciousness, or ultimate reality . . . .

It's here where I come up against some unexamined assumptions in the naturist's conceptualization of "reality" that highlight the fundamental impoverishment of this worldview. Naturism posits that the natural world consists *only* of what is external, what can be measured by science. In doing so, it dismisses entire realms of experience that are internal, that cannot (at least at the present time) be measured by any scientific instrumentation available to us, but that nonetheless are "real" in the sense that we experience them.

Herein lies a fundamental crack in the foundation of scientific reductionism: its dismissal of the *primacy of experience*. I posit that *anything that we can experience is real*. We know that it is real, because we experience it. That alone establishes it as real, and one could go a step further and assert that anything that is beyond the scope of experience, that cannot be experienced, may or may not be "real"—but we have no way of knowing because it is beyond experience.

Once we accept this postulate, that anything that can be experienced is real, then we can move on to the debate about the nature of that "realness." Is it material or immaterial? Is it "inside" of us or "outside" of us (bearing in mind that these are also loaded terms, heavily weighted with assumptions that are not immediately obvious without closer examination). So I am not making an argument that the experiences that characterize the "typical" psychedelic mystical experience, the sense of a normally unperceived dimension teaming with nonhuman intelligences, in any way demonstrates their reality independent of our minds and imaginations. But neither does it disprove it. They are experienced; therefore, to that extent, they are real.

And that fact—that these phenomena are experienced—points out the inherent incompleteness of the naturist worldview. The arrogant assumption that only what is external, measurable, and quantifiable can be considered real, forces us to dismiss great swaths of our experience. It's also worth noting that these internal experiences that naturism is so quick to dismiss are among the most interesting and personally meaningful experiences that people can have. And any system that purports to build a model of reality based on those criteria is by definition incomplete. In fact, this impoverished worldview is as much a "comforting delusion" as the most implausible metaphysical and religious fantasies. It's just that naturism happens to appeal to those who are most comfortable with the delusion that there is nothing more to reality than what is external and measurable. In doing so, naturism does itself a disservice.

Just as the telescope and the microscope are tools that augment our experience of external nature, perhaps psychedelics can be viewed as tools that expand our experience of the universe within. And just as these instruments brought unseen worlds of the microscopic and the cosmic within our experiential compass, and thus subjected them to scientific investigation, so may psychedelics be the lenses through which we apprehend new experiential realms. Internally experienced events—such as thoughts, ideas, hallucinations, visions, and mystical revelations—are all real. Again, we know this because we experience them, and any model of nature that dismisses them as somehow "not real" remains an incomplete model. If the goal of science is to understand and explicate reality, then it must expand the scope of its quest to include phenomena that are internally experienced.

One could take this one step further and assert that there really is no "reality" apart from internal experience. This is so because even experiences that appear to come from the "external" world are apprehended by consciousness through the various sensory/neural channels that bring information from (what we perceive as) external sources into our awareness. And awareness, our experience, at any given moment, is a reflection of our neurochemical brain states. The light of apprehension never directly illuminates reality. Instead it illuminates a model of reality that our brains construct, and that model of reality is characterized as much by what it blocks from awareness as by what it includes. Huxley called this the "reducing valve" and it is roughly equivalent to what is now called the "Default Mode Network (DMN)" in current neuroscientific parlance.[3]

This perspective essentially turns the naturist worldview on its head. It asserts that there is no extended, external reality that can be verified that is beyond the scope of what can be experienced. Such realities may well exist, but they are not apprehensible to us, and hence no more amenable to measurement or quantification than the interior of a singularity or a parallel universe (or the interior landscapes of our minds).

The same charges may be leveled at the insights gained from mystical experiences triggered by psychedelics. Namely that they are "comforting delusions" that, while they may relieve suffering and increase well-being, are fundamentally misleading because they "foist a comforting delusion on the sick and dying . . . making them believe in some comforting but implausible worldview according to which there is another reality, some ultimate or divine reality."[4] These are the same charges that could be laid against any number of religious or spiritual traditions. People usually find spiritual succor in religious beliefs that provide comfort in times of distress. They seek reassurance that their suffering has meaning, and that there is indeed something beyond this life, possibly survival after death, possibly the existence of an intelligent and compassionate deity that actually loves them.

If we are going to declare psychedelic mysticism as invalid, then we must similarly dismiss religious beliefs that depend on an alternate understanding of the nature of reality that is not consistent with "the truth" as defined by the naturist worldview. There are false assumptions behind this view. For one thing, it implies that the naturist, reductionist worldview is the only valid one, and that any alternative understanding of reality that does not conform to it is "delusion."

This is far from a settled question. In fact, this assumption is completely unscientific. Science, on which the premises of naturism are based, is a work in progress, and by its nature is meant to be subject to constant reexamination and revision. This is the very essence of the scientific endeavor: science seeks to develop models of reality that are based on the development and testing of hypotheses about aspects of nature. Those hypotheses are tested against observation and are developed and refined—or sometimes rejected entirely—based on available information. This is the great power of science: its ability to correct its assumptions as additional data becomes available.

While science has great explanatory power as a result of this self-correcting methodology, it is also prone to a certain arrogance. The assumption that "we've pretty much got this reality thing figured out" often permeates and, in my opinion, cripples the scientific endeavor. Fact is, we fully apprehend only a tiny fraction of reality. There is always infinitely more to be known, compared to what little we have successfully incorporated into our current (working, provisional) model of reality. Psychedelics are useful inocula against scientific arrogance because they consistently remind us of how little we actually know. In doing so, they remind us that the universe is a far more marvelous, mysterious, and astonishing place than our crude reductionist models would have us believe. In doing so, they remind us that the possibility to expand our understanding is effectively endless, even while knowing that the quest for complete understanding will never be achieved.

This may be depressing to some, because it forces us to recognize that we will *never* have "this reality thing" figured out. Personally I find this a reason not to give in to despair or depression, but rather to celebrate the fact that the universe is marvelous and fascinating beyond measure, and that our questing, curious minds will never reach the end of the exploratory journey. In fact, there is no end; there is only the journey.

And as we contemplate this fundamental insight, in our search for the miraculous we should take a moment to reflect: how, in the fullness of evolutionary time, on a backwater planet in some lesser arm of the galactic spiral, did it come to pass that organisms with big brains and complex nervous systems emerged that are capable of contemplating the infinitude of nature and our place within it? And not only that, but that the neurotransmitters that fire within our brains to create the warp and weft of consciousness resemble, and in many cases are identical to, the small molecules that mediate chemical communication networks across the biosphere? When these molecules find their way into our synapses from whatever plant or fungal sources, they can evoke worlds of wonder and unimagined vistas of the terra incognita of the mind. Is not that fact alone a miracle, and evidence of an intelligent universe awakening unto itself?

That is basically the genesis of my inspiration to found the McKenna Academy of Natural Philosophy: to foster expanded understanding of the myriad ways of knowing that are open to experience, beyond reductionism. The time is eminently ripe to rediscover the long-suppressed mystery school traditions for the generations to come. The "primacy of experience" that can be engendered when psychedelics are used appropriately suggests that they have an important if not essential role to play in this fundamental reenvisioning of the cosmos that calls to us in this time of great upheaval, difficulty, and opportunity.

The Beckoning Reckoning

Rachel Kann

KOHENET (ordained Hebrew Priestess) RACHEL KANN is a poet, ceremonialist, and practitioner of international standing. More of her brilliant work can be found at rachelkann.com.

• • •

Behold humanity:
so eminently capable,
so supremely gifted with
the capacity
for an infinity of possible decisions
that can cascade
into limitless
potential eventualities.

And yet—

the law
of cause and effect
is impossible to circumvent.

In this pivotal moment
of unprecedented consequence,

alone together
on the brink of extinction,
we are still wreaking utter destruction
with reckless abandon.

This ingrained inability
to withstand discomfort
has facilitated monstrous atrocities.

Captains of industry
on a sinking ship
of fools
pirated by greed—

there is nary a metaphor
that does not contain
at least a drop of poison
or much, much more—

This is the collapse.

Let it dismantle.

Capitalism
is done.

The industrial revolution
has reached its natural conclusion.

We stand in the aftermath's rubble,
still unable
to solve this hateful equation.

Meanwhile, birds fall from the sky,

meanwhile, unmarked graves gape
in the hateful prison of euphemisms,
meanwhile, the heating concrete
induces third-degree burns
on children's feet,
meanwhile, ancient forests blaze,
meanwhile, our sacred teachers, our holy pollinators,
the bees, face extinction,
meanwhile, coral reefs bleached
by sunscreen
have expired
in our poisoned oceans
meanwhile, the rain forest is razed,

and none of this is new information.

We humans: a whole species
of traumatized beings
continuing the cycle,
perpetuating hate,
fatally limited
by shortsightedness,
relentlessly violating each other,
indoctrinating our young,
abusing this beautiful planet,
that gave us a place to exist,
to create and to thrive.

Is it any wonder
we avoid our reflection
in the mirror?

We delight in our denial;
cram delusion down our own throats

because the truth is so hard to swallow.

And yet . . .

. . . even in this eschatological moment,
there is good reason to be hopeful.

There is so much possibility.

Powerful illness calls for powerful medicine.

There is no time for denial.
There is no place to hide.

Pump the brakes
on this unwell, oiled machine,
on this getaway vehicle—
there is no place to escape to.

What will it take
for us to come awake?

We cannot run
from the grievous damage
we have done.

We have been given
unbelievable reprieve,

been shown
unfathomable forgiveness

wrapped in boundless patience
by this sacred Earth,

who, beyond all logical reason,
has yet to post eviction notices
on our doors.

We have reached this point
together.

We can't go backward.

That's not how this works.

Let us go with the slowdown.

We have this last chance to
let us be like the trees.
Let us learn from their wisdom.

Let us collectively
cultivate empathy,
expand our capacity
for understanding,
build our stamina.

May we finally believe in
ourselves,

may we finally heal
ourselves,

so that we will stop breaking the hearts
of everything.

For the Barasana, their most profound philosophical intuition is the idea that plants and animals are but people in another dimension of reality.

WADE DAVIS

13

The Psychedelic Journey

Past, Present, Future

Wade Davis, Ph.D.

WADE DAVIS is professor of anthropology, and the BC leadership chair in Cultures and Ecosystems at Risk at the University of British Columbia. Explorer-in-Residence at the National Geographic Society from 2000 to 2013, he became a Member of the Order of Canada in 2016, and an honorary citizen of Colombia in 2018. His many books include *One River, Into the Silence,* and his latest, *Magdalena: River of Dreams.*

◆ ◆ ◆

IT'S DIFFICULT TO IMAGINE what initial exposure to the psychedelic experience would have been like for the true pioneers. We look back to Louis Lewin and Havelock Ellis, and certainly Aldous Huxley. But I'm drawn as always to the extraordinary cadre that gathered around Richard Evan Schultes, the Amazonian explorer from Harvard, and Gordon Wasson, an executive at J. P. Morgan who followed in Schultes's footsteps. Together, over a span of nearly twenty years, they pursued the mystery of teonanácatl and ololiúqui, the mushrooms known to the Aztec as the "flesh of the gods" and the "serpent vine," a humble but powerfully psychoactive morning glory.

It was such an extraordinary collection of characters. Dick Schultes, destined for a career in medicine, the first of his family to attend university, working for pennies an hour at Harvard's botanical museum. He was just eighteen when he stumbled upon the one monograph then available in the English language that described the stunning pharmacological effects of peyote: Heinrich Klüver's, *Mescal: The Divine Plant and Its Psychological Effects*. Schultes read throughout the night, enchanted by descriptions of visions of orb-like brilliance, delicate floating films of color sweeping over the imagination and transforming human consciousness. Medicine was forgotten; botanical history was made.

In the summer of 1936, together with Weston La Barre, an anthropology student from Yale, Schultes travelled overland to Oklahoma to live among the Kiowa. Studying at the feet of the roadmen of the Native American Church, taking part in nocturnal ceremonies that lasted into the dawn, this young lad from East Boston who had never before been west of the Charles River ate peyote three, four, sometimes five nights a week for eight weeks of his young life. Needless to say, he returned to Harvard a student transformed.

Two years later, following a clue discovered by chance in a letter attached to a herbarium voucher in the National Herbarium at the Smithsonian, Schultes set off for Mexico in pursuit of the mystery of teonanácatl and ololiúqui. In the end, he connected with Gordon Wasson, this curious banker who, with his beloved wife, Valentina Pavlovna—both enchanted by fungi—was convinced that somewhere in the world people worshipped mushrooms. Where, how, why, he wasn't sure. But then, through Robert Graves, he learned of Schultes's work in Oaxaca. They met not long after Schultes returned from the Amazon in 1953.

Wasson, encouraged by Schultes, travelled himself to the homeland of the Mazatec, and in June of 1955 became the first outsider to ingest the mushrooms in ritual context. Schultes and Wasson teamed up as they tried to identify the active compounds in both teonanácatl and ololiúqui, the former being a number of species of mushrooms and the latter, as Schultes also discovered, being *Rivea corymbosa*. And that brings Albert Hofmann into the mix—this extraordinary pioneer who had synthesized LSD and gone on that famous bicycle ride, the world's first acid trip.

So you had this fraternity of independent scholars: Weston La Barre, an anthropologist deeply influenced by Freud; Richard Evans Schultes, a botanical explorer with a unique appreciation of the genius of traditional healers; Gordon Wasson, a banker by profession, but by calling and dedication a wildly eclectic scholar of ancient mysteries; Albert Hofmann, a Swiss chemist with eyes wide open to wonder. All of them came to the psychedelic experience with no expectations.

Later, those who became serious about these substances—Timothy Leary, Richard Alpert, Andrew Weil—introduced the notion of "set and setting," stressing the importance of the mental state of the individual, the expectations brought to the experience, the psychological set, if you will, and as well the physical setting in which that experience would unfold. Hands-on research had shown that these two factors invariably mediated the nature of the psychedelic experience.

Today, for those who have used these sacred substances, the importance of set and setting seems obvious. But it wasn't always so. When these early pioneers took a psychedelic, they did so in a void of expectations. All they brought to the experience were their own minds. Schultes was fortunate to have been exposed to these powerful substances almost always in a traditional context, be it in Oklahoma with the Kiowa, or the northwest Amazon among the Barasana, Makuna, and all the other peoples of the Anaconda. But certainly when Albert Hofmann accidentally absorbed LSD on his fingertips and rode through the streets of Basel on that fateful day, he had no idea what to expect, no context to contain what was for him—as it would be for Wasson in the mountains of Oaxaca—a soul-shattering experience.

It's fascinating to imagine a time when the psychedelic experience was unknown, and thus free of expectations, impossible to anticipate, a blank slate if you will, on which might be etched images, impressions, and intuitions born in a completely different reality. A man like Schultes, for example, persisted throughout his life in saying, "I never get hallucinations, I just see colors." Someone a bit more reflective, Gordon Wasson famously said, "To try to explain the ephemeral nature of the experience is like trying to tell a blind man what it's like to see." Timothy Leary, following his first exposure, said something very similar. Returning from Mexico in the summer of 1960, having ingested the mushrooms in Cuernavaca, he noted, "Like almost everyone else who has had the veil drawn, I came back a changed man."

Of course, they were all coming at this from different points of view. Schultes was intrigued by the perspicacity of Amazonian peoples—hunters, for example, who could smell animal urine at forty feet and identify the source. They could do this not because they were *sauvage* in a Rousseauian sense, but because they were true natural philosophers who had, over countless generations, come to understand a forest homeland upon which their lives depended. Schultes was drawn to the study of these sacred medicines not simply because of their dazzling psychoactive effects but because of what their elaboration told him about another way of knowing.

He was the first, for example, to recognize that yagé, as ayahuasca is known in the Colombian Amazon, was not a plant but a combination of plants. These were the tryptamine-containing leaves of a shrub in the coffee family, *Psychotria viridis,* along with the beta carboline-containing bark of a woody liana, brought together to yield a powerful synergistic effect, a phytochemical version of the whole being greater than the sum of the parts. Tryptamines, orally inactive due to an enzyme in the human gut (monoamine oxidase), were potentiated by the beta carbolines harmine and harmoline, found in the liana *Banisteriopsis caapi.* Curiously, William Burroughs was with Schultes in 1953 when he first made these observations, and it was Burroughs who would collect the very first voucher specimen of *chacruna,* the critical admixture, *Psychotria viridis.*

What astonished Schultes at the time was less the raw effect of yagé—by this point, after all, he was becoming accustomed to having his consciousness awash in color—than the underlying intellectual question that the elaboration of these complex preparations posed. The

Amazonian flora contains literally tens of thousands of species. How had the Indians learned to identify and combine in this sophisticated manner these morphologically dissimilar plants that possessed such unique and complementary chemical properties? The only scientific explanation was trial and error, which Schultes recognized as a meaningless euphemism obscuring the fact that botanists have no idea how the people of the forest made their discoveries.

Schultes had always been interested in yagé, ever since reading the journals of his great hero, the Yorkshire botanist Richard Spruce, who first described the curious potion in 1852. Through the study of the preparation in the forest and ultimately in the laboratory, he was able to confirm all that he had been saying and writing about the genius of the shaman. Even more importantly, he came to understand that the study of such plants provided a portal into another cultural realm, and a totally different way of thinking, a unique vision of life itself.

And then you had Gordon Wasson, who was really on a philosophical quest. It wasn't an accident that he learned about Schultes from the poet Robert Graves. He devoted years to the study of the Vedic scriptures, speculating in his classic book that soma, the mysterious elixir of transformation mentioned in the ancient texts, was, in fact, *Amanita muscaria*. He would later explore the possibility that the Eleusinian mysteries were mediated by the consumption of ergot. Ergot is a fungal parasite replete with indole alkaloids, the very compounds with which Albert Hofmann was experimenting as he attempted to first synthesize LSD.

Or, again, we have Weston La Barre, who in 1938 would publish his classic book, *The Peyote Cult*. At a time when the use of the sacred medicine was under assault, La Barre and Schultes traveled to Washington in February of 1937. They planned to testify successfully against Senate bill 1399, the latest effort to outlaw the religious practices of the Kiowa. Schultes declared that the ingestion of peyote in ritual context was no different from the Christian use of sacramental bread and wine in Holy Communion, only if anything, far more effective and persuasive.

La Barre spoke of the agonies of the people, and the manner in which the Native American Church had flourished, sweeping the Great Plains in the wake of the collapse of tribal life. With the buffalo slaughtered, the warriors and great chiefs dead, peyote offered a pharmacological shortcut to distant metaphysical realms traditionally reached through the pain of ordeal—the vision quest—and the ingestion of the truly toxic mescal beans. Originating among the Tarahumara, embraced by the Huichol, peyote reached first the Comanche and Kiowa, the ritual practice itself being codified by visionary healer Quanah Parker, before spreading to all the peoples of Turtle Island. For nearly a century, the sacrament and the ritual were taken up by a new people every year, an extraordinary rate of diffusion that ultimately brought the Native American Church as far north as the boreal forests and the homeland of the Cree.*

Schultes remained in close touch with La Barre, even as his own work took him to the Amazon in 1941, where he would remain for twelve largely uninterrupted years, travelling down unknown rivers, living among unknown peoples, all the time enchanted by the wonder of the forest. When he returned to Harvard in 1953, perhaps as a tribute to his old friend, he kept a bucket of peyote buttons just outside his office door, available to his students throughout the 1950s as an optional laboratory experiment. It's unclear who and how many partook of the opportunity, but certainly by 1960, his beloved university had produced a new generation of scholars and psychedelic researchers, among them Timothy Leary and Richard Alpert.

Tim Leary, who famously coined the phrase, "Tune in, turn on, and drop out," became in time a pop icon, a prisoner of his own notoriety. But while still at Harvard in the early 1960s, he was a highly accomplished and widely respected social psychologist, as was his colleague, Dick Alpert. At a critical junction, both men had reached a turning point in their professional careers. A famous study had reported that no matter what the psychological ailment, and no

---

*The boreal forest homeland of the Cree is a large area in northern Quebec province in Canada. —Ed.

matter what the psychiatric or clinical intervention, a third of patients got better, a third got worse, and a third stayed the same. Not surprisingly, these results provoked in both men a professional and existential crisis. Just as they pondered the future of their discipline, Leary read in *Life* magazine Wasson's report from Oaxaca, which an editor had given the snappy title, "Seeking the Magic Mushrooms." The name stuck. Leary made a beeline for Cuernavaca, took the mushrooms, and, needless to say, came back a new man.

All of these individuals were pioneers, the original psychonauts if you will, scholars who took these substances at a time when there was precious little context, and few precedents to help them integrate the totality of the psychedelic experience. They were out there on their own, with a degree of psychic and spiritual exposure difficult now to imagine.

Among those who most effectively took up the challenge, making sense out of sensation, providing both a cultural and historical perspective, and a clear distillation of what these hallucinogens were all about—their promise and potential, their hazards and hidden shadows—was another Schultes protégé, Andrew Weil, a graduate of Harvard Medical School, whose first book, *The Natural Mind,* examined the very nature of human drug use. Weil noted, for example, that the propensity to evoke some technique of ecstasy—to momentarily shift consciousness—is so ubiquitous in the ethnographic record that it has to be seen as part of the basic human appetite.

Such an impulse begins early in life. In playgrounds all around the world, children spin and twirl until, dizzy with delight, they fall laughing to the ground. The anthropological lens suggests that this fundamental impulse can be satisfied through a myriad of techniques—dance, meditation, prayer, ordeal, and even, as Weil recounts in another marvelous book, *The Marriage of the Sun and the Moon,* through laughing fits and the celebratory ingestion of hot chili peppers. And, of course, there are many peoples, notably in the New World, who have satisfied this universal urge through the ingestion of entheogens, or as Schultes wrote, the plants of the gods.

One of the great anomalies of botanical science is the fact that of the 120 or more hallucinogenic plants reported in the literature, fully 90 percent are from the Americas or Siberia. There are, of course, noted exceptions such as *Tabernanthe iboga,* employed in initiation rites throughout Gabon and the Congo. Such rarities aside, most hallucinogens are found in the New World. There is a simple explanation. The use of these substances is firmly rooted in culture. The forests of West Africa and Southeast Asia are biologically rich and diverse, and the local people have long sourced biodynamic plants as toxins or medicines. In West Africa, the manipulation of plants as ordeal poisons* and for other societal purposes is probably the most ubiquitous trait of material culture. If they didn't assay the forest for hallucinogens, it's simply because in spirit possession they had found another doorway to the gods. As a vodoun priest, a houngan in Haiti, once told me, "White people go to church and speak about God. Indians eat their magic plants and speak to God. We dance in the temple and become God."

The shamanic art of healing—a medico-religious practice prevalent among small hunting and gathering societies—also accounts for the unusual distribution and concentration of entheogens in the Americas. While some of these plants found a place in the religious life of pre-Columbian civilizations, Chavin and Moche, Chimu, Paracas, and Inca, they are more commonly associated, at least today, with those small and isolated cultures where shamanism remains the fundamental spiritual practice. As the Huichol embark on pilgrimage, for example, entering the holy lands of Wirikuta, they invoke the language of the hunter, seeking the tracks of the sacred deer, which is how they refer to peyote. They do not harvest a plant; they unleash their arrows into the earth. The flesh of the cactus is seen as the flesh of a deer.

This convergence of the hunt, the shaman, and the plant is no

---

*Ordeal poisons: plants that when touched or ingested in sufficient quantity can be harmful or fatal to organisms because of their poisonous compounds. —Ed.

accident. Death is the first mystery, the edge beyond which life as we know it ends and wonder begins. How a people deal with this inexorable separation invariably determines the outlines of their mystical worldview. Religion is but an attempt to wrestle with eternity and come out on top. For those who have not succumbed to the cult of the seed, hunting myths, as Joseph Campbell wrote, honor the covenant that exists between predator and prey, allowing the hunter to rationalize the terrible fact that to live, he must kill the thing he loves most—the animals upon which he and his people depend.

In state religions, the role of the priest is to socialize a congregation into a flock that can be inculcated with a dominant religious ideology. The role of the shaman, by contrast, is to catalyze the individual's wild genius, allowing him or her to soar away on the wings of trance, reaching distant metaphysical realms and a direct connection with the Divine. The entheogenic plants are the vehicles of transformation, and hence their vital importance, which is why so many have been found, even as the search continues in tribal societies throughout the Americas.

As we anticipate the promise of a new era of medicine, with hallucinogens being heralded as the therapeutic instruments of a psychedelic renaissance that will transform the treatment of mental health, there is much to learn from those who first brought such botanical treasures out of the forest and into our collective repertoire as a species. Andrew Weil—who spent time in the Amazon and paid close attention to how Indigenous people use these substances—asked an obvious question. How had these cultures been able to use these powerful plants so effectively, doing no harm, while we in the industrialized world remain tormented by drug problems that only seem to get worse?

He came up with a template that remains valid to this day. For one, he suggested, they use their substances in natural forms. It's an adage of pharmacology that the purer the drug, the greater the potential for abuse. The first morphine addict was the wife of the man who invented the hypodermic syringe. Tobacco did not become a serious problem until the invention of the cigarette machine and the development of mild strains of tobacco that allowed for the direct inhalation of smoke into the lungs. As late as 1910, a surgeon at Washington University in St. Louis famously ordered all his medical students to the amphitheater to witness a rare pathology, something, he assured them, they would never experience in their careers. The disease was lung cancer, virtually unknown until the cigarette, and today the cause of death each year of 480,000 Americans.

Andy also noted that all of these Indigenous societies recognize that the desire to change consciousness periodically is not an aberration but a natural aspiration, something fundamental in the human experience. At the same time, they acknowledge the power of the plants, their ambivalent potential for good or evil, at times a template of light, in moments a tunnel of darkness. Hallucinogens are not pharmacologically dangerous. The lethal index, the difference between an effective and a lethal dose of a drug, remarkably narrow in a drug as common as aspirin, is impossibly vast for LSD. A couple of aspirin for headache is fine, but if you swallow a bottle, you'll be in trouble. Acute toxicity from LSD would imply exposure to more than five hundred times the effective dose.

Pharmacology aside, the psychological impacts of these substances can be daunting, a negative turn to fear and even terror that Indigenous people anticipate and acknowledge. This partially accounts for why the use of these substances in traditional cultures is less an individual quest than a collective journey, with each ritual gesture serving as a prayer for the well-being of the entire community. Ritual provides a protective cloak, insulating the individual from the dazzling pharmacological effects of the plants.

Consider, in this context, both the traditional and contemporary use of ayahuasca, the Amazonian preparation that has become in only a few short years a truly global phenomenon. The potion, known in Colombia as yagé, first entered Western pop culture with the publication of *The Yagé Letters,* a small book that featured the letters that went back and forth between William Burroughs and Allen Ginsberg, beginning in 1952. This was the year that Burroughs headed for South America in search of the ultimate mind-bending high. In Bogotá, he meets Schultes, a classmate from Harvard. Eventually Schultes introduced him to yagé in Mocoa in the Putumayo. Burroughs had a horrific experience and escaped as soon as he could, convinced that the shaman leading the ceremony had a business on the side, a rare specialty that involved the killing of gringos.

The Yagé Letters drew any number of young travelers to Colombia, with some finding their way to the *curanderos* living and working along the road from Sibundoy to Mocoa. In 1974, I took yagé for the first time in one such place, where a self-professed healer serviced local people who came to him with any number of ailments, from physical pain to economic challenges to marital problems. The whole idea was that the healing ceremony could set things right by reestablishing a certain equilibrium. These were individual curing sessions, with ritual practices that invoked both Catholic and pre-Columbian beliefs and imagery.

Such syncretic rites thrive as well on the coast of northern Peru, as the Canadian cultural anthropologist Douglas Sharon has documented, with the San Pedro cactus serving as the Holy Host, a symbol of the Divine. In Huancabamba, a small town in the mountains of northern Peru, the office of the mayor maintains a log that lists by name the many hundreds of individuals who arrive each year from all over Latin America and the world. The healing ceremony involves the ingestion of the cactus by night, followed by a ritual pilgrimage that brings the patient by day to a sacred lake, where the seeker is baptized by holy waters and released into the realm of the healed.

In the northwest Amazon, among the Barasana and Makuna on the Río Piraparaná, something quite different is going on: ceremonies in which the entire male population ingests yagé for two days and nights. The men enter through dance the liminal space of the gods, donning the feather coronas, which are not symbols of the sun. The yellow plumes are the actual rays of transformation that allow the individual to *become* the ancestor, setting off on the wings of trance to alight at all the points of origin that mark the territory of the people.

What they recall through the visions is the primordial journey of the culture heroes, the four *ayawa,* the "thunders," who at the dawn of time came up the Milk River from the east to bring order to the world. Through ritual, the ancestors come alive, a constant presence that reminds the living of their own responsibilities as stewards of the forest, charged for all time with the task of maintaining order and harmony in the entire natural world. For the Barasana, the role of the shaman is neither that of a physician nor a priest. He's more like a nuclear engineer, as the social and cultural anthropologist Stephen Hugh-Jones has written, who periodically enters the heart of the reactor to reprogram the world. The Barasana cannot simply go into the forest and hunt. The shaman must journey there first, to speak to the animal masters and seek permission for the kill. Barasana mythology and cosmology serves effectively as a complex land-management plan determining precisely how a people should live in the immense upland forests of the Amazon.

In this context, the ritual use of yagé has little to do with the individual, his health or well-being; the focus is on the collective, with each participant benefiting as a member of the community. Each dancer moves to the same rhythm, arm in arm, surrounded and supported, the entire male cohort at his side. For two days and nights they dance, pausing only to take another calabash of yagé, which they all do as one. They recognize that the potion is not for the fainthearted. It's not about the twiddling of thumbs. The Barasana describe the experience in graphic terms. "You can be nursing at the breast of Jaguar Mother," a friend once told me, referring to the power of the plant, "and then she rips you from her tit and flings you into a pit of vipers."

In the lowland forests of Ecuador, I once took ayahuasca with the Cofan in a strictly ritual context. We built a hut in the woods. No women could be near us, nor any man who had a wife who was menstruating. We drank several bowls, several rounds through the night, of a particularly potent brew. In the morning, when we returned to the community, I unabashedly told my companions that the experience had been terrifying, with visions of demons and jaguar and a horrific sensation of disappearing into the depths of the Earth, enveloped only in darkness. I was astonished by the response. We were speaking in Spanish, but some of it my friend Randy translated to Cofan, at which they immediately said, "Well, of course you were frightened. That's what it does. That's the entire point. Don't you get it?"

We have this notion that these substances are expected to be benign, and maybe in some cases those expectations may render them benign. But my experience has suggested otherwise. As the late ethnobotanist Tim Plowman once told me, "Ayahuasca is many things, but pleasant isn't one of them."

All of this brings us to the astonishing growth of ayahuasca tourism, notably in the Peruvian Amazon, in cities such as Iquitos and Pucallpa. Iquitos alone is said to have as many as 120 lodges catering to the trade; there are even restaurants in town with specialized menus catering to the dietary needs of the seekers. Those leading these retreats range from the spiritually inspired to mail-order mystics, con men and psychedelic grifters that give the business a bad name. Indeed, one could be forgiven for coming away from Iquitos convinced that there are more Shipibo shamans in the area than there ever were Shipibo living in the forests of the upper Ucayali. In such an unregulated market, with so many strange scenes, wisdom would urge caution before placing your psychic well-being into the hands of a stranger.

Such perils aside, the psychedelic experience remains one of transformative promise and potential. Just consider what we have witnessed in a generation. Women have gone from the kitchen to the boardroom, people of color from the woodshed to the White House, gay people from the closet to the altar. When I was young, just getting people to stop throwing garbage out of a car window was a great environmental victory. Nobody spoke about the biosphere or biodiversity. Now these are terms familiar to schoolchildren. The notion of Gaia, the Earth as a living entity, an interdependent network of biological life, a concept inconceivable to our great-grandparents, is today evident and obvious to anyone with the eyes to see and the heart to feel.

And yet as we try to account for these astonishing social movements, this recipe of cultural transformation, there is one ingredient consistently expunged from the record. This is the fact that millions of us lay prostrate before the gates of awe, having taken one of these revelatory medicines. Truth be told, I wouldn't think the way I think, write the way I write, understand culture or the natural world as I do, had I not, along with so many friends, embarked on the psychedelic journey. Often it seems, within minutes of meeting someone, I can sense whether they've ever tripped. There's just something about the way one approaches the world, a twinkle of curiosity in the eye. Back in the day, fathers and mothers everywhere warned their children that if they took hallucinogens they'd never come back the same. Our parents failed to understand that coming back transformed, never to be the same, was the very point of the exercise.

This is not to suggest that these substances are panaceas. They are powerful and potent, again not always for the troubled or faint-hearted. There are many who, for any number of reasons, would be wise to stay clear. God knows Charles Manson was a fan of LSD and we all know how that turned out.

Those who do elect to experiment should always keep in mind what Andy Weil noted so many years ago—take them in natural forms, with a good set and setting, enveloped in your own protective cloak of ritual, whatever that means in your life. I would never advocate the use of psychedelics or encourage any person to experiment with them; these are deeply personal decisions. I can only say that in my life these substances were catalysts, in a very positive sense, opening my eyes to possibilities that in my youth would have been beyond all imaginings.

One's experience with these substances can shift through time. As a young man, psychedelics helped me deconstruct a world that had been imposed upon me by birth. But as I grew older, entering what the Vedic tradition refers to as "the householder phase of life"—building a career, having a family—I lost all interest in having my day-to-day life challenged, an edifice so carefully constructed shattered. So I went through a long hiatus. I was, at any rate, very much in that school of Alan Watts, Ram Dass, and George Harrison, "Get the message and hang up." I'd learned what I had to learn. Often the plants have a way of sending you a signal. For years, for example, mushrooms may provoke a purely benign experience. But then you begin to notice a little bit of paranoia slipping into your experience. That's probably a good time to stop. These things have a magic of their own, with messages one needs to heed.

All of this brings us around to the question of the day. What can these substances really do for us, in this moment, in the wake of Covid, with the world on fire, rivers running dry, oceans rising, and hurricane winds battering our every shore? I come down to three things. The first practical application is surely basic therapy. Not to treat those suffering from serious physical-psychiatric challenges, from schizophrenia to manic depression, for these are major afflictions that have to be treated with enormous care. But there is so much that clouds our lives. We dwell in a world in which science, as Saul Bellow wrote, has made a housecleaning of belief, in a society driven by a purely materialistic imperative, an extractive economy, a culture in which the individual has been liberated at the expense of the collective, giving the individual great freedom but also taking away the comfort that community implies. We have all these little traumas and neuroses and confusions. Psychedelics can be helpful there, particularly a substance as benign as MDMA.

In a whirlwind of despair and obscurations, one certainty remains our greatest fear, and here again these potent substances can help. Each of us is born to die. The terminally ill are just those who have a clearer sense of when they will check out of the world. Each of us will surely follow. Buddhists spend their lives getting ready for a moment that *we* spend all of our lives trying to ignore, as if it doesn't exist. But death comes to everyone, in all its fury. Psychedelics can provoke both understanding and acceptance, allowing death to become, if not something to look forward to, something that becomes approachable, understandable, less frightening. In that sense, in terms of hospice and palliative care, the judicious use of psychedelics can be very helpful for those facing the end, allowing them to embrace the inevitable in a space of acceptance, without fear.

Aside from hospice care and personal therapy, there's a third category that is perhaps the most important. All societies are culturally myopic, faithful to their own interpretation of reality. And all are products of their own history. During the Renaissance and leading into the Enlightenment, as we sought to liberate ourselves from the tyranny of absolute faith, we tossed aside all notions of myth, magic, mysticism, and above all, metaphor. When Descartes wrote that "All that exists is mind and material," in a single phrase he de-animated the world. The Earth was reduced to a stage upon which only the human drama unfolded. Plants and animals were but theatrical props. The idea that the flight of a bird could have meaning, that a mountain could be a deity, a forest the domain of spirits, was ridiculed. We take this as a given. Extraction and consumption is the basis of the global economy. A child raised to believe a mountain to be but a pile of inert rock, a forest mere cellulose, does not hesitate to rip open the mountain, tear asunder the forests.

Viewed through the ethnographic lens, this way of thinking about the Earth is highly anomalous. Most societies celebrate not extraction but reciprocity, some iteration of the basic idea that the Earth owes its bounty to humans, but humans in turn owe their fidelity to the Earth. That has profound consequences in terms of the ecological footprint of a people. For the Barasana, their most profound philosophical intuition is the idea that plants and animals are but people in another dimension of reality. The *mamos,* the sun priests of the Kogi and Arhuacos, truly believe that their rituals and prayers maintain the cosmic balance of the world. They say that the blood flowing through your veins is no different from the water running down a river. And they are right. We are all part of the hydrological cycle, each of us destined to die, our blood draining away, slipping toward the sea as surely as the rain.

The mamos tell us that we must change our ways. Their beliefs, their very existence as a people, puts the lie to those in our own culture who say that we cannot change the fundamental way in which we inhabit this planet. How are we going to make that change, a change that we must make? How many years of therapy, how many seminars and workshops, how many rules and regulations would it take to bring us to a visceral understanding of our place: one species sharing the planet with millions upon millions of others, each worthy of life, each inspired by the Divine? Truth be told, it couldn't be done. One can't *think* one's way to revelation. If words alone could forge a new dream of the Earth, the deed would have been done long ago. Transformation comes as a spark of insight, and perhaps these powerful plants can offer a way.

Over two thousand years before the Inca empire grew to embrace Tawantinsuyu, the Four Quarters of the World, the first of the great Andean civilizations was born in a small valley on the edge of mountains where the rivers run together and fall away into the Amazon. In a flowering of culture and art unprecedented in South America, the people of Chavín came to power not by war, but through the triumph and dissemination of a religious idea. Shrouded in mystery, the cult of Chavín arose from an oracular shrine. This shrine was a temple of stone that cradled and then brought forth a new belief—a spiritual conviction of unknown character but of such authority and power that within a century its worship had spread north and south, encompassing all the central Andes and reaching west as far as the sea. A clue to the origin of this ancient vision may be found today, inscribed in low relief at the site of Chavin de Huantar. This vision is of a were-jaguar clutching in its claws a stalk of Huachuma, San Pedro, the cactus of the four winds. San Pedro is a magical plant, loaded with mescaline and employed to this day by healers the length of the Andes.

Arguably the most powerful yet benign of all the sacred medicines, San Pedro opens the eyes to wonder, leaving one spinning in the sand, embraced by the glory of the natural world. You find yourself staring at a blade of grass emerging from the desert, understanding as never before the miracle of photosynthesis, not to mention survival. This simple formula of life is something every politician should be able to recite: carbon dioxide coming together with water, sparked by photons of light from the sun, yielding the food that we eat and the air that we breathe. Anyone who suggests that economy is more important than ecology should try counting their money with a plastic bag over their head.

San Pedro is the antidote to such thinking. Nothing taught in schools, distilled from scripture, or heralded in policy or polemics can ever achieve what this plant can deliver in a morning—an emotional and spiritual catharsis, visceral, even sensual, that leaves one prostrate on the ground, touching the soil, overwhelmed by the miracle of life, the simple blessing and good fortune of being alive, a sentient being, just one of millions, all basking in the light of a radiant sun.

Mama Ganja's Role in World Building

Minelli Eustàcio-Costa

MINELLI EUSTÀCIO-COSTA was born in London of Nigerian and Congolese parentage. She is a Two-Hundred-Hour and Accessible Yoga certified instructor who, in 2012, discovered her love for the ancient practice of combining cannabis and mindful yoga. She guides cannabis-infused yoga classes with an emphasis on self-observation, nonjudgment, and embodiment. Minelli creates space to experience the ways that plant medicine supports mindfulness practices, acting as a guide to our most authentic self. She received a Cosmic Sister Women of the Psychedelic Renaissance grant to write this chapter for the book. Minelli's website is: yogawithminelli.com.

◆ ◆ ◆

CANNABIS, GANJA, BHANG, MARIJUANA, HASHISH—these are all names for a powerful plant that provides so much for so many in the world, whether it's growing wild in the African Serengeti or cultivated in a highly controlled indoor space in California. Cannabis has become popular recently as a recreational substance, but she is a sacred plant medicine that has historically been used in rites of passage, religious offerings, marriage unions, as a means of uniting with Divine spirit, mind-expanding ceremonies, and treating illness.

My experience with this plant has, fortunately, been rooted in exploration, deepening understanding, and connection with others. I have been replicating some of Mama Ganja's oldest uses without knowing it, finding my way home through intuition. My earliest and most potent memory with cannabis is of my partner and I sharing a joint packed with Sour Diesel flower, and watching Neil DeGrasse Tyson's *Cosmos*. It was an awakening. My eyes opened for the first time to knowledge of the universe and my position in it. I witnessed a notable shift in my way of thinking; a switch turned on in a dark room. The information I received in this elevated state stimulated much curiosity, discussion, and creative thinking of new ideas, a trait I quickly learned was one of the many blessings ganja could offer in the appropriate setting.

My mind became more malleable. I asked questions with true interest in discourse and solutions. It felt like I had, for a time, returned to my true nature of childlike wonder. All human beings have a capacity for this level of openness and way of thinking. We are all children in the sense that we know little about the world and universe around us, and our species as a whole is very young compared to the billions of years some planets, plants, and creatures have been alive.

Since this mind-altering experience, cannabis has become a staple in my mindfulness practice, a maternal hand gently coaxing me back to myself. My yoga and meditation sessions are typically preceded by a quiet rolling of flower, a blessing, an inhale, an exhale, then a drop into practice. This ritual has evolved into an offering to my community, a way of guiding others back into their true nature and enabling all of us to walk back home together.

As I guide cannabis-infused yoga classes and sit alone with the plant, the thing that has become most apparent is that cannabis is a unifier. She connects us to ourselves and our communities. They become indistinguishable from each other. When we are less self-centered; there is space to think about the wellness of the collective and see that what best serves us is what serves all beings. This is a challenging lesson, as many of us are looking for instant gratification and individualism.

Cannabis's ability to change the way we preserve ourselves and our environment makes it a medicine that can heal the most common sickness in today's world: a corrupted and confused ego. Individuals place themselves above all other beings—including other people and the Earth that so generously provides all life-giving resources—to the detriment of themselves. This condition favors an unsustainable and self-centered pyramid over a self-renewing circle of life. Cannabis can uncloud our perception. She turns a narrow view that's limited to personal experience into a wide-angle lens that incorporates other stories and truths beyond our own.

BALANCE AND REST:
KEY TO COLLECTIVE LIBERATION

We live in an unbalanced society, which in turn leaves the body, mind, spirit, and our relationships to one another, nature, and ourselves out of balance. Cannabis creates homeostasis in the body, maintaining internal stability that helps us survive external conditions. This facilitation of equilibrium can be replicated in our communities.

That being said, cannabis is also a tool, and any tool can be mishandled by ignorant users. Medicine can become poison if taken without care or knowledge. In a culture that tends to overindulge, whether through unsustainable extraction processes or excessive dieting, greed can and does spill into cannabis use.

It's easy to spoil ourselves with anything that brings pleasure, especially the kind that ganja can bless us with at the end of a grueling work week. A small puff, bite, or droplet can offer a remnant of respite after a day of surviving late-stage capitalism. But there's a big difference between a mentally soothing smoke experience and one that leaves you couch-locked and of little use. Cannabis is a nurturing mother plant that excels at helping us feel held and happy, exactly where we are—a feel-good sensation that can be addictive. I believe the distinction between medicine and poison lies in the ceremony preceding each sit with cannabis.

Ceremony is in all moments. Before consuming cannabis, ceremony can look like an expression of gratitude, an intention-setting or prayer, or a deep breath and pause. Mindful consumption brings a healthy relationship with and awareness of the plant, how it got into your hands, and the Earth's giving nature. Have you ever thanked the Earth before bringing medicine to your lips? Or asked how you could serve the plant—getting out of the colonial mentality of taking and never giving? Have you thanked the stewards of the land who allowed the cannabis plant to grow? Have you thanked yourself for preparing the herb with love?

A deeper connection, a moment of pause and thanks, can help us see the connectivity in all things and get out of the human habit of forgetting that no one and nothing exists in a vacuum. We all rely on each other, and the more we feel that palpably in all moments, the faster we'll come to the realization that the destruction of one thing will ultimately lead to the destruction of all things.

Beyond rites of passage and ritual, cannabis is commonly used in our modern age to combat stress and promote relaxation, two key components in our collective pursuit to heal and save ourselves before it's too late. When we are rested, clearheaded, and thriving rather than simply surviving, we can make room for creative solutions to steer away from our current path of self-destruction.

Revolution and evolution do not come from a state of exhaustion and depletion. Cannabis is a joy-giver, the poor person's heaven, a soother of grief and discomfort, and an accessible medicine many of us, especially people of color, women, and queer folk, use as a means of finding relief in a society built to bury us. You cannot pour from an empty cup, so I encourage you to light up a joint, take a nap, and awaken ready to make shifts in the world from a rested space.

CANNABIS ILLUMINATES

The spirit of cannabis is freedom and knowledge, but not all knowledge feels good to receive. As a mothering soul, cannabis can choose to bring us face-to-face with the awkward, jarring parts of ourselves we try to hide— the shadow self. She can pull our worst nature to the forefront, making it uncomfortably apparent and unavoidable. This is why some folks dislike the plant, but they're missing the blessing in discomfort. Rather than blindly pushing the shadow away, it can be useful to ask what it's trying to show you. When a difficult sensation arises, let your guard down. Listen deeply. You might find there is a potent lesson just beneath your unease.

A healed society is vulnerable, able to question and give and receive critique without making any individual disposable. When we can sit with our own shadow without rejecting it or feeling guilt (an emotion that has little to do with inciting change and more to do with centering on the self)—as cannabis can force us into doing—we can learn to do that for other beings. Collective healing will not happen until we let our guard down and accept change in our thought patterns and ways of being.

Introspection and inner work are the foundation of activism. We must reflect on our own blind spots, biases, and projections. As the adage goes, be the change you want to see in the world. It's easy to see the flaws in others, but what happens when you shift the mirror to yourself and see these "flaws" as opportunities to create a new narrative? Cannabis is the softness around the hard edge of reality, allowing us to do the required work without harshness, self-judgment, and other ego-filled distractions.

A MOMENT FOR DIVINE PLAY

In the loss of our true nature, we've forgotten how to dream and play. We have all been falsely told we must earn pleasure by overworking, and that creating lasting change is a grueling task. Unlearning these ways of thinking and taking on the idea we all innately deserve to have fun just because we are alive is key to a collective consciousness shift that is sustainable rather than a bursting firework that fizzles out as quickly as it is lit. Creativity and play are left to the children, making it impossible for adults, those responsible for destroying what could be a perfectly symbiotic relationship with our planet, to imagine a world different from the dystopian science fiction we're hurtling toward.

Cannabis releases anandamide, rightfully called "the bliss molecule," in our brains. We can use her to bring more bliss into change-making, and turn activism into a form of divine play, a Hindu concept known as Lila, which embraces being a part of the cosmos and exploring our conscious bodies in all ways, even through hardship. Play is adapting to the moment, being present enough to create something *right now* and step outside of our comfort zone. Just watch a group of children playing. They make up the rules as they go along, and when one rule stops serving the intended purpose, it's quickly disposed of and forgotten.

Cannabis creates space for play, pleasure, daydreaming, deepening thoughts, and world building. Consuming cannabis while sitting outside in nature is a great way of moving ideas from the mind to a place of integration and practice. Try it. Reflect on a topic that seems to have no solution. You might daydream about what a world without police would look like. What does a world without inequality look like? What could you personally do to leave this Earth better than when you came into it? Let this be an exercise in play and curiosity.

Thinking about solutions doesn't have to be a wretched job, and you don't need to have all the answers. Sit, smoke, or eat, and daydream of a sustainable world with a friend. What does it look, feel, and smell like? Share your insights, listen deeply, and collaborate. The easy and predictable path is to lament the ways the powers that be will never change, giving all our agency away. It's time to do away with that. The opportunities we take to daydream and create new worlds and ways of being in our daily lives can inform the ways we move and interact with the world.

This is what change looks like—slow and unassuming, rippling into our communities through direct action until it suddenly becomes the standard.

*So everything contains knowledge, and knowledge contains
information that, in our way of looking at things, is Spirit.*
TYSON YUNKAPORTA

15

The Tether

Tyson Yunkaporta, Ph.D.

TYSON YUNKAPORTA is an Australian aboriginal academic, arts critic, and researcher who belongs to the Apalech clan in far north Queensland. He carves traditional tools and weapons and works as a senior research fellow at the Indigenous Knowledge Systems Lab at Deakin University in Melbourne. The ideas and principles discussed here are fleshed out in Tyson's brilliant and necessary book, *Sand Talk: How Indigenous Thinking Can Save the World.*

◆ ◆ ◆

EMERGENT CULTURES OF
TRANSITION FOR OUR DESCENDANTS

Before your trip, some information. We need to know how we got here before we go an inch further. And we need to understand the rock beneath our feet before we go charging off to commune with the cosmos, before we orgasm across galaxies in all our transcendent splendor. Here is story. It's lore for changemakers, whether you look to change yourself or change the world, or just *be* the change you want to see in the world. It's not a fable of hope, but a vision of belonging and emergence.

The crises and meta-crises that have developed since my birth in the early seventies have seen the annihilation of 60 percent of the world's biodiversity. The externalities created to provide a sanitized, nonviolent, technocratic space for a tiny minority of the world to live in have been horrendous for everyone and everything living outside of those entropic bubbles of privilege. Including individuals indigenous to these ravaged lands and communities in the sharing of some of the spoils from this extractive system in its final moments of decline does not represent justice and sustainability to anyone remotely connected to reality.

Our failure to respond effectively to this existential threat is grounded in theories of misdirection that cause us to see correlations as causations. We have been led to believe that systemic injustice and ecocide are caused by the aggregate of our poor attitudes and lack of awareness. So we direct all our efforts toward changing attitudes and raising awareness, trapped in the illusion of democracy as if a collective shift in ideology will remove caste systems and extractive practices and corruption and oligarchies.

We apply ointment to the rash when we need to be treating chronic candida in the gut and the blood and in every inch of our flesh. We self-actualize and amplify and organize to change culture while our physical reality crashes around us.

Racism and inequality are not the cause of our problems; they are effects of liberalism and the global machinations of the Anglosphere. They are preconditions for making the extractive economic system work, whether you are capitalist or communist, which are two sides of the same demonic coin. You can't have a growth-based economy without having a caste system in place and without having at least half of the people missing out on the goods and services needed for surviving, let alone thriving. We must have people missing out on that in order for anything to be priceable in a growth-based economy. Demand needs to exceed supply, and all goods must be limitable and excludable. This includes land as capital. Thus are most of us excluded from our habitat in order to make that capital stable and increasing in value.

The concept of nationhood is just over a century old. It's a form of social organization that takes away regional identities and places a uniform identity over millions of people who are supposed to be alike in thought, word, and deed. Basically everywhere you go in the world, everybody has to have a nation in order to have the right to exist. In recent decades, many First Peoples have made moves toward changing their group identities into this idea of nationhood as well. This is about survival; if you don't have a nation with recognizable, liberal symbols and institutions, then you lose the right to exist and will soon be eradicated.

This system of perverse incentives and competitive dynamics and self-terminating algorithms can't just be tweaked a little to make it feel more fair and eco-friendly. We can change our language, we can change our social norms, we can amplify marginal voices all we like, but in the end everything will die on this Earth if that system remains in place. Given this, it's probably better not to just paint over the ants in the walls in the name of hope. That isn't hope at all. It's denial.

True hope would reflect a pattern of emergence—people flocking and schooling in breathtaking dances moving in the direction of living within their bioregion as part of that sentient system. This means building family relationships that balance autonomy and collectivity and are scaled to neighborhoods, then to communities, and then to regional identities, economies, and systems of government. Solid communities in those places would then be networked and interdependent with all the other bioregions, exchanging energy, matter, and information in dynamic relationality. This then scales to states and continents and beyond. The structures are already in place, but the flows of power are all being directed downward, and the flows of value are being sucked upward, when these flows need to be reversed.

Emergent cultures of transition for our descendants will require people to be reasonably mobile. Our elders say that if you don't move with the land, the land will move you, because Creation is always in a state of flux. Ecosystems aren't just sitting within these lovely parks where God put them for the duration of some weird cosmic computer simulation. They're constantly moving around and exchanging energy, matter, and information with other systems—even those quite far afield from them. If we follow these laws of the land, they will give us the patterns of governance and trade that we will need to transition to regenerative systems.

Every complex system has to dump entropy, but the only way to make that sustainable is for your entropy to become another system's lunch, recycling in closed loops with other systems. You could imagine that in very simple terms. If you're a complex system, you have to make "poop." And that poop goes into the system of the ground, and the plants eat it and grow and give you fruit, and that cycle continues.*

Civilization operates on open loops resulting in static piles of entropy outsourced to marginal lands and peoples, and static piles of value stored in the centers of illegitimate power. Even with the "free exchange" of information in cyberspace, data is mined and hoarded in open loops of extraction.

In the few ways left to us in our limited living spaces, we as a species need to be occupying our ecological niche, or at least keeping the memory and story of that way of life alive for future generations to reclaim. *Our ecological niche is that of a custodial species.* We range across a lot of systems and we have a parasitic or symbiotic relationship to everything within all of those systems. We are supposed to be spread out across the landscape. Landscapes that don't have us in them are impoverished and sick. There's this idea that wilderness where no man has trodden is a healthy landscape, but this is a myth. Biotic systems need us there to help them along and to caretake those systems.

I think there is enough carrying capacity, at least in the midterm, for the amount of people we have on the Earth if we all spread out a bit, walk off our cellblocks, and start reclaiming lifestyles that would be a lot more satisfying. This would involve being in these landscapes and managing our food production more locally, while also exchanging with other systems and remaining mobile as our landscapes change and shift in increasingly rapid cycles. This is a Deep Time way of being. Sea levels rise and fall. Mountains rise and fall. You do need to move, and it's only an apocalypse if you try to sit still in your bubble of ill-gotten gain.

---

*This and a number of other terms that Tyson uses in this chapter, and that are perhaps less familiar to the layperson, are briefly defined in the glossary at the back of the book. —Ed.

No matter what your level of privilege, look us in the eye and tell us you wouldn't rather be free again. It's just a matter of who takes the first step, who divests themselves of their competitive advantage while trusting that others will do the same. (It's no fun streaking when you look back and see your fully clothed friends laughing at your wobbly white butt.) And so we wait.

This is not the first apocalypse we've experienced. In Australia there are many stories about previous cataclysms, and a lot of them are supported by the geological data. They're quite survivable, so if people are looking for hope, that's a good place to start. It just means we have to change a bit. I don't know why so many cultures view change as an end. Systems only end when they cease changing.

However, it is difficult to see this pattern through the lens of reductionism—that cultural and academic perspective of zooming in and focusing on just one thing and studying it in and of itself to the exclusion of everything else around. Industrialized, or industrializing, cultures tend to domesticate people and train them into focusing solely on the task in front of them. They're on a production line and don't know what happened to that object before it came to them and they don't know what will happen to it when it moves on. How can you act outside the box when you can't even *see* outside of it?

HIGH-CONTEXT CULTURES: EVERYTHING IS IN RELATION

The cultures that are being created in these industrialized nations are low-context cultures. When you look at the world, you're not looking at complex systems and viewing things holistically—seeing a pattern and making predictions based on that pattern of all these inputs, and knowledge, and story. Instead you're thinking in quite a linear way of how to get from point A to B. What's the cause? What's the effect? What's the action? What's the reaction?

High-context cultures look at the universe and everything in it as being in relation. And everything you know and you've heard of and you've seen and you've done is all connected to entities that you're in relation to. Thus you're sitting in the center of a web of relations (or even better, your cognition is distributed throughout it) and seeing the entire system and making your decisions and your predictions based on that, and your actions are coming from that demotic system in your community.

We are demotic in the same way an ecosystem is biotic. If you think of biotic as being the emergent properties of a biological system, demotic describes the emergent properties of a human social system that is patterned on the landscape. It's not about one person inventing a hashtag and then that takes off because they have a cult following. It's the wisdom of crowds. It's what emerges from the collective conscious and unconscious working together. The demotic is just the everyday, lived culture and practice and habits and norms that emerge organically from a group of people in response to evolutionary pressures of the environment and the systems around them. There's selection going on and, as with all evolution, some things are useful and some things are not. There are mutations occurring all the time, and in the end, the majority of mutations are generally beneficial to the system, and the nonbeneficial ones are managed by custodians.

This means that solutions are not tinkered or engineered by people narrowly looking at aspects of the system and then designing little interventions here and there. Instead of that, one needs to foster emergence. Phenomena in self-organizing systems will always emerge to balance the imbalances. Systems are autopoietic and dynamic, and will throw up something almost like an immune response to a pathogen. You don't have to tinker with that; just make sure you're eating enough citrus in the right season.

Emergent properties elaborate and develop from different combinations throughout that system all the time. That's why for any system to work and be healthy there needs to be constant flow and exchange between all the parts of that system. There needs to be velocity of every unit of energy and information within that system. This gives rise in human systems to the demotic, and in biological systems, the biotic. In an Indigenous worldview those two things aren't separate. They follow the same totemic pattern.

This pattern of distributed energy is replicated within each of us as individual organisms. The human as a social mammal is patterned to resist any kind of social grouping that isn't mostly heterarchical. We're happy enough for temporary hierarchies to emerge in order to manage something that needs doing quickly. Yet this idea of permanent hierarchies, of individuals who are elevated above everything else, creates a revulsion and rage response in most human beings at the molecular level.

We don't have centralized control or institutions in Indigenous societies (although occasionally tribes have been known to experiment with this, as all humans do from time to time until they are reminded of the consequences. The champions of command and control are always eager to point out these examples to dismiss our advice on decentralization). Our elders and knowledge keepers do have authority, but they don't have much power. There is a difference. Authority is something you earn through knowledge, and it cannot be used to command. There are no bosses. We don't have centralized institutions because those things inevitably fall apart even if they have the best intentions. Power is distributed throughout the community.

There is a concern in the changemaking community that this model cannot scale enough to be useful today. Game theorists cite the Dunbar number of one hundred and fifty to two hundred people being the maximum limit of a community that is transparent enough to maintain enough trust for a healthy commons. Everybody knows everybody and what everyone is up to all the time. You can't really try to game that small system, but you can when it grows large enough to provide you with anonymity. That's the tragedy of the commons, also known as a "multipolar trap" in which bad actors can gain a competitive advantage and force everyone else to behave the same way or else be outcompeted. Then nobody can stop until the commons is destroyed.

In a properly functioning Indigenous community you can't have bad actors, because everybody knows who they are immediately. You can't have pedophilia. You can't have violence against women. You can't have domestic abuse and all these things in a community that's self-governing and embedded into the landscape. And these communities can indeed scale. You can have networks of autonomous systems that can scale infinitely, as long as the core principle of every relational pair (balance between self-interest and collective interest) is replicated fractally throughout. Each group can't grow beyond its limits, but you can have as many of those groups networked together as you like.

The problem is that this can't work without transformation toward high-context cognition, which is difficult to recover once a mind has been domesticated. It takes very good teachers, and there are not many of these to go around unless you include nonhuman teachers. You can work with wood, fiber, stone, river, mountain, air, or any entity in right relation through ritualized practice to achieve flow states, peak performance states, transcendental consciousness, or whatever term you care to apply. When I describe this to young people, I describe it as any state that feels like no time has passed at all.

Most Indigenous cultural activity falls into that category, particularly material, cultural activities of making, doing, singing, dancing, walking in the country, hunting, fishing—all these activities that put you in a timeless state of mind. A lot of incredibly complex thinking can happen in that state where you're not just mind and body, but you've got a haptic connection out to everything else, all your relations, the landscape, and beyond. All of that crystallizes and you can see the big picture all in one go, but you're not trying to hold onto it. You're not even seeing the pattern—you're just *being* the pattern. All your solutions and actions and all you need to do come to you in that time.

I achieve that through my carving practice. I don't use power tools or anything. I'm just chipping away at wood and it takes a very long time and I find myself coming into that way of being. I get into a state where I have a sense of direct communication and guidance from my ancestors, and all entities, and the lands and waters and skies. I'm being guided by all of that spirit. Once that's switched on in me, that's it. It only needs to be turned on. Some people turn it on with assistance from plant teachers.

NOT LIKE A TRIP AWAY:
PROPER RELATIONSHIP WITH PLANT MEDICINES

Most Indigenous cultures have traditions of assisting or enhancing cognitive transformation with plant medicine for important purposes. You must have plant medicines that you're in relationship with, within totemic and biological kinship. You do that for a purpose and you go over to another place while you're still strongly tethered in this world. It's not like a trip away. And you really only need do that once, or at most once every fifteen years or so, like with some people who are really transcending into deeper and deeper levels of knowledge at different stages of initiation. For most of us this is achieved with the psycho-technology of ceremony and does not require chemical assistance.

A lot of people today are tripping balls once a week, because they aren't in right relation and are stuck in an ecstatic loop of entropy. They have no tether to a place, no kin, and no purpose for the work, so no work is delegated to them. I was introduced to my overseas brother San Pedro cactus about fifteen years ago when I needed to act above my pay grade and access higher cognition for a task I'd been given. That was before I met Old Man Juma, the man who gave me symbols to share with as many people as possible. I saw them first with San Pedro years before I met Juma, in preparation for receiving that ritual technology. I had to change my hardware to run that software. It was very hard on me. The trip lasted about twelve hours and I went through all of the pains of labor so that I could appreciate the importance of motherhood and the sacrifice that women make, to understand the centrality of the kinship pair of mother and child for any sustainable society.

I also saw a symbol that shows a model of time. I saw that entity of how time-place works, and I looked at that for eons. But basically, I only needed to do that once and I'll probably never do it again because I'm still working with everything that came through that ceremony. I've got a lifetime of work to do from that one experience. I don't want to jump back in; it would be more than I can handle, not to mention greedy. There aren't enough hours in the day in my whole lifetime to work through all that. Again, if you're going in and saying, "Oh wow! I'm a child of the universe with cosmic consciousness!" and then you feel you've got to go in again shortly after that, you're probably not doing it right. You probably need better story.

ANCESTRAL MIND AND
THE IMPORTANCE OF STORY

Story is a collection of metaphors that puts you into a state of optimal cognition when shared. That doesn't mean telling a fable, or invoking a legend, or creating a film synopsis, or anything like that. It's not that kind of narrative. It's like a collection of metaphors where there are different layers of meaning. This brings you into a relationship with place and entities of place. You might not be connected to all the same entities that the storyteller is connected to, but they're bringing you into that universe. It's working on you as a listener, but it's also working on all the natural and spiritual systems associated with that story.

For example, if I start talking about Brolga (crane) story, that's connecting to water lily and other kin, but then that's connecting to Emu and the tension and conflict between enemies, between those two different ways of being, almost two different ontologies. But it's bringing you into an association with place and a series of places from the coast up into the river country and along the savannah. And then it's connecting you to a series of totemic images that are related, like a black cockatoo, a mud shell—which is a mangrove sort of shell—water lilies, a whirlwind, and an ironwood tree. There are all these entities and totems, even body parts, that are totems in that relation, like knees and shins and feet and hands and blood and urine.

You're using metaphors to bring somebody into relation with another ontology, and with the ontologies of every entity within that system, because each entity has its ontology of what it knows to be real in its universe. But it has to be suprarational. It's bringing you into an ancestral mind space. *Yarning* is the English term we've taken up for this practice, which can be quite casual, day to day. But then it can be a bigger, more ritualized thing as well. Yarning has that exchange, that flow that you find in self-organizing systems. But it's also highly ritualized and it brings you into that state. It brings all these ontologies together and forms a lot of different viewpoints looking at the same universe. That gives you a more holistic point of view where you are all-thinking-feeling together with one belly/mind.

You get into that state, like when you're engaged in a conversation with a group of people, and it's really flowing. That really energizes you. You come into that ancestor mind state. But you're sharing it together collectively and creating a larger mind on narrative maps of place. That mind can do amazing things. That's what informs your collective decision-making and your collective governance. Thus it's quite an important action. And story is an integral part of that.

Unfortunately, in this context, I find that for the past ten years or so it's been very difficult to do these things. It's a very powerful thing to do together, and inevitably somebody with that "greater than" urge will be there. People will start to separate and think, *This is great. Who is going to be the boss of this?* And they'll hijack the process, thinking *I can take that for myself.* So somebody starts monologuing and everybody gets bored and it breaks up. Or somebody starts to cut people off, debate people, or rebut people, rather than allowing things to flow, for all the ideas to coexist together even if they're contradictory. They're supposed to coexist because they're all different facets of one truth. But then someone says, "No, my narrative, my story has got to be the dominant story that others will follow."

That never lasts long. Usually one narrative will become dominant, then people will sense the power in that and they'll start to cluster around it. It becomes an ideology almost. They'll keep repeating it within their groups and eventually it will break up and splinter. It's a continuous fracturing. People are building their brands and their unique identities and then defining themselves around their differences or reified trauma or their rejection of other narratives. This has accelerated over the past decade to a very destructive point, as you can see.

Everyone knows about echo chambers, virtue signaling, policing each other ideologically, and all the rest of it. There are so many narratives out there now jostling for position. Everyone's got their own story and their own facts. It just goes around in endless cycles. This comes from a disconnection with land, a way of being that sits in a placeless place of abstractions in the clouds. We need to reconnect with the non-human sentient entities in our local place to break this curse.

EVERYTHING CONTAINS
KNOWLEDGE AND INFORMATION

Consider that everything has an ontology, every physical thing, even man-made things, which is basically their experience of the world—what that thing knows to be the reality. A rock knows quite a few things. It knows things from deep in the ground where it came from. It was born out of that ground. It came together from several different things coalescing. It knows the sky. It knows the people who might use that rock for different things. Everything in Creation contains and carries knowledge. It is information, molecular structures if you like, that hold these rocks together, because otherwise in terms of physics that thing couldn't maintain its shape and would crumble to dust. At the end of its long life span that will certainly happen as it develops a kind of informatic dementia.

Everything contains knowledge, and knowledge contains information that in our way of looking at things is Spirit. No scientist knows how to quantify or measure it. No philosopher knows the substance of what information or knowledge is made from. But most humans know at some level that everything is sentient, though whether this becomes useful to you is a matter of whether you can be consciously aware of the effects that these things are having on you, the information they're passing to you. You are in a web of relations with all kinds of entities constantly exchanging energies and information with you. It's to what degree you can come into an awareness of that.

If you're using substances to come into that awareness, the next time you're tripping balls get your mind off the trip and start to look for what's holding you to the real world and pay attention to that. Because that's your tether, and it's where you're going to find all of that information coming from your entities of place. You'll find what you're connected to. You'll find the web of relations that is your ontology. And you'll find a lifetime of work to be done within that web of relations.

What you're looking for when you trip is not what's on the other side. It's what is *here.* If you can turn your gaze away from the infinite and back to the place you're connected to and understand your connection to that place and that web of relations, then you'll know what you're here for and you probably won't need to do that trip again for at least fifteen years.

THE RIGHT WAY AROUND:
RESPECT, CONNECT, REFLECT, DIRECT

There is a simple process for your practice that comes from Doris Shillingsworth, a Murruwarri elder. It's the order in which you do things properly. Respect, connect, reflect, direct. It's a protocol for how you come into relation with a place or any kind of relationship you want to form. You can start with respect. Let's say you wanted to use a rock for something. The way that people often do it is in reverse, as in direct, reflect, connect, respect. That's the wrong way.

A lot of people would approach that rock and say, "I want to use that rock to decorate my hallway table!" for example. They go straight to the plan or action—*direct.* They pick that rock up, take it home, and start working with it. Then things start going wrong, so they *reflect* on it and wonder why. Then their attention goes to the rock and they think maybe they shouldn't have taken that rock out of its place. Then they *connect* with the rock and realize they probably should have approached it in a different way. They take the rock back and make that connection. And then finally they end in *respect.*

That's the wrong way around. You need to approach that rock and that place with *respect* to begin with. You have to respect that rock as being sentient, or at least part of a sentient system. In that way you're also coming into relationship with that rock and that place. You ask permission from the custodians of that place. You find the story of that place and *connect*. And then you need to *reflect* on, "Why do I want to use this rock? Is my use of this rock going to be in proper relation to this place and will it be enhancing Creation or will it be detracting from Creation?" And then you can do the *direct* aspect, the practice of actually doing something with it, or maybe you choose to walk away at that point.

That's the proper way to come into relation and begin to transform your cognition. That's the proper way to interact with communities, with other human beings, with a tree, with a rock, with everything in life. That's the way Mumma Doris says it. I translate that into: *Spirit, then heart, then head, then hands.* That's an easy way to remember it. You start with that Spirit, then that heart—coming into proper relation, then head, where you do the thinking about it, and then you know what to do with your hands.

I strongly recommend getting very good at this protocol before attempting to make relationships with plant teachers. Make sure you have a good story of the world and all the systems that nurture it but also the ones that are destroying it. Make sure you are grounded in right story and strong kin relations, so you understand the damage of extractive systems and economies and therefore aren't bringing that entropic pattern into your communication with Spirit and place. Above all, be prepared to take on the work that will be delegated to you. You might be disappointed to find that it's nothing special and does not make you fabulous or exciting or fuckable, but still you will have to see it through.

16

Save a Dragon, Slay the Grail

Laurel Sugden

LAUREL SUGDEN is a writer, plant witch, and Ph.D. candidate in ethnobotany at the University of British Columbia. In 2020, with Josip Orlovac and Felipe Pereda, she cofounded Huachuma Collective, a nonprofit in Peru that cares for the sustainability of San Pedro cacti through planting and community-led projects. She splits her time between Montana, where she was born and raised, and the Andes. Her photos and writing from the field can be found on Instagram @laurel.sugden and @huachuma.collective.

◆ ◆ ◆

THIS IS A STORY about dragons. Dangerous ones. Teeth, fire, hypnotic powers—the works. Dark green leathery skin that shimmers blue at dawn and sets off red-orange and deadly spikes. Golden wings that catch the sunlight, so they can reach their dwellings high in the cliffs of river valleys. Their bodies are thick as anacondas, and they drape themselves heels-over-head across the hot rocks, almost fifty feet long. These are the wild San Pedro cacti of Lima, Peru.

Fierce countenances and strict, every one of them. You cannot misrepresent your intent to them. Too many have tried: some looking for gold, some for women, some for enlightenment.

But the Andes have kept their secrets well-guarded. Cities of gold were never found. Many of the men who chased them ended badly. But the men didn't stop coming—wave after wave of them. When they had exhausted their quest for gold they turned to the treasure in the souls of the people: shimmering, many-colored threads that weft and warp in some of the most beautiful textiles on Earth. Lovely adornment, the men must have thought, for their own rather bland god. The genocide was cruel and bloody and the end of the world for nearly everyone, including the dragons. It was hard on dragon tamers, too: the women and men who had, over lifetimes, forged alliances with those greatest of creatures and learned their power. Five hundred years of witch hunts later, few dragons survive. The best hidden of them persist, though they have crept every year further up sheer cliff faces and into less traveled river valleys.

By a colorful twist of fate, I am married to one of them. Josip Orlovac Del Rio: part human, part cactus, and part dragon himself. His name comes from his Croatian father, a World War II refugee to Peru, but the cactus that runs green in his blood comes from his maternal grandfather, a dedicated herbalist and political revolutionary from the Andes.

So it is with San Pedro today: the maestros are mixed, Indigenous and European; the ritual is mixed, Indigenous and Catholic; even the plants are mixed, hybridizing rampantly and resisting all attempts at categorization. In any case, no purely Indigenous tradition of San Pedro shamanism survives. The plants draw power and symbolic utility from both worlds, and for this the dragons and their tamers have survived.

Josip lives on the land where he was born and raised in the Rimac Valley, downriver from where the fiercest of the remaining dragons dwell. I often live there too, along with our four wild cats and upward of four thousand San Pedro plants at last count, many of them over twenty years old. Their abundance and Josip's foresight in planting mean that all the medicine we work with falls naturally from mature plants. Every fallen head of cactus is replanted or gifted in a cycle of endless regeneration.

But this practice is the exception rather than the rule. Few cactus gardens on this scale exist yet, and the vast majority of San Pedro that people drink in Peru and around the world is poached from rapidly declining wild populations.

We are acquainted with a few of the dragon slayers. Their trucks filled with cacti pass our house at night after the forestry service checkpoint has closed, bound for illegal export from Lima—or for Cusco, the modern hub of San Pedro tourism. It would be easy to blame the people cutting and selling the plants for what is happening. However, most often, they are Indigenous community members whose ancestral connection to the medicine has been lost because of colonialization. It would be easier to blame the shamans in the Cusco area who order wild San Pedros by the hundreds for their ceremonies. They pay dirt-cheap prices for plants whose homeland they have never bothered to visit, while planting only a few token cacti at their retreat centers. We could even blame the thousands of tourists who pay to drink irresponsibly harvested San Pedro each year and call it "mescaline."

But it is a way of thinking that is destroying the plants—more than a person or even a group of people.

It is the quest for the holy grail that leaves dragons slain by the wayside.

It is the enormous and repeated doses of medicine designed to shatter egos and ram through the fortress walls of modern consciousness. It is the fetishization of transcendence at the expense of embodiment. It is the conviction that the answers will be found "out there," and we just need to push the limits a little farther. It is the very idea that life is a problem to be solved, and that there is an answer to the mystery, and if we had the answer we would know how to live. It is the cold, straight, upward path to enlightenment.

Answers. Endpoints. Solutions. Ascension. Fountain of Youth. Princess. Holy Grail.

Anyone can break an ego with psychedelics. With the right dose of the right synthesized chemicals, it takes less than a minute. Modern psychedelic science has become a veritable ego-dissolving, mystical experience generator. Unfortunately, if "ego death" were all that was needed for enlightenment, the most reckless among us would be the wisest.

It's easier to break shit than make shit.

Building a healthy, embodied, connected, fulfilled sense of self takes a lifetime. And that building process is what San Pedro is invested in. Will the plant blow the doors off the hinges of your psyche and show you the light of God? Maybe. If it's what you actually need.

More likely it will start by taking out the trash. Trauma and fear. Not comfortable nor pleasurable nor full of pretty lights, and a reason why some people discount San Pedro after a dud of a session or two.

Later it will teach you to live beautifully in the realms you already have access to. Grace them with your presence, your warmth, your texture, your gifts and power. Pour into them the fullness of who you are. Belong yourself to them with small, meaningful actions: a flower gifted to the river, a greeting to the sun and the birds each morning. Simple work, done well. In doing so, the dimensions that once were beyond reach to you will unfold themselves as you are ready for them.

You are here because your heart holds a question. Pack it in your coat, close to your body, where it will stay warm. Come, walk with the medicine.

We are going upriver. We are going to the water's source. Up to a spring-fed creek above the main valley. It is farther than it looks. Feel your lungs strain in the thin air; feel the sweat spring to your brow; feel your question grow heavy in your arms. Welcome the cactus spines that tear the legs of your pants and leave bloody furrows like cats' claws.

Climb community trails that line the creek and greet the farmers harvesting their prickly pear fruits in the desert sun. Buy a few to eat on your way. Consider what they remember: that in their own lifetimes, the Rimac ran with the blood of parents and friends and neighbors who were victims of terrorism in the 1980s. Today it runs with heavy metals and toxic waste from mining.

Rio Rimac, *rio hablador*. "River that talks," they call it.

Hearing this, go with respect. Hold the truth in equal measure with the beauty. Carry fruit: lucuma, chirimoya, paqay. Carry dry beans, root beer candy, seashells, *detentes* for Santa Rosa, coca leaves, Coca-Cola. Share with the children you meet. Then share with the land.

Touch the water. Introduce yourself.

Tip a drop from your cup of San Pedro into the pool. Drink the rest, quickly, before the bitterness gets to you. Drink it down.

Look to the mountain under your feet. There are the red-earth shards of a thousand years of ceramics. Pottery jugs of fermented corn beer, called *chicha,* were shattered here on the mountain as offerings. Run the fragments through your fingers. Feel their sharp edges. Find a larger piece, one that preserves its painted pattern—black-and-white geometrics, lines, dots, and if you're lucky, tiny figures that might be animals. Study it with all your senses.

Unwrap your question. Place it gently in the curved shard. Drop it into the water.

There, you see the same painted patterns reflected in liquid and stone? And yet, it is not a hallucination—it is the natural way that the water moves here, witnessed and recorded by an ancient artist, revealed by San Pedro. The plant surges in your blood. Nods yes. You close your eyes. The hairs inside your nose prickle with the scent of coming thunder. Electricity fizzes through the air.

The painted patterns pulse, pulse, and begin to feel like a certain drumbeat in the bones—a rhythm both ancient and deeply comforting. Listened to, the beats grow stronger, the rhythms more complete, and one may hope to catch strings of melodies rippling to the fore. The wind picks up.

Take my hand. Don't forget yourself to this power. It can only show you what you are ready to know—do not ask for more. This music asks us to stay together.

Caught, felt, entered, sung along with, the melodies unfold into scenes across space and time, and together we might—might!—be fortunate enough to meet the ancients there, whether they speak with human voices, or animal, or mountain.

If we can do this—follow the spiraling stories of stream and wind to the place where the ancestors dwell, and be unafraid—we might hear from the mouth of one of those ancients, or from the rising water seeping from Earth's depths up the base of your spine, water that shines with a timeless mineral light. Starwater—an answer. Not an answer for the brain, but for the heart. It's an answer that feels like déjà vu. It sounds like this:

> *We know how to fix this.*
> *This has happened before.*
> *We can see further than you.*
> *We've prepared for this.*
> *We want to prepare* you.

They may teach you to wake up those hidden pockets of Starwater in the Earth, circulate them like blood. May stroke each of your cells with golden fingertips to crackle the old sparks that burn in them. Blow sweet, straw-scented air on those sparks and watch them glow. They may also, given time, take our hands and lead us again into the sacred groves, into the lands on Earth that sing for us, the mountains or plains or forests or coasts where we belong.

They tug on the colorful threads that tie us together, and bump us laughingly into those we love. They know how the love between people and land creates a special center of gravity—no groups of believers or stairway to heaven or mirror houses of enlightenment, but the steady hum of people cooking together, taking care of each other, laughing, lovemaking. The generative tension of diversity balanced by the warm sun of belonging. Sweet like honeysuckle.

The world has ended before, in many ways, in many times and places. In the Andes, the end of a world and a turning over to a new era is called *pachacuti*. Pachacuti is enormous, inevitable, and decided by earthly forces much greater than humans. Humans cannot solve it, shift it, or change it once it has been set in motion. We can only listen, deeply, for the impulses rippling out from the center of the Earth, impulses that move us, that move all listening things.

What will be our bedrock? What can we hang on to as the world turns over? Their laughter feels like earthquake tremors underfoot.

How about actual bedrock?

These are no designs of sun gods on high. They are no machine elves or aliens or robots from the future. They care nothing for ascension, and everything for embodiment. They are warm, like volcanic water bubbling up from the depths. Solid like black forest soil beneath our feet, soil that is composed entirely of the bodies of the dead.

As are we.

As are we.

They are as ancient as the seasons, spinners of the wheel, shadow movers of Starwater. Were we to name the thirst we have for that substance, we may call it nostalgia or wistfulness. It's the longing for the garden before the Fall. The longing for the place we were before we were born.

Dip your cup and drink wild water, right from the spring. Splash it over your neck. Rub your eyes.

Look.

It's here, and you can hold only a cupful. But here, today, you can drink what you need and be nourished. You can have the answer your heart needs now. Tomorrow, you can have tomorrow's drink and tomorrow's answer.

But *they* hold all of it, forever. They always will. When Andean people connect to their ancestors through springs, caves, and highland lakes, they are not dealing in metaphor. The dead are the blood and power of Earth; they are our power and our blood.

Many "psychonauts" go out looking for the Starwater and its source. They may drown in it without bringing home a drop. They go out alone, unprotected by culture or true ceremony, and hell-bent on *understanding*. They are propelled by the sterile rocket fuel of synthetic psychedelic drugs. Or else they're propelled by untold doses of plants or mushrooms, bridled and ridden like straining horses, by the determination to go out farther, seek higher, and ultimately retrieve truth from some far-off land. Perhaps they're moved by some dimension "out there" that knows more about the reality of *here* than do the birds and rivers, the remnants of ancient glacial lakes, the clouds gathering in the east, the night-blooming cactus flowers that shine white like moons.

Do the machine elves have something more useful to our human experience than to the beings who live here, or lived here? Do they belong here the way the loon belongs to the lake? Can their insights be grounded, or are they an endless mirror of all that we long for but cannot attain?

Our minds alone are poor portals to truth.

Tip the grail. Spill it out. Watch the stars freed there sparkle before they sink into the Earth and disappear.

As will I.

As will you.

You never change things by fighting the existing reality. To change something, build a new model that makes the existing model obsolete.

BUCKMINSTER FULLER

Are We Alone with
Our Fate?

Bruce Damer, Ph.D.

BRUCE DAMER is an astrobiologist at the University of California at Santa Cruz, and chief scientist at the BIOTA Institute. With his colleague David Deamer he has coauthored a leading new hypothesis on the origin of life and tests it with teams worldwide. He has contributed two decades of mission simulation and design to NASA and other space agencies. Damer has also built an extensive collection of computing artifacts chronicling the rise of the digital world. He is a follower of the evolutionary edge of culture, an occasional wanderer on the path of plant medicines and elixirs, and the curator of extended archives of figures such as Timothy Leary and Terence McKenna. Many of his monologues can be found on the Levity Zone podcast, www.levityzone.org; his science, space, and personal projects at the BIOTA Institute, www.biota.org; and his personal website, www.damer.com.

◆ ◆ ◆

ARE WE ALONE WITH our fate? It is reasonable to believe that our future is dependent solely on us humans taking action and *getting it all just right.* Perhaps this belief is the source of our despair, for we know in our gut how fallible we are. When have we ever *gotten it all just right?* And yet, throughout our history we have been pulled forward through seemingly insurmountable natural disasters and catastrophes, some of our own making. Perhaps there are other forces in the world that will carry us forward, not to an inevitable crash of our civilization, but into a brilliant future?

PROLOGUE

My life's primary work has been a quest to reveal the bottom-up chemical and informational mechanism that powered life into existence on the early Earth some four billion years ago. I began this journey back in the mid-1970s as a "spectrumy" teenage kid. Shortly after my birth I was given up for adoption. I believe I was indelibly shaped by missing the connection with my birth mother, which is so critical in the first weeks of life. I came home to my loving adoptive family but I was averse to making eye contact. My mother described me, even as a newborn, as being "in your own world." I was definitely deeply inward, perhaps in a state that would be diagnosed today as autistic. From my earliest memories, I *realmed* to hyperdetailed worlds of the imagination, later learning how to draw them in vivid detail. I also loved nature, spending countless hours exploring the sagebrush hills near my parents' house in British Columbia.

At age fourteen I knelt down to study a mariposa lily emerging from the recently frozen ground. I wondered, *How did this beautiful and complex flower emerge from a simple bulb?* I stood up and cast my mind wide, asking: *Where did all these plants come from? Did they arise from a single, original seed long ago?* Pondering this "original seed" question while walking back across the hill toward the house, a vision appeared hanging in front of me. I stopped. As I was an Albert Einstein fan, I assumed this was an example of a "thought experiment" similar to his famous sprint alongside a beam of light. The sixteen-year-old Einstein used the insights and questions from that vision to later develop the special theory of relativity.

The vision appearing to me was that of a seething bundle of molecules in rapid motion. I decided to engage it. Looking for repeating patterns in how its parts were twisting and turning, I mentally posed the question, *How can these movements somehow assemble into the first living thing?* Instead of a reply, it retorted with its own question: *Figure out how I made a copy of myself!* I thought back at the bundle: *That's an implausible question; you can't make a copy of a machine without a bigger machine, and I don't see a bigger machine anywhere around you!* It winked. I took this riddle as the challenge guiding my central intellectual pursuit. And for a very nerdy kid I was pretty excited, for I knew I had found one of the coolest questions to commit my whole life to.

Early in my twenties I was introduced to computers and began to explore digital space, coding some of the earliest user interfaces available for 1980s personal computers. I experienced the pleasure of weaving tapestries of pixels that enabled users at big organizations to design documents on screens with the click of a new device called a "mouse." In my thirties I helped a nascent tech community birth a brand-new medium for human communication and community on the 1990s internet. These were the first virtual worlds—graphical cyberspaces inhabited by users represented as "avatars." This very exciting and pioneering work led to a decade developing serious virtual environments for NASA to simulate space missions. I was then tapped to help design missions to asteroids and the moon.

In 2008 I decided to return to school to earn my long-delayed Ph.D. For the thesis work, I felt ready to ask another big question, *What is the formula by which the universe complexifies?* Thus, the EvoGrid was born. It ran on a dedicated supercomputer stack for a year until, with some tweaks to our algorithm, the data began to trace out a distinctive, staircasing plot on our charts. First, we noted the numbers for volumes in which two bonds were formed, then three, four, six, nine, thirteen, and on upward. Like a mountaineer making his way into foothills leading to great peaks, each plateau represented a resting point from which higher maxima of complexity could be scaled. We had a clear signature of the "stochastic hill climber," a universal mathematical principle that seems to underlie the emergence of all things novel, from ever heavier elements forged in stellar furnaces to the evolving shapes of finch beaks observed by Charles Darwin in the Galapagos. It was also a well-characterized optimization proof and earned me my doctorate. Today I like to call it the "cosmic wiggle," a candidate for the universal formula of complexification, the emergence equation. Armed with this result, and having just met my future collaborator, David Deamer, I was finally ready to work on the riddle earlier posed by that persnickety bundle of molecules.

I now realize that, all through my early life's journey, I was in training to become a follower of what I now call "the Endo way." Endo is a practice that invites altered states of consciousness delivered from endogenous (internal) sources, not requiring the use of any ingested (external) psychoactive substances. I discovered that Endo is a phenomenon experienced by many people. It is characterized by receiving extraordinary visual downloads to clearly posed questions, usually while wide-awake. I realized that many great discoveries in science, including relativity theory, world-changing inventions, and visions behind profound works of art, were described as being fully formed, wakeful downloads.

To activate my own Endo machinery, I would load my mind with a key question and some fragments of design approaches, including reasoned and fanciful notions. I would then keep it in the back of my mind, holding onto the confidence that a solution would eventually be forthcoming. Sometimes stepping-stones would appear, specific actions that I knew I had to take. After patiently waiting for weeks or months, a detailed download would come. These downloads felt like I was sitting in a movie theater as a feature film flickered to life and poured off the screen. Pencil and paper at hand, I would begin to sketch. The download would last twenty minutes to an hour and then run out of steam. I would never try to influence or embellish what was playing out by bringing in my own imagination. When in Endo, I found it best to turn off judgment and other filters and just pay attention. The Endo way has never failed me; instead it has delivered in spectacular fashion over the decades.

Through my twenties and thirties I had skirted around the edges of psychedelics or mind-altering drugs of any kind. Barely taking a puff off a joint, I was reticent about messing up the machinery of my Endo system. For me these "Exo" or exogenously (externally) enabled experiences seemed like a crude shotgun approach, overcharging or dulling delicate brain tissues. I worried that they might invite in misleading ideations or perhaps consume me with destructive delusions. Meeting Terence McKenna changed all that. I concluded that "this guy was nowhere *near* whacked," and I liked his questioning scholarship and style of thought. I also noted that he was able to bring back some solid, and certainly very entertaining, stories and insights from the psychedelic netherworlds.

We first met in person in 1998 at my farm in California and again at his jungle hideaway in Hawaii. We agreed to a swap and a kind of experiment: I helped him experience avatar cyberspace for the first time, and he did me the great honor of opening the door to my first *psy-space* journey with psilocybin mushrooms. We then compared notes on our mutual "tripping" experiences in these two different immersive worlds. We also talked long into the night on questions such as: How does the universe build complexity? Could a form of intelligence inhabit the internet? And what is going on with all of this accelerating novelty? Sadly, our burgeoning inquiry was cut short when Terence was taken, less than two years later, by a rare form of brain cancer. I decided to continue to work on the questions we posed that night. To support that, I undertook an exploration of the full range of psychedelic "medicine" (although I sometimes prefer to use the more mysterious and less medical term *elixir*). I spent ten insightful years refining and ultimately combining my two visionary practices: Endo and Exo.

By my fiftieth birthday, I felt ready to bring one of the big questions of science to them: How did life begin?

FIRST COMES THE HEALING

I felt the calling to ayahuasca and joined a seasoned group on what would be the first of several trips to the Peruvian Amazon. When ideas crowded into my consciousness the night before my first ceremony, I admonished them: *First comes my healing!* There was that hard, painful knot in my gut. I had carried it with me since boyhood and it was the source of many physical and emotional struggles. It had isolated me from *feeling* other people and indeed, from feeling myself. In my first encounter with "Mama Aya" she flowed her tendrils around the knot. After providing me an extraordinary view of humanity's collective knot, she had me "look down, look into yourself now!" I witnessed an inner kindergarten that was out of control, with children in conflict, crying, or sitting in sad isolation. It was a shocking scene, and I shouted "time out!" The children all looked up and went completely still. For days I was acutely aware of these little ones. They now sat calmly on my bus, and I was finally able to serve as their caring driver. I was liberated.

After half a lifetime of not making eye contact, I became interested in how people felt, ticked, and booted up into their own version of "HumanOS." After several more trips to the medicine, I had established a good working relationship with Mama Aya. From my first moment of ingesting a powerful entheogen, I had carefully safeguarded my Endo machinery, mentally powering it down to protect it from the storms and high weirdness I was unleashed into. After dozens of sessions I had evolved a new practice, which I called "winding the vine." I would start the evening by taking a very small dose of the medicine. Next I would enter into a silent and alert presence, turning off all mental faculties and simply listening. Any sounds, shapes, or feelings that showed up served as my guide as to where to focus and what to do.

It was October, 2013, and my healing journey was ready to take a truly supernatural turn. Out there in the night I noticed a long, curved shadow. A glowing object beneath the curve caught my eye and I focused on it. It was a 1950s automobile with the interior light on. Lying across the back seat were a man and a woman. They were my parents making love beneath a suspension bridge in North Vancouver. *Become it, become it now,* was the voice that came into my head. I summoned up the courage to do what I knew my role required.

I now had to show up as the lead man in the drama of becoming me. Despite a self-conscious resistance, I clasped my hands over my head and formed my body into the shape of my father's sperm, ready to be injected into my mother. Now swimming among millions of fellow sperm, I rushed forward and became the first one to meet her egg. From the egg's point of view, I was the only one, and I was invited in. I was made. The egg began to divide and, as a blastocyst, it entered the portal of her uterus. In utero I grew past the threshold of embryo becoming baby. Surrounded by her amniotic fluid, I felt my mother's love for the first and only time.

I savored those moments, but then everything started moving very quickly. I heard a series of whispers, glanced over to the door of the ceremonial maloca I was sitting in, and there was a silhouette of two people. I struggled to understand them, but then knew that they were my parents deciding to give me up. Suddenly and wrenchingly, the heart connection with my mother dropped. From that point on I knew I was on my own. Psychically reorganizing, one part of me took on the task of protecting the delicate, emerging soul deep within: the little *petal*. The form that protection took was to hold the petal tight and take him on journeys around the universe.

Now to the knot. Two excruciatingly beautiful nights were spent birthing it. For the knot was an implanted, fetal form of me that had never wanted to leave the womb, yet the womb had left *it*. Softened and nurtured, the knot reconfigured and emerged as a beautiful baby boy. I took him out into the moonlit jungle and we danced. I had reparented myself, become whole, and learned a core practice in the healing arts. The knot dissipated, never to return. From that point on I was ready to receive and give love in an entirely new way. I had become comfortable making eye contact. Together with a heart that was now online, I was remade for the future.

AND THEN COMES THE REVEALING

In retrospect I now understand that the medicine wanted me to undergo this kind of fundamental healing before I could become a bearer of the knowledge that followed. Visionary revealing follows body healing perhaps as the medicines transmute into the elixirs. The knot was gone. I was engaging with other humans, and I had finally read my own boot-up code. I was ready to explore questions of the mind. To prepare for this new level of inquiry I sensed that an advancement in technique was required. For years I had been curious about the common bonds between Endo and Exo. Did both practices involve flushes of the same chemicals? I found that Endo trips deliver a vividly visual immersion but operate at a more subtle level than your classic hyperdriven Exo journey.

So what is Endo and when does it manifest in your life? Most people nodded their heads when I shared that when I was nine years old and went to bed after a stimulating day, I saw flashes of color behind my closed eyelids. It seems this is a pretty common experience. I quickly determined that these flashes were not lights in my bedroom but were coming from within. I learned that if I stilled my mind and just observed them, they turned into strobing red washes that then opened into technicolor worlds. I worked from that point to keep this "color TV mind channel" broadcasting, and have tuned into it ever since.

I now realize that this tuning in was the fundamental tech of Endo. How similar or different was an Endo show to the Exo broadcasts like those Mama Aya streamed in from the jungle every night? To find out, I dialed back my dosage to such a degree that our shaman used to joke about it, looking at me and saying to the group: "Tonight the rule is, a full cup." Taking a few drops of this tasty black castor oil, I then held myself in a grounded presence for over two hours. I waited for my microdose to manifest, and finally, there it was: sinewy lines of flowing geometry entering my field, eyes closed. Without losing signal with the subtle Aya channel, I carefully took down the mental firewall that for years had isolated my Endo system from anything psychedelic. With the touch of a wish, I felt a flush of Endo juice surge within my body, percolating up my spinal column to reach my brain. The visual field was suddenly filled with familiar, red fractal washes. The fractals flowed upward, touching the sinewy geometries reaching down. Aya and Endo had met.

The primary psychoactive compound of ayahuasca has been described as the "spirit" or "dream" molecule: dimethyltryptamine, or DMT. Did my experience of the visual field confirm that Endo and

Aya both induced flushes of DMT? It was just one data point, but what followed was truly remarkable and seemed to suggest the affirmative. My hands began to tingle, then vibrations moved throughout my body. My intuition said: *full activation*. Minutes earlier, my session with the shaman had resulted in a total healing through the song of his *icaro*. I was clear, and an open attractor. Energy began to move along my spine. It felt like kundalini and moved up through my crown. I sensed another energy entering the room, the inquisitive aliveness of the surrounding rain forest. Endo and Exo swirled, pulling a multibraided cord of different systems together and winding them into a thicker, ropy vine in my mind.

It felt potent and ready.

For one final threading, I invited Mama Aya herself to merge with me, assuring her: "It's easier this way; we can travel as one." It was now time to give her my special gift, a journey to the beginning of all of life. Stronger than any single medicine, the collective elements of the vine pulled and launched us onto a reverse transit through a trillion, trillion generations of ancestors. The egg and sperm of my parents rapidly receded as my consciousness raced back along lines of human and animal ancestry joining, joining, joining . . . back, and back, and back. The thick cloud holding three billion years of fungal and microbial lineages lay between us and my goal, but with a cool head we punched through.

Dropping through brown clouds floating in a pink sky over a hostile, alien Earth, my observer was about to arrive at the presumed time and place of life's birth four billion years ago. Beneath was a large volcanic peninsula hosting steaming geysers feeding interconnecting hot spring pools. Suddenly, my observer plunged into a molecular soup that was stirring in one of these pools. I was surrounded in all directions by vast numbers of silvery objects, and I recognized them as protocells, the lipid compartments containing other molecules that we form in the lab. I knew from our research that they could form from organics released by meteorites and dust landing in these warm little ponds. Looking around, I noticed one protocell lit up by squiggly, glowing, neon threads in its interior. I sensed these threads were polymers like those we also assemble in our experiments. A voice came to me with a familiar commandment: *Become it, become it now!* I moved my observing eye cautiously toward the neon protocell, and then I blacked out.

The ticktock of time resumed and I returned to awareness, now fully embodied as that protocell. My arms and legs were gone, replaced by an undulating sack made of lipid membrane. I was a mess of moving molecules. I felt a scream rising up inside me as my gelatinous body began to split asunder. My emotions raced, but my observer coolly watched the complex process of division. A part of me tore off, forming a spherical bud floating away. It contained nothing but darkness, and the word *death* came to me. It was a shocking feeling and I recoiled, turned inward, and noticed a brighter light in the surviving part of me, and I felt much more alive.

While the semichaos of the division was unfolding, my observer had been studiously recording the undulating movement of a particular glowing thread. It was a polymer, a molecule built up like a row of keys on a piano. Its segments moved up and down as though an unseen player was tickling out a tune. I realized that this unseen hand would return to play again and again. And through each death, each failed division producing a black bud, a little more of the composition of life would be written. When that song was played to its final movement, the first cell division would produce two daughter cells, each with their own independent futures. This was the final stage in the origin of life. As it was in the beginning and remains true today, death writes the song of life.

I sat back and took a pause. The room was quiet as our group was on a silent break. I checked in with myself. This had been the single most intense ten minutes of my life and yet I felt clear, with energy to spare. I sensed that rather than being overtaxed by the Exo elixir of Aya, my Endo system had generated most of what I had experienced. With a small dose, Aya was a player but not the star of the show.

Perhaps there was another act to come?

MECHANISM MEETS MAGIC

The question now consuming my nerd mind was: *The unseen hand playing the keys of the polymer, what was it and how could a precise, repeatable score emerge?* The particular sequence of keys, the base units composing the first genetic polymer, would have to encode all the steps to make the first cell division possible. Science tells us the composer writing that code would have been none other than the earliest version of Darwin's natural selection. Even before life emerged, this "computer" was already in operation, driven by cycles of energy and self-assembly processes to animate nonliving matter, molecule by molecule. Wherever in the universe the conditions are right, this engine will fire up and churn away, climbing the hill to life traced by the cosmic wiggle.

Fair enough. My reasoning mind concluded that the mechanistic answer was fully explanatory, if a bit mundane. I therefore concluded that this was "the machine that made us." I thought it was a done deal, but there was more to come. Months later, while revisiting my embodied experience of the protocell division, I fell into a powerful Endo trip. It was the bookend to my jungle download, the completion of the solution. I was shown that the little protocells undergoing the first faltering attempts to divide were enabled within a communal matrix of fellow protocells. This matrix was the *progenitor* for life, the actual cradle of Creation.

The progenitor also directly addressed the riddle and the wink offered by that bundle all those years ago. The answer: a collaborative web of little machines can collectively lift a bigger machine into existence. It then struck me that the scenario of life's origin within this cradle was fundamentally *cooperative.* Darwin's Victorian science considered nature "red in tooth and claw," a slave to the dictum "survival of the fittest" in a winner-take-all world. Yet, in the simple protocell world that begot life, there *could be no competition.* These flimsy molecular entities simply had no tools to compete and could only survive and grow as a member of a larger, sharing aggregate. Life really had to arise through a deeply codependent, collaborative mechanism.

I thought, *Perhaps this mechanism still lies at the core of all life today?* To be clear, competition is a potent vehicle of evolution on Earth and is clearly at play throughout the human world. But the takeaway might be that collaboration made competition possible, and that they operate as a partnership. Our fear that our fate will be sealed by some terrible dog-eat-dog scramble for dwindling resources could therefore be tempered a bit. *We are wired to get along.* Like Einstein's discovery of relativity, which so was transformative to society in the 1920s, this new finding from the hard sciences might carry a similar, transformative power in our time. The deeper you grok it, the more meaning the mechanism starts to take on. This download about our communal origins completed the model, which was published in several widely cited scientific articles.

Until recently, I have lived most of my life "in my head." Yet my heart and my whole being craves another reality: traveling in a space of awe and wonder, with no map and no explanation. The *magic* of the Endo and Exo journey keeps drawing me back. I am comfortable to leave the reassuring world of logical problem-solving behind and just receive. Having one foot in the world of these mysteries gives my life much more shape and color and is as core to my being as breathing. And yet I still seek explanations: *Where do these experiences come from, and what entity or system delivers them so elegantly and vividly?*

Sitting in the maloca during another trip to the Amazon, I asked: *Was it the DMT molecule itself that orchestrated this, or was it something greater, an intelligence far larger, way beyond the capacity of our mind to figure it out?* I sensed that the intelligence needed me to cocreate it. It was clearly running on the OS of DMT and other molecules flowing through my synaptic gaps. Yet the experiences often seemed foreign, imported from a distant reality well outside my life experience to that point. Was it all generated internally through Endo, or did it disembark into my consciousness from some psychic flying "exosaucer"?

What if it was both?

Every culture and religious tradition share the belief in a greater intelligence inhabiting our world. We like the idea that this intelligence listens to us, and perhaps shapes our future. Some call it "God"; others refer to a nonhuman "synchronous field"; and still others talk of a "planetary mind," like the famous French Jesuit priest-scientist Teilhard de Chardin's noosphere. During experiences of *ecstasis* perhaps we really do come into contact with that intelligence. Human history is full of proscriptions about how to facilitate such encounters. These were once rare in our history, and avatars such as the Buddha were among the first to report on a complete merger with this intelligence. Experiencers describe the end of suffering, entering a great emptiness inhabited by a mind both all-seeing and accepting. They emerge embodying a powerful form of peace, and practice unconditional love with a wisdom of discernment. With the tools of Endo, Exo, and other practices, millions of us are entering this realm and are changed. By our example we will reflect this light into the lives of others and provide hope and courage to a world in crisis.

Sitting there in the maloca as our silent break was coming to an end, I was marinating in a sustained state of bliss. I still felt the presence of that guiding intelligence close at hand, so I thought: *Quick, there is more work to be done!* I dove back in and posed the following rather bold question: *If what I experienced was the machine that made us, where is Spirit in that?* The reply began to flow in as I became surrounded by colonies of the first living cells, spreading from pool to pool. They were beginning an unpremeditated collective labor that would transform a toxic planet into a garden world. I looked up and there towering above me was a translucent spire—stacked cellular innovation built layer upon layer. It was a single sculptural vision, four billion years high, of the origin and evolution of life and consciousness.

The spire sat on a volcanic hot spring landscape underlain by the blast of the big bang that created the universe and caused the heavier elements to form rocky worlds. The spire grew through life-forms capturing the daily shower of energy from the sun. Bacteria and archaea begat eukaryotic cells and then fungi, animals, and plants, and ultimately, us.

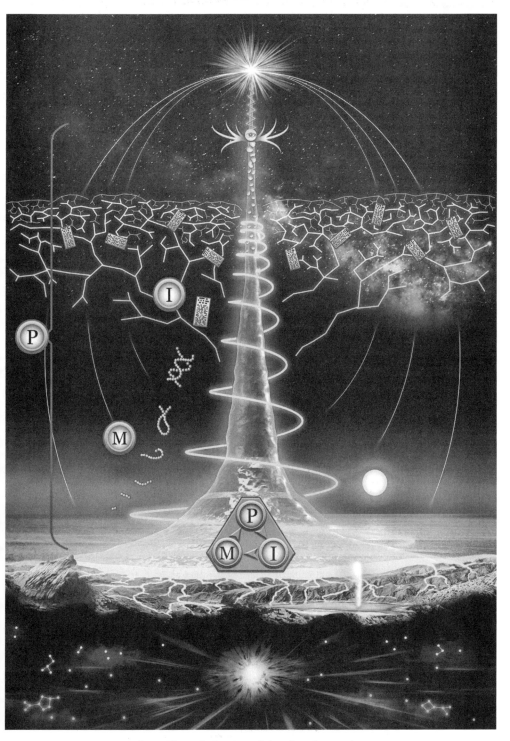

The "Silver Spire," a vision by the author
Concept and sketch by Bruce Damer, rendering by Ryan Norkus

The combined actions of their probability-shaping chemical encounters (P), network interactions (I), and the storing and reading of genetic memories (M), had created a machine I named PIM.

Operating within life at all scales, PIM's spin was weaving something else, an invisible web that surrounded the spire like a haze: the "field." PIM propagated and vastly increased the inventory of connections, memory, and the probability-shaping capacity of that field. The field in turn accelerated the growth of the spire. As I traveled along its length, I observed microbes turning into multicellular organisms. Body and brain sizes grew. Out of this milieu toward the top of the spire, an eye opened, looking out over its world and then back on itself. It heralded the coming of self-awareness in animals such as cetaceans, birds, elephants, and primates. Only one animal was capable of toolmaking. Culture, science, technology, and humankind began to rock the planet. Our presence put evolution into hyperdrive, and within a hundred generations we remade the world in our own image.

Looking further up, beyond the eye, a quickening series of zigzags told of a highly energized, unpredictable near future.

The zigzags wound up to a point where the spire seemed to pinch infinity. From that point a brilliant flash of light emanated. The light cast tendrils reaching down, back four billion years toward the light emitted by the big bang. Was this emanation the coalescence of the field into an all-embracing, planetary intelligence? Or possibly was it a beacon marking the sublime summit where the Buddha and other awakened beings sat? Perhaps this light might grow ever brighter as more of us touch and are touched by it? The light helps us in exposing the long shadow of humanity. This shadow is clean and full, telling of our pain and fear. Once we engage it in communal healing, we will turn to face into the light for our collective revealing.

This majestic vision was a response to my question: *Is there Spirit in the machine that made us?* The machine is hardly a simple mechanism. For it lifted all of life, scaled up an unfathomable enormity so potent with probabilistic potential that it could yield miracles exceeding all genius, paint any scene of exquisite beauty, and grant us any form of experience of the mystical we might seek.

The machine and the magic were one.

ONE MORE QUESTION!

I felt a tug. It was time to come down from this exalted state, to rest. Not knowing when I would ever return to this place, I beseeched into the night: *I sensed a mind, an intelligence behind the undulating keys of the polymer. This is implausible: an intelligence present before life began— don't you need to have life before you can have intelligence?*

I turned and faced into the dancing energy of the field. Imperceptibly at first, then resolving out of moonlight reflecting off the palms in the jungle canopy, began a stream of light. The stream resolved into the most ancient of star clusters, surrounded by immense sheet walls of dust. Multicolored stellar nurseries ignited and birthed countless new worlds. Galaxies arrived in their billions and packed the deep field. I recalled years before sharing with Terence the story of my first Exo journey: the near-death and transmutation of the universe by consciousness. This time the newborn cosmos rushed toward me, impacting my consciousness with a force that knocked me back. The answer provided was clear: *The universe was born and grew large enough to permit the probabilistic pathway for human beings to come into existence!* In that moment I felt the presence of a truly vast intelligence, the totality of the All. The Creator was all that was in Creation.

WE ARE NOT ALONE

As I was growing from embryo into baby, I became entombed into a deep well of aloneness. And yet today, I no longer feel alone. Time and time again I experienced a force, an intelligent presence, which brought me to a state of healing. With each healing I was provided a revealing, which carried my life's work to a point I never thought possible.

When I consider the question we posed at the outset of this inquiry, I feel I can now answer with certainty: *we are not alone with our fate.* Our very existence in this universe is extraordinary, and despite the challenges we face, we are riding an accelerating forward vector of miraculous actualization. This leaves me with no doubt that there are forces all around us and within us that will carry us to and through that brilliant passage into our future.

18

Plants and Subjectivities

Learning from Plants

Ailton Krenak, Ph.D.

AILTON KRENAK is a thinker, environmentalist, and one of the main voices of Indigenous knowledge. Along with Dantes Editora, he created Selvagem, a cycle of studies about life. Ailton lives in the village of Krenak, by the margins of Rio Doce, in Minas Gerais, Brazil. He is the author of the books *Ideias para adiar o fim do mundo* (*Ideas to Postpone the End of the World*); *O amanhã não está à venda* (Tomorrow is not for sale); and *Vida não é útil* (Life is not useful).

◆ ◆ ◆

THE WORLDVIEW CONSTITUTED by the massive and broad influence of the logical thinking of the West establishes the separation between culture and nature and teaches all children from the earliest age that the two do not mix. This worldview can express disorder, and it represents a regressive backtracking of humanity, which can be characterized by disorder. It denotes a distinct difference between the "civilized" and the "wild ones" who are not. *Wild* in this context means everything that emerges from the natural world, in dynamic contrast to all that is born from the culture of humankind and has been "tamed" by it.

Beyond climate change or climate crisis, the twenty-first century

---

This chapter was translated from the Portuguese by Sofia Reis and Laís Furtado.

announces this abyss between culture and nature that has revealed itself. Many millions of people now live in urban areas of the planet, isolated and literally separated from the Earth, fearful of contagion or any proximity to nature. We have brought about the Anthropocene in a declared separation of the human from non-human.* The non-human here is everything that involves listening to the voices of the Earth and her constellations of living beings, which is infinitely more diverse and vast than mere human speciesism. The Anthropocene asks us who can guide our reconciliation with life beyond the limited scope of the human.

When I started reading Western literature, I discovered an idea from other traditions that surprised me: humans are complete unto themselves, and they can control and subjugate nature and history. Such a thing does not exist in my tradition. Instead, we are *part* of important events, not *apart* from them. Despite living and relating for a long time with the facts as recorded by the clock's calendar, I look to preserve this original memory within me. My appreciation of history has to be careful to follow the path and vision of my ancestors. We understand that we are capable of moving a stone that may be creating a blockage on the edge of the *igarapé* (stream), but we know we cannot change the destiny of the waters. Again, we are part of events; folded into their very fiber. We step in or interfere with them from our virtue and our knowledge, from our interaction with that place, but we cannot act as beings external to those events.

EPISTEMOLOGY AND WILDLIFE

Unlike a moral calculation or division between civilized and wild beings, I see the wild *as* life. The expression of life *is* wild. Life does not seek our species, it moves *through* our species. That's why a tree was once a stone and a river was once a cloud. It's wonderful—you look at

---

*The Anthropocene is the current geological age during which human activity has been the dominant influence on climate and the environment.

a cloud and you can see a river! This is evolution in action, but not in the same way it was conceived of in the twentieth century as something that happens outside of us. For a seventeenth-century naturalist, to be wild was not the opposite of being civilized. For them, to be wild was to embody that natural truth of the life they sought.

Where did such a profusion of life come from? Had it sought existence in the Himalayas, in the African deserts, in the Andes? Humankind has been looking for the fountain of life and to follow the thread of life wherever it might be found. We might deem the seeking of the origin of life to be a childish human endeavor, and it's interesting to observe that we judge that quest in this way. However, and again, life is what speaks *through* us. Naturalists were hunting life. But we already *are* this life—we don't need to look for it. This is powerful because it gives us confidence—a firm confidence that life is greater than any reflection we can create, including a reflection that incorporates the world of science in its purview.

Good words are those that pacify us, and we have songs, or chants, that are short and that feature such good words. These songs are an expression from our soul, from the depths of our being, which opens other connections. They enable a special type of interaction where we can pause our mental activity and let our spirits establish communion with the environment, with people, with everything—even if we are inside a closed room or a book.

For a long time I ran away from school, and in adult life I prevented the children of my village from going to school. I wanted distance from schools, any of them, because I knew we already had the best school possible. I resisted government schools as much as I could. I don't recommend anyone taking their young children and handing them over to something called "school."

The Krenak people understand that we must protect our children from negative contact with the so-called "educational" system, because to educate is to domesticate. We want to preserve our wild soul. We still want to be able to react and to be able to move with the changes. If we settle into an education that trains us for a certain kind of survival, when the sky falls on our heads we won't know what to do. This has happened a few times. In our history, heaven has already fallen on our heads at times, and our ancestors had to create a new world again. In our very old narratives with the first humans, their world ended and they then had to reinvent other worlds: a second or third edition of the world as it were.

Maybe this brutal colonization that has hit the planet in the last millennium is the sky falling in over our heads, messing up our convictions. But if we—those who keep the memory—continue clinging to that memory, we can find our place on Earth again and restore the way of life we love and value. We love and want to continue living in the natural places that we treasure.

Many of our territories have been transfigured, but we still know who we are. This is my vision. Of all the promises the white men made, the only one they kept was that they would take our land. This seems to be common the world over. It makes our battle around the world a constant claim for our lands, either because we can't hunt or we can't have the use of the water. Any restriction means we don't have autonomy, we don't have full access to natural resources, and we are being contained. It is against this situation that Native peoples all over the world are standing up. The oldest expression of colonial assault is the assault on our homes, and the current worldview of the north has only served to deepen the assault, which we must resist.

LIFE MANAGEMENT

We live in times of disillusionment with a kind of life-management that has left people without direction. Life moves through everything. It is in everything, including us, of course. The process of evolution that Darwin described is not limited to the nineteenth century. It happens to us every day, like a butterfly in the backyard. Life is always being re-created. It never ceases to exist, it just moves around. This is the example I have in mind—the caterpillar and the butterfly.

There is a life-celebration narrative among the Desana and Tukano

Amazonian peoples that says that these bodies in which humans are configured today were, in another time, bodies of water, amphibians, or fish, and that this transformation of water to land life took place within the "transformation canoe" story. This would be the event that completes the understanding, the cosmovision, and the memory of these peoples about the origin of life: the snake canoe came through the waters, sailing rivers and seas, and was manned by fish-people. Different from fish, a multitude of species were configured as human bodies later and now inhabit the forested areas. Beyond the observable metamorphosis happening in the beings around us—in plants or animals—our idea of the body comes into play. Body is what we identify as anatomic, meaning that a being has previously and can again in the future be housed in the form of a different body, a different type of entity.

The idea of a life power implies that everything that exists on Gaia—this wonderful Earth organism—is permeated by this sense of life as a creation that did not take place in a remote event, but instead was and is generated each and every moment. This metamorphosis expresses the constant creation of life. It is similar to what the Brazilian anthropologist Eduardo Viveiros de Castro calls "perspectivism." According to this idea, form and content are transforming over and over again. *Content* is the life that runs through us, while the *forms* can be many. They may range from plants to organisms we consider to be more active than a plant—like a cat or dog we see jumping around that makes us realize they're interacting and full of life.

Species like a Sumaúma (Kapok) tree can live two hundred to three hundred years on the side of a river, where many generations of people can pass by and feel a presence there. But there are many other beings living in the gigantic Sumaúma. In fact, some of these Amazon cultures believe that that tree is inhabited by an infinite number of living beings. This is another metamorphosis scenario, where a certain form can exist for a while, but its contents keep changing. It's this principle of the re-creation of life. What I mean, quite precisely, is that we are nature, unlike what they teach at school or what I read in the world's literature—this belief that we have a body separate from nature. We, our bodies, *are* nature.

THE PLANTS AND US

Plants have a special relationship with humans, as they function like forms interwoven with the content of life. Take, for example, the body painting that Amazonian peoples do with the genipap plant. I would like to reflect on the use of plants in traditional Indigenous medicine, based on this idea expressed above about how content moves through different forms, how life moves through our bodies, and how we are nature. In these practices, they do not think of the use of teas or the active principles of plants as herbal medicines only. It goes beyond that, and works with the perspective of the associations of masters who use the healing power of plants in practices that affect human subjectivity.

We are used to thinking that if we prepare a bath, or a tea, or if we extract the active principle from a plant, it is possible to produce medicine. But what I'm inviting you to think here has to do with the different uses that physicians of Indigenous medicine make from the association between humans and plants. Some people, through their connection with plants—or more precisely, with the masters or owners of those plants—are able to summon these extraphysical qualities of plants to act as auxiliaries in therapeutic care practices. That is—in practices that go beyond the therapeutic.

Without necessarily making a direct application of any active principle of that plant other than its symbolic expression, these practices I'm referring to could begin, for example, with taking a genipap tincture bath as part of an initiation rite that can open new insights for the healer. From this bath you will be able to count on the help of this plant, genipap in this case, when it is working to take care of the person undergoing treatment.

A body painting, an impression on the body with these marks, will summon the healing nature of this plant to reestablish balance, to activate some self-healing principle within the patient, who is the recipient of the cure or treatment. The healing relationship between the plant and the patient takes place in a different dimension from that of the active biochemical principle.

Plants can also act as aids in healing through dreaming with these plants, or to be more precise, through their manifestation in dreams. Here they take the place of masters in the treatment of different disorders or of different mental and physical states. In these states the recipient of the healing starts to establish communion, a connection with the nature of this plant, recognizing its personal quality.

The plant is an active subject, and the patient who relates with it develops an affection for it. That's why, before the healer looks for them, plants usually choose their healer, the agent who will look after them. A person initiated in this knowledge can be visited by a plant in a dream. However, he could also be walking along a forest trail and be surprised by the presence of a plant that is not endemic to that place. This might be a plant that shouldn't be there on that riverbank or on top of that hill but that appears to him nonetheless. The initiated person will recognize that plant because they will be touched and will feel the plant communicating to them. Of course, this would be a person already open to this kind of contact, already initiated in this relationship. It is very uncommon for a person totally blocked in the senses to be surprised by a plant talking or to have a diet (*dieta*) prescribed for them. But plants do have this communicative power.

The relationships that plants establish do not occur in physical forms, but with the subtle body, which is imprinted on the body, like a tattoo or a drawing. Take the genipap, for example, placed on the arm of a Kayapó painting. It's on the arm, but it's also somewhere else, in another place you're not aware of—your subtle body. Some other medicine practices—such as Ayurveda, acupuncture, and what they call Chinese medicine—also take into consideration this subtle body sensitivity. These pertain to the functions of chakras and other vital centers that balance the energy circulation of both the physical and the subtle body.

The subtle body is like a sensitive layer of the physical body. It's more active when we are children but becomes disempowered with the development of the intellect and other nervous reactions in the physical body. If we call it a sensitive body, we would say it is something that is organically related to the head, trunk, limbs, and even the senses. But the subtle body, in the way we're referring to it, is the ability to keep the senses activated throughout one's physical development. For example, when someone gets scared, or has an accident, it's very common for them to experience what psychoanalysts call "trauma"—an emptiness, a degree of detachment from this sensitive body, from a sense of balance or well-being. Everyone has their physical, mental, and subtle alignment, which we could call "psychological" or "spiritual," but for this purpose we'll call "subjectivity."

The first relationship with the plant is through subjectivity, such as how it manifests through body painting. But it can also be established (though not manifested) in different, other ways. These other ways include picking up the plant, activating it, and leaving its essence in the air, in the environment, and with people passing by. For example, if you take the leaves of citronella and rub them, it creates an aura, a beneficial relationship with your physical body. It gives you a good sensation, which you're inhaling, exhaling, and feeling, thus amplifying the frequency waves of your physical body with the subtle body.

Of course, for someone who has been experiencing the pressure of the "reality" field for a long time, this surrounding reality that forces them to think about time—counting the hours 24/7 and always paying attention to routines—limits their recognition and enjoyment. A person living like this has an obstructed subjectivity field, greatly reducing the flow between the physical and the subtle body.

This stage of our relationship with plants that I'm referring to is prior to the direct use of the active ingredient of the plant, whether through the ingestion of tea, or any other application. It is about expanding the understanding that *all* plants are plants of power. There is no list of plants that are not of power: again, all plants are of power.

Many Native people in the northeast region of Brazil have a traditional ritual use of the *Jurema* plant. In the Amazon, we find peoples making use of other plants, ayahuasca for example, and these mark two very distinct camps. From the point of view of culture, these relationships are informed by the cultural heritage matrix of each group. Among these communities we can find a vast repertoire of indirect uses of the healing power of plants. These uses range from cotton—for restoring the physical body affected by an accident or illness—to the use of some plants simply to invoke their power as a blessing. The term *blessing* became common to many cultures, perhaps because it is the easiest way to communicate what actually happens, given that it's a subtle application of the plant and not a direct one.

When you bless someone with a twig of rue, for example, you don't have to order the patient to eat the rue, or order him to drink the rue tea. When blessing with rue you are invoking the power of that plant, its healing power to communicate with the subtle body of that person.

To bring this perception closer to the most common understanding, it would be possible to say that just as in the Afro-Brazilian tradition there is this reference to the owners of plants—the *orixás*. In different Indigenous cultures the owners of these plants are other beings who have this domain, and grant access of the knowledge to selected humans. These plants choose those people as affiliates. The plant likes the person and then manifests itself in several ways. It will appear in the person's path, in their garden, and in their dreams. It's different from going to pick up a plant in a botanical garden, nursery, or herbarium. Instead, the plant can leave its own domain to make contact with you. It takes the role of master, acting as a caregiver, together with the human. In this sense, the plant is not working *on* the person, or in any other way, but is effectively calling humans to work *with* it. That is wonderful, because it opens up to the perspective that these other beings have their own agency and their own fields of action and domain.

When one's perception opens up to this field of subjectivity, the human being opens up to all these possibilities of interaction, communion, and contact. In the case of plants, this is true despite the long history of resorting to plants to produce drugs in the creation of the entire drug industry. This is based for the most part on the use of the active principle of plants, and also from animal sources, minerals. Many of the medicines that people consume on a daily basis come from plants.

The colonialization of nature is done with minerals, which comes from the rocks, from the mountains, and other sources in the mineral kingdom. This relationship of colonialization with the mineral kingdom also occurs with the plant and animal kingdoms. These are distinctions made in the field of Western science. But in this other type of plant interaction with the subtle field, it's the senses that are affected. Some humans are able to activate the subjectivity of the plants, just as the plants themselves affect those people. They relate to and affect each other.

This means expanding the field of subjectivity relations between beings beyond this anthropocentric colonizing use—the colonization, for example, of corn and tobacco by modern industry. Tobacco has such a history of being representative of this plant agency, which is a story of the Mbya Guarani. Families of these people moved through the vast region of territories. When they felt welcomed, the first sign they had that they could make the Tekohá—their sacred place of life—was the instruction that Ñanderu (the Creator) gave them. This instruction posited that they should open a clearing and camp in the woods—not settle down, just make a *tapiri* and stay camped in the forest. After a few days of camping there, they walked through the *coivara* (cleared area) into a place where the trees had already been felled.

As they walked, they looked carefully for where the fallen trunks were to see if a tobacco plant, the *pety*, had sprouted. (The *petyngua* is the bowl for burning tobacco, while *petai* is tobacco. For us, in the Krenak language, tobacco is called *kumã*, meaning smoke.) If the little plant spontaneously appears in the clearing, you can build the maloca (the *opy*, or house of religion). Then you can start a farm and build a home.

This is a balanced settlement model, obeying the principle of Ñande Rekó. The settlement is born from the Earth. It does not implant itself on the Earth, it sprouts *from* the Earth. If we were to speak in the language of the subtle field, we would say that the land demarcates a place for us, not that we demarcate the land. It is the land that chooses who it wants; not who wants it and appropriates it. This is another kind of communion, of contact.

Let us close with this beautiful story. I have mentioned the example of tobacco, but there are others. My dear friend Nixiwaka tells me that when the Yawanawa in Acre established themselves in the village of Seringal Kaxinawa (the New Hope) below the Gregório River, for a long time they didn't visit the old village up the river. Once, when Nixiwaka was walking in that Kaxinawa village, he was surprised to see a captivating little plant calling his attention. He got close and saw that it was a *muka,* a kind of shamanic potato that didn't exist anywhere else and that nobody knew where to find anymore.

This muka plant chose to appear where an old house was located. It then activated a hidden or sleeping field of subjectivity for him and for his relatives. In this, it provided a real rebirth in the culture of the Yawanawa and in the training of new doctors, of new *pajés* (healers). These new doctors and healers then began to receive dreams, songs, music, and paintings. It was a true renaissance of something they already had, because their ancestors had this knowledge but the people had not been applying it. The Yawanawa then began to apply this entire body of knowledge that the plants had kept for them for so long time, waiting to deliver to them there in the sacred village of the Seringal Kaxinawa.

Indigenous people are the original sentinels of Mother Earth. This means that we have an intimate, informed, and practice/evidence-based connection to her.

SOLANA BOOTH

19

First Aides

Indigenous Stories to Heal
Our Relationship with Mother Earth

Solana Booth

Solana Rose Booth, Tsymsyan, Mohawk, Nooksack, lives in the state of Washington, where among her many skills and responsibilities she is a storyteller, filmmaker, lineage medicine keeper, and community leader promoting, cultivating, and integrating Mother Earth and ancestral teachings employing Indigenous healing modalities.

◆ ◆ ◆

As you are reading this, I pray that you are in good health, and that this finds you in your highest self. I want to thank my relatives who also contributed to this book. It is an honor to be in this space with them all.

ALLOW ME TO INVITE YOU to radically accept that we as a human family and Mother Earth have been in an unhealthy relationship, and that this relationship is causing us to have an unhealthy relationship with ourselves and with one another. Regardless of which happened first, we are all in tough times, we are in *the thick of it* (a term used when we are referencing a tough time during a plant ceremony). This book is a testament to humanity and Mother Earth. This is what we are all asking for, and also what Mother Earth is asking for.

Indigenous people are the original sentinels of Mother Earth. This means that we have an intimate, informed, and practice/evidence-based connection to her. It's knowing that we are both made of the same elements—mostly water. Here is the first story of how deeply connected we are to Mother Earth as a human family and how we can reframe the dysfunction happening among all of us right now.

This story starts long, long ago. And when I say, "long ago," I mean before computers, before radio, before television, before the written word, before mental health diagnoses, before prisons, and before borders. It was so long ago that sometimes folks didn't always speak to one another with words. Sometimes they communicated without their mouths. Sometimes we could just feel each other and we knew. We employed other intelligences, such as awareness, connection, and deeper authenticities. This story is from *that* long ago.

These people had a special protocol and lived in a special way. This village community of Indigenous people traveled with the seasons. At certain times of the year they would be by the river. At certain times of the year they would be farther down by the valley. At certain times of the year it just depended on what was happening outside. It depended on what the people needed for their homes and for each other, on what resources they needed to gather, such as when the berries were ready. Or when it was time to harvest salmon. So you could say that these people had a strong relationship with Mother Earth and that they were living the best they could.

One day the chief of the people was so very blessed to receive his daughter, his beautiful, precious daughter. But sadly, he lost his wife in childbirth on that very same day. The chief and the people then had to come even closer together to help his daughter, to help tell her those stories about her mother in the hope that she would remember her mother, hoping that she would remember how special and precious she was. The community would share stories of her mother's leadership and how she foraged for foods and medicines for them. They told the young girl how she loved being pregnant and how she celebrated her pregnancy daily. Her mother would say she was carrying a future matriarch, a leader for her people, a future grandmother. It was said that while she was pregnant, the young girl's mother prepared and planned many good things for her daughter, to fulfill a good, long, and fruitful life. Her behavior as a pregnant person was common in those days. That's what mothers did back then. That's what they did for us.

You could say that the people were emulating what Mother Earth does for us the way they cared for this precious girl. This manifested in the way they told her these stories about her mother singing and harvesting and foraging for food for the family, about her masterful weaving of cedar bark, and about partnering with the cedar trees. The young girl grew up listening to these stories about her mother. When she first started to speak and use her words to the people, she talked about her mother as if her mother was around all the time. She talked about remembering when her mother was a young woman. She talked about stories that the people didn't tell her. It's as if this young girl was still very connected to the spirit of her mother. It's as if the young girl was very much awake in generosity, awake in humility, awake in such a divine wisdom that at only fifteen winters old she sometimes surprised the people with her responses to the leadership. And that was okay with the little girl.

As this young woman got older, she began to sense things that were going to happen. She began to sense exactly when the berries would be ready. She began to sense what kind of teas to prepare to prevent sickness of the freeze. She began to feel the salmon as they were coming back home. Her people supported her in her connection to Mother Earth and the spirit of her mother. One day the young woman decided to share that a big fire was going to come, and it was going to wreak havoc on the people, and that people might lose their longhouses, their canoes, their food, their territories, and their livelihoods.

It was difficult for her to share what she was seeing in her mind and in her heart. She was convinced by this vision—so convinced that she begged her father and some workers around the village to help build her an underground chamber. Finally, because they wanted to appease the daughter of the chief and make her happy, she got her underground chamber. As soon as she got it, she began to stockpile it with certain dried goods, salmon, teas, and plants to aid sleep and bring good feelings. Her vision of the fires just kept coming, visions of the fire taking away her family just kept coming, and she kept calling for her mother in her sleeping space, in her dreams. She imagined her mother there with her the more she had the visions of the fires coming.

Soon the young woman began to feel emotions that she hadn't felt before. She began to feel worried and confused because the people—including her father—weren't adhering to her warning. They weren't taking her seriously, and that confused her. She knew she had to stay true to what she foresaw in her visions. She was convinced the fire was coming.

It was getting close to fall time, the time when the salmon would be coming back home. At that time of the year the young woman was joyful, she was excited, she seemed even more motivated about life during this moon. She began to sing some of her mother's songs to the people at this time in hopes of showing them how serious her visions of the fire were. She wanted to build chambers for her people and bring the people into their own chambers to keep them safe. She wanted them to take her seriously.

In her vision of the coming fire, she thought, *Maybe if I get my mother's song down they'll believe me.* You see, at that time no one was teaching her mother's song. There is a whole other creation story about songs and how important they are to the people. There is a whole list of protocols that go along with bringing a family song out, a lot of work that must be done when you share a song. Just as the salmon were entering the river to spawn, the young woman's feelings that this fire was coming were getting so strong, just as her mother's spirit told her the fires were on their way. So she locked herself in her underground chamber and didn't come out for ten days. While she was in there she ate, had teas, and slept. She was safe in her chamber.

When she came out of the chamber on the tenth day, no one was there. She could smell burnt houses. She could smell an awful stench of burnt foods and of burnt loved ones who had been taken by the fires. Mostly ashes were left of her village and territories. She could feel the warmth of the burned-out fire and the crisp of the fall season's arrival. Devastated and utterly alone, she began to weep. She felt previously unknown pains and uncomfortable sensations. The pain was coming from the area around her belly button and went up her back into her shoulders. The young woman wept deeply through all of this emotional, physical, spiritual, and mental pain. The spirit of her mother helped her remember her father and the people who had perished, by singing memorial songs and weeping over the remains. This memorialization lasted four days around the territories of her beloved father and people.

The young woman now began to take inventory for herself. She was thankful for the food she had in her chamber, but she knew it wouldn't last much longer. She understood that she needed help. There were no more cedar trees for her to gather bark and weave a coat. There were no more plants or roots to dig to sustain herself. Every day she would go to the river and cry. She would sing remnants of her mother's song, the parts that were coming to her really strongly. She couldn't wait for the salmon to come back. She couldn't wait to feel them again. She cried her mother's song to the river as best she could.

To bring levity and love to herself, she would remember her auntie's laugh and her little cousin's jokes and all the curious attitudes people showed toward her when she would talk about this mother who wasn't there. And she remembered the embrace of her father—those hugs, his strong hands, and those tender moments with him. She brought all those memories to the river and cried some more. But then in that grief, she noticed, she heard, and she felt the salmon finally coming home, coming back up the river. She held her spot at the river and began to sing the salmon back home in joy and happy tears.

The Chum King then came to greet the young woman. You see, as all of this was happening the salmon were aware of the fire, aware of the devastation that these people had suffered, and aware that the young woman was alone and needed to be taken into a family soon or she would perish. The Chum King was awarded the privilege by the other salmon to go and help the young woman. He needed to go and see what he could do for her. So he met her at the river and invited her to go with him and be his wife. He wanted to show her the river as a salmon. He wanted to show her how to adapt from freshwater to the saltwater of the ocean. He wanted her to become one of the salmon people to survive and learn the ways of the waters.

The Chum King taught her how many moons it would take to enter the saltwater ocean from the freshwater river. He showed her how cold and how comforting the water could be. As they swam, he explained the emotions of the flowing river and its banks and told her about the bigger sea mammals that were out there after them. He also explained how sometimes the people would fish for them and how to avoid people since only certain salmon people are allowed to be taken by humans. He described how when they come back to the river to spawn, sometimes the bears and other mammals come after them. He then talked about their own protocol—how when they get back to their river, they must share all their narratives and stories of their travel with the cedar trees. He explained that the cedar trees are the generous ones, the rememberers and the wisdomkeepers for both water and land relatives.

The other salmon saw how the Chum King explained all of this to the young woman. Eventually they got married, began their travels, and adapted back into the ocean. Sometimes he had her swim in circles to practice strength and endurance. They swam and lived together with their salmon schools and families. Before long the Chum King and the young woman had had twenty-eight children. They were together in the water for almost forty-eight moons before the young woman began to remember her old life on land as stories of her people started coming back.

She then began to feel her mother's song ever so strongly. She knew it was time to go back home to the river where her people used to live. The Chum King understood that his time with her was over. He also knew that what they had had was very special. He had learned so much about the young woman, about her mother's song, about the people, about what they did on the land and with the cedar trees, about their relationship to one another and how they followed the rules of Mother Earth, and about the nurturing ways they were with one another.

It was the best relationship the Chum King could have ever wanted or imagined. He prepared to bring her back home to where he had met her. As he prepared to let her leave him and to let his twenty-eight children go with her, they promised each other many things. They then swam a little bit faster and higher up the river heading home. There was a different motivation now that was present among the Chum King's first family.

Sooner than expected, they arrived at the riverbank where the Chum King had first met the young woman. She said goodbye to her husband there and came out of the water with her twenty-eight beautiful children, back onto land again right where she'd first started, where she'd been born, where she'd lost her mother and her people. Right away she realized her children had nothing to eat. She saw that there were no resources here, that everything really had been burned down in that fire, and that there wasn't much at all on the earth floor anymore—so little to harvest or forage. Realizing all that, she began to cry again. But this time she cried and sang her mother's song. Her children gathered closer to her and she sang that song as loudly as she could.

As she sang, she began to walk and dance, and as she was dancing the song, she was calling back the plants and designing a sustainable organization of where they would go. The first plants to come from where the ashes lay were the mushrooms, the fungi. Memories and emotions of what she knew from her life immediately downloaded into her.
. . . She knew how treacherous the fire was and that people couldn't breathe in the fire and the smoke. She knew what it felt like in her body and what the fire did to her lungs and her breath. She knew about having babies and what pregnant people needed. She knew about not having a physical mother in her life. She knew how much love the people shared with her. She knew her father's love and respect. She knew about caring for children who were not her own. She knew there were certain plants that would help you when you had a baby in your tummy. Since

marrying the Chum King, she knew more about the waters and the emotions of Mother Earth, and more about the cedar trees as rememberers and wisdomkeepers. And now she also knew about relationships, about marriage, about trusting community, and about sharing information.

She was singing and dancing her mother's song, walking up and down the mountain, dispersing plants. When she came back down onto the flatter lands and into the valley, she was singing two different plants to be of a certain service. She called upon flame-resistant trees to protect the forests as vanguards. She commanded very special fungi to hide in certain locations and during certain times of the year. Her children learned this song and learned about her relationship with the plant people. They called the plant people, their teachers, "Mother's Breath." Before her mother's song was finished and before the plants completely covered Mother Earth again, her children acknowledged and praised their Mother's Breath. They got to witness that invocation and that creation and the dance and the grandmother's song in their own mother. Her twenty-eight children practiced many protocols from the Chum King that she showed them, protocols she remembered from her days in the underground chamber, teachings from her beloved father and from her connection to her mother's spirit.

I'm going to end the story there and say that that story is from my lineage. I am a descendant of that young woman with the earned privilege to sing the plants back for her twenty-eight children, Mother Earth, and the salmon people. I am a descendant of that young woman who understood that because of all these things—the traumas, the fire, being born, being motherless, and planting medicines—that certain plant people and plant medicines are Mother's Breath. The young woman knew that at some point we are going to be needing these ways and this reminding—for the human family to partner with Mother's Breath, to acknowledge and respect the life-giver, to heal our spirits, to heal our birth wounds, our emotional selves and mental selves, to heal our relationships, and to heal our relationship with Mother Earth.

Maybe some of these plants—some of Mother's Breath—are not just the well-known entheogenic plants like psilocybin, ayahuasca, peyote, and the toad medicine but also include plants such as osha, nettles, bear root, sage, sweetgrass, and cedar. There are many other plant medicines that aid our partnership with Mother Earth. We enter partnership with ourselves to be able to go into ceremony, to be able to truly be present when we're asking Mother for the mushrooms' psilocybin, when we're asking for Mother's spiritual help, when we're asking Mother to help heal others. It is in trust that Mother Earth nurtures us and offers us her breath, her medicine, and this opportunity to reconcile our wounds.

You see, for a lot of us in this work, our helpers are the plant medicines—the true and first healers. I invite you to check yourself or remind yourself or radically imagine an authentic relationship to Mother Earth, to radically imagine a reconciliation—not only to your first two traumas, which are being born and having your umbilical cord cut. I know you have these first two traumas; we all do. A reconciliation with Mother Earth and acknowledging her breath is necessary. So another aspect of remembering Mother's Breath is that she and the human family are made from the same elements: earth/physical, air/mental, fire/spirit, water/emotions. We're created the same way, from the prayers and wishes of our ancestors and the star beings.

I am saying that there is an order to the system in humanity just as on Mother Earth. You see that my eyes are up here on my head; they're not on my feet for a reason. You see my heart and my lungs are up here in my upper chest cavity and they're not on my legs for a reason. There's a rhythm and an order to where the parts are on our bodies, just like Mother Earth, just like how certain rivers go into the ocean, how certain species of cedar trees grow in the Pacific Northwest but not in certain parts of Alaska, how certain four-legged animals or winged ones are only found in certain parts of the world.

Not all parts of Mother Earth are the same, just like us. We all have our unique design. But we're made of the same things, and that means we're capable of the same things. And *that* means it's our job, and this is an invitation to advocate for what's true. You see, to heal and move further and progress in remembering Mother's Breath, advocating for decriminalization of these plants needs certain elements. These elements are applicable to us as a human family and likewise to Mother Earth. And that makes it true. That makes it all-inclusive. That makes it extremely diverse.

Perhaps these truths can be added to, but none of these virtues can be taken away—none of these virtues of trust, of vulnerability, of visibility, of truth and transparency. So when we go back to that creation story, you must know that the young girl, that young woman, was motherless. And how vulnerable is that? How vulnerable is it to not have a mother? In the animal kingdom, when new babies are born, they can't be physically too far away from their mothers or they'll die. Their system, their breathing, everything shuts down because that's how much they need their mothers. Some of our mothers surrendered us for adoption. Some of us have been in the social service system our entire lives (on one side or the other). But those details can be irrelevant because what's true is that we've all suffered traumas and so we are all invited to reconcile with Mother Earth. You are invited to acknowledge and respect her and love her. She just wants to be visible; she just wants us to see her without objectifying her; she just wants us to partner with her without exploiting her; she just wants us to trust her.

I know from experience that when I've partnered with certain plant medicines, they've told me to trust them, and I've heard this from many people. In doing ceremonies with certain plant medicines, it's all about trust. I invite you to employ that trust, and acknowledge and witness Mother Earth's visibility. She needs that and she wants you to see how vulnerable she is so you can truly feel her strength, so you can truly pay respect to her vision. This is a vision of you finding your highest self, her vision of you listening to your spirit, listening to your truth, and standing in that, and speaking to that.

The second "remember when" story I have for you is to support the first one of the little girl. I will leave you with an example of how I listen to the plants, leaning into them for various reasons. I have recovered indigenous plants from thousands of years ago, and then learned that this is where Western medicine got its synthetic steroids from. The elements and the medicine of this plant helps aid our mental health and treats high blood pressure in pregnant people. As a historical trauma expert, being in the thick of it can happen many times for individuals and communities. We have been in the thick of it since before the COVID-19 pandemic. This is not to say that precontact or precolonial times were all rainbows and butterflies. Though the goals weren't to control or have power over Mother Earth, we Indigenous people had our own wars among each other and our own warrior societies. We had to barter and trade, nation to nation, and sometimes this wasn't so friendly.

There was a protocol for healing certain parts of our psyche—our minds as a people—that had to be established because people also got hurt when they were hunting an animal, or when they were off on their own foraging for plants and foods for the community. Ailments and injuries were prominent, though not like the diseases of today. But there were and are a lot of plant medicines that were applied topically or ingested through teas or mixed into our foods, and they helped alleviate ailments and injuries. What we understood as Indigenous people is that *we heal ourselves.* That whole shamanistic idea is a bit dubious, because as a human family our bodies heal on their own, and furthermore our bodies *want* to heal.

You see, when you cut your finger, you don't get to tell your finger to swell up, and you don't get to tell your white blood cells to multiply to fight infection, and you don't get to tell your skin to scab over. As Indigenous people, we've known that our bodies are really smart. We've known the different parts inside our bodies and what our bodies needed, and what kind of plants we needed to partner with. We listened. We had an obedience in relationship with our plant people, with Mother's Breath—honoring her and knowing that our bodies want to heal themselves and that it's our job to listen to what our bodies need.

Trusting this plant caused me to stay in humility for my life. I decided to drink the fresh tea made from her roots while she whispered what she does and how she does it. She goes by many names, and her power is one great source. She's a heart plant and root source found at the highest elevations. She and my ancestors have been in close relationship since time immemorial. Practicing with her has been so uplifting and has been providing depths of so many simplicities for me and my family, my community, and my work. She's the one I found, or she found me—*in the thick of it*—during the pandemic. That is the second story.

There is a lot of discipline and a lot of trust and a lot of obedience to our natural protocol. As the original sentinels of Mother Earth, we Indigenous understand natural laws best. We did have an unmatched and beautiful relationship with ourselves, each other, Mother Earth, and her breath (plant peoples). I invite you to consider that parts of this story I've shared are true. And I invite you to reconcile with yourself and with Mother Earth as a partner in relationship again, as it once was. For Mother Earth and for ourselves, it's about preservation, it's about that partnership or that relationship, it's an invitation, a call to action, it's about reclaiming, and it's about the spirit.

You see, these plants alter us. They get into our emotions. They get into the physiological, spiritual parts of ourselves. There's a movement of believing this, for sure. But if we don't decide to trust that movement, if we don't decide to acknowledge that power and the relationship that the plant has all on its own, that Mother's Breath constantly carries, then there's no point. There's no respect for even yourself, for your highest self, the self that goes into that plant, the self that gets to see the sacred geometry, the self that is seeking those answers. Because it's not just your brain, it's not just your mind, it's not just your physical self or your emotions that are moving you to these plants. It's something bigger. It's beautiful. It's your spirit that wakes her breath. It's her spirit, her breath inviting you because it's what you asked for. It's your emotions that you sense from her breath. It's your mind that she trusts to partner with, and it is her breath that we expect to "help" or "save" us. . . . She deserves trust and so do we. She deserves love and so do we. She deserves visibility and so do we.

20

Pure Consciousness
Is at Play

chad charles

CHAD CHARLES is a therapist-healer-teacher using 5-MeO-DMT (5) with a nondual yet personalized approach with individuals and groups in his trauma-informed practice, which is in Montreal. He supports other 5-MeO-DMT-assisted practitioners globally via his guidance program and direct mentorship, based on unceded Indigenous territory in the city of Tiohtià:ke (Montreal, Canada). More of his writings can be accessed via his blog: chadcharles .net/blog.

◆ ◆ ◆

CHANGE ON EARTH is currently occurring at an exponential rate and the rate itself is about to begin accelerating exponentially.* The remnants of ancient wisdom are more accessible than ever and yet, as far as is consensually known, no previous chapter in the human story parallels these contemporary pages that are being flipped through at exponential speed.

---

*Exponential change is familiar to most of us, and yet change at an exponential rate can be difficult to grasp. For this I recommend the work of Ray Kurzweil, especially his book *The Singularity Is Near.*

Enter 5-MeO-DMT (5).* Here is an actual, bona fide entheogen.† When applied and ingested in an efficient way, it can bring an earthling up to date at a rate that may be able to match the speed at which the story is unfolding.‡

Wow! That was fast. Let's unpack that a little more in-depth.

At the Source of everything (the experience that can be *directly* revealed with 5) there is no time.** Yet with a limited biological lens— through human eyes—it can seem that disruptive events are happening at greater frequency than ever before. The tender, soft, consciousness-wielding vehicle that is the human body can only operate so fast. *Consciousness medicines* may be serving as a cosmic, toroidal scope through which we'll need to look so as to best perceive our place at this time.††

To actualize ancient wisdom so that it does not become antiquated we can reach back and learn what has already been professed by few. That's a way. Can it be a way forward? The multidimensional being may need to become transhuman in order for consciousness to be *fully* actualized through us. This is where biology meets technology, which I like to think of as the embodiment of multidimensionality. This idea is dif-

---

*For the sake of brevity, throughout this chapter I will refer to 5-MeO-DMT as 5. It is a very versatile substance yet, for the purpose of this book, I am focusing principally on the efficiency of its psycholytic application in a therapeutic context.

†From Greek, "becoming the Divine within," coined in the 1970s by an informal committee studying the inebriants of shamans. It has come to mean all consciousness medicines and yet I agree with Martin Ball that 5 may well be the only substance that actually evokes the true meaning of this word.

‡*Effective* or *efficient*? I think the distinction is crucial here. According to the New Oxford American Dictionary, both of these words express approval of the way in which someone or something works, but their meanings are different. *Effective* describes something that successfully produces an intended result, without reference to morality, economy of effort, or efficient use of resources (the drug is more effective in treating ulcers than its predecessors). *Efficient,* on the other hand, applies to someone or something able to produce results with the minimum expense or effort, as a result of good organization or good design, and making the best use of available resources (staff offer efficient and unobtrusive service).

**Please see "5-MeO-DMT: 'The God Molecule'" in chapter 2.

††With a nod to Françoise Bourzat's naming, I use this term to refer to psychedelics, substances, sacraments, entheogens, earth/plant medicines, etc.

ferent from transpersonalism. This is more than beyond the personal identity; I speak of beyond the physical limitations of the human body.*

An expansion of awareness is effectively accelerated by 5. Awareness and perspective are interdependent (or, have a close relationship). I perceive what I am aware of. I am aware of what I perceive. This is all-abiding awareness. The perceiver sees the world through the filter of itself. Expanded awareness brings more information into the picture—perspective enhancement. Think empathy, compassion, discernment. Increased capacity. Capacity is to "be able." To "banxiety." There's more to be aware of. It's getting more and more complex. Indigeneity would seem simple. Yet that's not what paradigm we're in.

WHAT IS A PARADIGM AND HOW DOES IT DIFFER FROM A TRADITION?

A tradition is a set of customs and/or beliefs.† Traditions allow for certain beliefs and customs to remain intact over time. Traditions are ways of doing things. Their continuity relies on an adherence to a belief-custom that is held as sacrosanct. Traditions attempt to "stand the test of time." There is a beauty in their lasting power, like an old building or temple that has been preserved and maintained. However, anything unchanging can also risk being stagnant and rigid. It is debatable whether a tradition is adaptable or not.

A paradigm is less of a belief and more of a recognizable pattern. It's more a model *of* something than it is the thing itself. A paradigm is less of a way of doing things and more of a perspective or worldview. Paradigms model and describe ideas, theories, and assumptions as well as realities, happenings, and actualities. A paradigm isn't adaptable. Rather, it is disrupted and then a new pattern is established.‡

---

*Again, Kurzweil's work expands on this very well. To me, the singularity and nonduality are rough synonyms.

†A definition of tradition: "a long-established custom or belief that has been passed on from one generation to another" (Lexico.com).

‡Paradigm shift: a fundamental change in approach or underlying assumptions.

GOD IS ALIVE, MAGIC IS AFOOT.
MAGIC IS AFOOT, GOD IS ALIVE

Whenever traditions are modified or paradigms shift, a change in identity is afoot. It is possible to hearken to ancient ways of doing things, to cling to a tradition. Even if it were to be seen consensually as a best practice—a better way—a tradition is nevertheless rooted in what *was*. A paradigm doesn't necessarily bring about the idealized sense of something that once was but, rather, observes that something that once *was* no longer *is*—modern-day flatlanders notwithstanding.

Highlighting the difference between traditions and paradigms isn't to suggest that what is currently happening is ideal or to be idealized. Rather, it's to say that if it were to be recognized, that *what is happening* is unprecedented, then a tradition may not be suitably relied upon to meet the "now." In other words, ancient bodies of wisdom—and the epochs in which they were conceived/birthed—may not be the bearing to which our compasses need to point. What paradigm will we enter into from here on in? Thing is, we can't know. Yet we can observe the rate of change. And, I observe, what *is* happening *is* new. Will old ways of being equip us with the necessary resilience, the capacity to adapt?

Also new is 5. What it reveals is not new but the way it reveals it *is*.* It is not here on the coattails of a tradition. Instead, it is emergent; it is upon us now. Now, in this time—in this time of exponential newness, the time that is happening. A time that challenges not just the way of the person/individual, but the way of the human.

HOW DO YOU MAKE GOD LAUGH?
TELL HIM/THEM YOUR PLANS

I think that the prevalent paradigm in contemporary human culture is anthropocentrism. At least that is what is implied when it is believed

---

*This is true, although pockets of wisdom have espoused nonduality over the past few millennia.

that human activity (which implies population) is the dominant influence on Earth's well-being, or that the universe exists by virtue of our ability to observe it (anthropogenic). For many, the planet is currently perceived to be ill and in critical condition. Allowing for that, it could be said that there's a crisis. Most crises lead to revolution. Revolutions are typically the harbingers of paradigm shifts. If this is indeed the case, I can't think of anything more apropos than the efficient use of 5.

Yes, but what about the others, one might ask? What about the ayahuasca, peyote, iboga, yopo, the mushrooms, LSD, the TIHKALS, the PIHKALS, for instance? One response is that because most of these substances, new and old, are visionary, there's a problem. I think this is important for this reason: any vision *seen* by the human is *interpreted* by the human. The interpretation of visions is tricky. I'm not talking about what can be envisioned when one has the visions that inspire transformation; I mean the visions themselves.

Best suited to the current malaise, rather than revealing visions, 5 reveals what's at the source of anything that can be seen, read, and interpreted. It interacts with the human with a directness that is transperceptible. Why is this important? Because amidst and across this increasing frenzy of change, humans will have to adapt quickly. We may need to get to the point. What *is* the point? It may very well be beyond us.

POST-ANTHROPOCENE: ZOE AND THE AGE OF LIFE

What could be beyond the human? Well, what persists when the body expires? Life! *Zoe,* in Greek. Life exists without the human. Consciousness! Consciousness exists without the human. Have you ever felt the palpable life force in the pulsing flesh of a freshly caught fish being filleted without its head? Have you ever heard the breath emanate from a human body that has been labeled brain dead or comatose? Life prevails despite us.

How can we be in service to life? Not just human life. Not just the livelihood of sentient beings. Not just the life of Earth, but life itself?

It is to feel it. And not just sensation or emotion, but the feeling and awareness of the all-pervading and ever-present energy that signifies existence, consciousness, life force: to feel It-Self.

How? Well, yes, it is "to go beyond" identity. Not for the sake of transcending via some sort of hack-bypass; I'm not suggesting we dissociate from our humanness. I suggest that it's the blind attachment to that identity—self-importance—that obscures and veils the feeling (of) It-Self. So as humans, we can serve life. I believe we can be grounded, functional humans and still intersect in unity.* At a certain *point,* we are cis-human and multidimensional.

With the scale and speed of change afoot, I think that unparalleled shift and transformation is upon the human story. To become expeditiously awake and aware to that transformation is a function of 5. I dare say that its emergence at this time of unprecedented change is its sublime design and raison d'être. Not only timely and relevant, its emergence is part of the convergence. Adapting is to respond to change, and 5 is part of the response tool kit.† It is the optimal entheogenic key to this current metaphysical portal.

hap·pen·ing | ˈhap(ə)nING
noun
a partly improvised or spontaneous piece of theatrical or other artistic performance, typically involving audience participation
—Oxford Languages

What's happening is that change is accelerating; 5 is accelerating fast. It acts fast and it's happening. It's happening now. Instead of bracing for change we can embrace 5.

---

*Without expounding too much on what we imagine "intersect" to encompass, I drop a few lines here: the Fourth Way, critical race theory, multidimensional stratification, quantum physics, and so much more. All converging and re-Sourcing at the event horizon, the source of duality, the All, the One!

†A nod to Rak Razam for extending this conversation in sublime ways that he describes as and within the simulation.

I am not issuing a clarion call. There is no 5 bandwagon that I think needs to be jumped on.* I don't pretend to know what the meta plan is. I am listening, however. I'm observing and recognizing what's happening: the patterns of incidents and occurrences, the co-incidents, the concurrences. I am tracking, tracing.

Humans are trackers, tracers. At once way-finders and trailblazers. And as we track, humans also leave traces. So who's tracking us?

The thing being sought,
will its footprints be found?
Did it stop in its tracks,
or is the seeker gaining ground?

The thing is It-Self.
Who's tracking whom?!
What's playing what!?
One's being one, too . . .

Either way, I say,
pure consciousness is at play.
We could resist it with dismay,
but I think we'll have to give way.

Reader, I take the time here to relate to you what I am seeing in and along the way. When the clouds are cleared, the sky is blue. I call it "blue." I don't know how I came to call it that. It's just how I call what I see t/here along the way.

Do you see what I see? T/here, on the path?

How do *you* call it?

---

*An informal definition of the word *happening* as an adjective is "fashionable; trendy" and in this discussion suggests perceiving the transformation that can occur in the human when it answers the proverbial call (Oxford Languages).

It is up to each and every person on this planet to decide how we can be most fully in service in this moment.

THE TEAFAERIE

21

Mamafesta

The Teafaerie

THE TEAFAERIE is a writer, flow arts teacher, *ruespieler,* toy inventor, app designer, street performer, and party promoter. She regularly volunteers with the Zendo Project, as well as several other organizations that provide psychedelic peer support and integration services at festivals and events around the world. Her popular column "Teatime, Psychedelic Musings from the Center of the Universe" was a regular feature for almost a decade on the preeminent psychoactive information site Erowid.org.

◆　◆　◆

INTRODUCTION

This sincere prayer to my ancestral grandmother was originally composed on about an eighth of mushrooms at the National Rainbow Gathering in 1999. Every year on the Fourth of July ("Interdependence" Day) thousands of hippies gather in a communally selected national forest to pray for peace.

There are no official leaders at the gathering. It just sort of assembles itself. There is an open Vision Council in the springtime that chooses a site by consensus, and most of the harder core tribal affiliates begin to show up there around the summer solstice and set to work. Nobody is in charge, but there are folks that know the ropes. This has been happening for half of a century, after all! There is a strong sense of familial *communitas* amongst all of the usual suspects, many of whom have grown up within the gathering milieu. Kitchens are like the Rainbow version of theme camps, and within a week there are dozens of kitchens that are spread out over an area that is as big as Black Rock City. Some are large and well-established institutions that can feed hundreds of people a day, which is great, because people just keep on arriving.

By the last week in June there are thousands of us. At which point the party has well and truly begun, of course, but the swarm still continues to build stuff at an ever-accelerating pace. An elaborate theatre is constructed, which is where I tend to plug in. (I also serve tea at Teatime, the pirate teahouse that is widely understood in Rainbowland to be the Center of the Universe, and from whence comes both my nom de plume and the title of my long-running column on Erowid.org.) Everywhere happy hippies are digging shitters and firepits, setting up dishwashing stations, chopping wood, carrying water, and otherwise making it happen.

And then indeed it does happen! Or at least it feels like it is happening. Rainbow is actually very similar to Burning Man in this respect. The vibe changes radically as the frenzy of the build gives way to the juicy fullness of the event. The stuff that we've worked hard on is as operational and awesome as it is ever going to be, and we get to enjoy all that's been wrought by our entire community. The population seems to double every day. Synchronicity begins to spiral out of control. And then on Burn Night the entire event shifts into a new gear that the uninitiated would be wholly unable to anticipate if they had not been informed. Yeah. Well, Interdependence Day is like the Man Burn and the Temple Burn combined.

The communal prayer is the main event around which the gathering coheres, and the surprisingly well-maintained silence that begins at dawn is a powerful call to internal reflection. Almost everyone in camp begins to gather around a central Peace Pole in the main meadow fairly early in the morning, and we all pray or meditate together until about noon, when the children's parade from Kiddie Village arrives and makes its way into the center of the circle. Then there is a many-thousand-throated Om, which eventually breaks into a sustained cheer; and thus begins the daylong psychedelic celebration that is the peak of my annual cycle of communal *ecstasis*.

I took my eighth ounce of *cubensis* when the sun rose, which was barely the beginning of my battle plan that year. (I was a psychedelic jackass in my twenties, and it was the tradition for all of the faeries at Teatime to take as much acid as they were offered until they could no longer name the nine kinds of tea on the rail and also keep the patter snappy.) I had resolved to write throughout the silence because while I sincerely desired to participate, I had abandoned my childhood religion at the age of eleven, and I had always felt kind of awkward around the subject of prayer.

I wrote the following on a couple of dozen tiny notebook pages, which I rolled up like a scroll and bound with a bit of fabric torn from my fraying skirt hem. I finished just in time to leave it as an offering by the Peace Pole before the children's parade marched into view, and then I promptly forgot all about it. Everyone was beginning to move to the perimeter to join hands for the Om circle, and I had to hustle to collect my little things and find my people. The epic day that followed was particularly memorable, and my fragile and state-dependent morning's musings never even made it off the clipboard into my longer-term memory storage.

Imagine my surprise when I rediscovered that my little scribblings were printed out in full in the following year's guide to the gathering! Whomever opened it up and went through the not insignificant trouble of decoding and transcribing my nearly illegible tripper scrawl is responsible for its continuing to exist so that you can read it today, and also for engendering the notion within my heart that I might someday be able to write stuff that could touch and inspire (or at least potentially amuse and entertain) my fellow humans.

I hope to someday discover the identity of the responsible party, and to party responsibly but enthusiastically with them. They unknowingly set my feet upon the path that has defined me, and through which I have racked up the vast majority of my admittedly rather modest score for the home team in the epic battle to transform our collective consciousness in time to redeem the human enterprise. Whoever you are, beloved stranger, I'd like to take this opportunity to thank you from the very bottom of my heart, and to formally salute you for helping me to discover my true calling.

MAMAFESTA

I find that I want to pray, but not to the deadbeat God of my childhood; that reckless progenitor forever tossing down rules and promises but never apologies, and never explanations. What use has immortal perfection for offspring? Amusement? A balm to loneliness? The child of a sheep grows up to be a sheep. The child of a human being grows up to be a human being.

Life moves directionally through time. It must renew and replace itself. It bootstraps itself from lower order singularity to higher order singularity through multiplicity. It's what this machine does. It evolves. I cannot be made to worship a higher power whose engendering and birthing is but a pale mockery of our own; a god who cannot create something greater than itself, or who fears to, and must content itself with mud golems endlessly enacting a tragic farce scripted in the inexorable Fall of matter. To whom then, am I to address my prayers? Should I broadcast my dreams and my soul's unrest wideband, hoping to chance upon the frequency of some benevolent intelligence?

My great-great-grandmother was the last of her line taught to pray to her ancestors; the last born free before the change and not indoctrinated by the victor's violent, fearful, and self-hating memes. While I cannot bring myself to expect succor from the dead, I find that I do resonate with the impulse to call back to that life of which I am the natural fruit.

Therefore, Grandmother, I address my prayer to you. Perhaps it will come as sudden thunder after four generations of silence. In truth I expect to be heard by no one but myself. However, there may yet be some link of identity between you and me that is unbroken by time's transforming illusion.

I am your daughter.

You were successful. You passed the torch of life into the future, as did your ancestors before you. It is now incumbent upon me. I am the body of life. I see now the infinite gift that this is, and also the burden—so heavy that it can only be borne by my own children. I see the tunnel of life as it points away into the insentient past. I see all the travails of those who manifest on the event horizon separating Math and Story. I see the fire of language kindled and multiplying out of itself like a thing alive. I see the drumming breaking out in Africa, the rhythm, the rhythm, the rhythm patterning the blank template mind. More and more the thought matrix bound us; made us possible. We ask, *What are we? Why continue in this absurdity? Why bear this life—its sweetness and savagery, the infinite indignity of it, the irony, the wild joys that take us and are taken from us? Why do we die for our children?*

Yes, it is the Impulse to Life, that song that called us down from our ancestral trees and points us toward the stars in a desperate, insatiable drive to persist. To be! To be! To be! It is this that brings human beings together in ecstasy amid death.

Oh Grandmother! I reached the age of understanding and I did not understand! I was raised amongst lost souls imprisoned by their own elevating symbols. I thought myself filthy and I was, weak and I was, powerless and I was.

I am your daughter, and I have been made to feel ashamed of being a woman. I have been ashamed of my humanity. I was raised in a culture that perverted the worship of the Spirit into a weapon of fear to extract tribute and impose control.

I am your daughter, and I find myself made manifest in a time of crisis. Here the fetus has begun to soil the womb. Here we must catalyze the metamorphosis or be reabsorbed by the Mother to await a more perfect incarnation. We are great with our pregnancy; with our fullness and our fear. Our expectancy. Clearly it is a time that must give birth to heroes.

The eternal myths that the fractal pattern has enfolded everywhere within itself are of course as much prophecy as history. The time has come again for true avatars of the Impulse to Life to step forward and challenge the Great Sea, or rather to accept its awesome challenge with the courage and passion that is born of necessity. We have all been told legends of past glory; past victories of the human spirit against overwhelming odds. We say to ourselves, *Had I been in that story, I would have done likewise. I would have taken up arms! I would have left my family and my lovers and borne great hardship and done terrible battle!*

I see now that I am in the same story, and have always been so. I am living in the story that began with the Word and will end with the Silence, the only tale there is to tell. Here has been the endless pageantry of the human enterprise. Here millions upon millions have chosen to give themselves into the service of that which they were collectively above, that which they were individually—again and again sacrificing *even experience itself* in order to advance a flag, or to promote an ideology.

If ever within the divine play some struggle within the plot merited the dedication of the actors' lives, surely it approaches the irrelevant when held up against the effort to transform the collective consciousness in time to ensure the very continuation of the tale itself! Will we survive into our racial adulthood and carry our story on to hundreds of worlds for millions of years? Or will we founder and die, unfit to survive? The events of the coming century will bear heavily upon this question.

I am your daughter, and I have been denied my rights of passage. How can we mark the end of our cultural adolescence when we each remain unconfirmed as individuals, our allegiance to the human cause unsworn? How can we free ourselves from superstition if we cannot bring ourselves into accord with the truth about our existential predicament?

Here we are. That's what it comes down to. Again and again here we are. Again and again we are ourselves; suffering, ephemeral, bound up in a universe that defies expectation and transcends metaphor. So be it. Our only tenable position is to say yes to it, whatever it is.

Very well, then. I'll take it! It is what there is to be taken. I accept those terms of existence that I cannot change. I give my retroactive consent, and take up my adult status of my own free will. Bring it on!

I find that I do not yet resonate with the desire to end the cycle of birth and death. Life is more than a bridge between nothingness and nothingness. It is the perfect figure that dances upon that perfect, unmanifest ground. It is what is before me, and I will seize it with both hands. I am a part and product of this life, no more stuck inside of it than it is stuck inside of me.

What great spirit has ever walked the Earth who would not have gladly traded places to be me? Staggering miracles are my daily fare! But far more importantly, I am onstage for the climax! (Or *a* climax, anyway.) I am alive and capable of taking action at this most critical and exciting of all possible moments, when the fate of the human species—and perhaps of the entire Gaian matrix—hangs precariously in the balance. I am the very luckiest of the luckiest of the lucky! The time is here, the game is on, the curtain is up, and every chip there has ever been is on the table. This is the time when we either make it or we break it. It's now or never.

I used to say that if you are alive now, then you are drafted. But a volunteer is far more noble than a merely hapless draftee. It is up to each and every person on this planet to decide how we can be most fully in service in this moment, and to try our hardest to be worthy of the great honor and stupendous responsibility that has devolved upon us. Or that we have evolved our way into.

Grandmother, Impulse to Life, Logos, Creator, Inner Self—this is my prayer. Help me to free myself from the bondage of self-centered and inefficient thinking. Help me to transcend the useless fear that has shackled my spirit. Help me to conquer my ignorance, apathy, and cowardice. Grant me the perspective, focus, and dedication requisite to the task at hand. Inspire me. Wash me with love. Let me be undaunted by the overwhelming complexity of it all, and the seeming uselessness of individual action. Remind me that I am never alone. Remind me that the tale has its own inner artistry, and that probability, as we perceive it, is not the only factor at play. We shall surely succeed, for all that action is needful to make it so. Grant me faith.

Thank you, Grandmother, for sending life into the future. Everything that I have and will experience, richness beyond counting, beauty unimaginable—these gifts have passed through you to me. In gratitude, indeed in reverence, I wish to help ensure that the flame does not gutter and die at this crux, but burns on.

It is yet possible that the Impulse to Life could prevail. It's really pretty tenacious. It must evolve or it will die, but that has always been its story. It is the challenges we face that re-create us. They make us better.

Perhaps one day a young woman will stand with her feet firmly rooted in the soil of another planet, and she will call back to me across time with a joyful and impassioned voice, crying, "I am your daughter! I am a Chieftess of a free people! I have reached the age of understanding and I do understand! Thank you for my life!"

I need no more reason than this to persist—the beauty that I experience, and the beauty that my experience makes possible. It is sufficient.

Glory be to our Mothers and Fathers, as it was in the Beginning, is Now, and Ever shall be, Worlds without End.

An old islander fella once told me to get my eye off myself, share freely, and it will all be taken care of. I'm still struggling with that, even though I know he was right.

TYSON YUNKAPORTA

22

Bringing It Home

More Inspirational Quotes for the Path

One does not discover new lands without consenting to lose sight of the shore for a very long time.

ANDRÉ GIDE (1869–1951)

Where there is ruin, there is hope for a treasure.

JALĀL AD-DĪN MOHAMMAD RŪMĪ (1207–1273)

Even a wounded world is feeding us. Even a wounded world holds us, giving us moments of wonder and joy. I choose joy over despair. Not because I have my head in the sand, but because joy is what the Earth gives me daily and I must return the gift.

ROBIN WALL KIMMERER,
BRAIDING SWEETGRASS

All healing is essentially the release from fear.

A COURSE IN MIRACLES

Thought is responsible for fear.
J. KRISHNAMURTI (1895–1986)

Put your thoughts to sleep. Do not let them cast a shadow over the moon of your heart. Let go of thinking.
JALĀL AD-DĪN MOHAMMAD RŪMĪ (1207–1273)

He who does not know the secret "die and become" shall remain forever a stranger on this earth.
JOHANN WOLFGANG VON GOETHE (1749–1832)

Every situation properly perceived, becomes an opportunity to heal.
A COURSE IN MIRACLES

There is a point when you have to decide and to allow yourself to fly into the unknown.
BELINDA ERIACHO

To be hopeful in bad times is not just foolishly romantic. It gives us the energy to act.
HOWARD ZINN (1922–2010)

This work is about relationship—with sacred medicines, self, loved ones, community, humanity, and the miracle of life on Earth.
ZOE HELENE

Through time, prophecies have foretold that the moment of humanity's transmutation would arrive, and that women would be at the forefront of this process. And here we are, bringing our seed.

GRANDMOTHER MARIA ALICE CAMPOS FREIRE

These spirits are real. If you believe in them, they'll help you. That is what those medical doctors don't understand.

GRANDMA BERTHA GROVES (1923–2019)

All plants are plants of power. There is no list of plants that are not of power.

AILTON KRENAK

A spirituality that is only private and self-absorbed, one devoid of an authentic political and social consciousness, does little to halt the suicidal juggernaut of history . . . On the other hand, an activism that is not purified by profound spiritual and psychological self-awareness . . . will only perpetuate the problem it is trying to solve, however righteous its intentions.

ANDREW HARVEY, *THE HOPE*

So the unwanting soul sees what's hidden, and the ever-wanting soul sees only what it wants.

LAO TZU (CIRCA 571 BCE), *TAO TE CHING*

Everything here seems to need us.
RAINER MARIA RILKE (1875–1926)

You are the indispensable agent of change.
ARCHBISHOP DESMOND TUTU (1931–2021)

The secret of change is to focus all of your energy, not on fighting the old, but on building the new.
DAN MILLMAN

A precious miracle is hidden within the pain of our time of great transition—a whole new life is being born.
DUANE ELGIN

Everything I understand, I understand only because I love. Everything exists, only because I love.
LEO TOLSTOY (1828–1910)

Unlike a moral calculation, or division, between civilized and wild beings, I see the wild as life. The expression of life is wild.
AILTON KRENAK

The medicine of the future will be music and sound.
EDGAR CAYCE (1877–1945)

Stop acting so small. You are the universe in ecstatic motion.

JALĀL AD-DĪN MOHAMMAD RŪMĪ (1207–1273)

Acalma o coração *(Calm your heart)*

FROM A SANTO DAIME HYMN

Be completely empty. Be perfectly serene.

LAO TZU (CIRCA 571 BCE),
TAO TE CHING

There is an ancient peace you carry in your heart and have not lost.

A COURSE IN MIRACLES

23

From Lead to Gold

Alchemy across the Arc of Time

Ya'Acov Darling Khan

YA'ACOV DARLING KHAN has been studying and practicing shamanism all his life, and has been recognized as a practicing shaman by elder shamans of the Sami (European tradition), and the Achuar and Sápara peoples of the Amazon. Together with his wife, Susannah, he is the cocreator of Movement Medicine, a contemporary, dynamic shamanic practice. Ya'Acov is the author of several popular books, including the bestselling *Jaguar in the Body, Butterfly in the Heart,* and his most recent, *Shaman: Invoking Power, Purpose, and Presence at the Core of Who You Are.* You can find him on Instagram (@shamanyaacov), and at his website: www.darlingkhan.com.

◆ ◆ ◆

INTRODUCTION

First, let me briefly say how privileged and grateful I feel to have been asked to share my contribution among such a diverse and inspiring circle of human beings. To be invited to perceive the way things are from so many perspectives is a blessing. Second, I want to share with you my favorite quote, in order to give you a sense of my approach to the kind of learning I believe we are going to need to adopt if we are to evolve as a species:

Knowledge is only a rumor until it's in the muscle.
ATTRIBUTED TO THE ASARO TRIBE
OF PAPUA NEW GUINEA

My intention is to help you to know that it is within your power to transform the lead weight of past trauma into the gold of here-and-now presence. After more than three decades of working with people all around the globe, I know that if your heart is beating right now, who you are and what you carry within you matters. Although we cannot change the past, we can all develop our personal power to the extent that we recognize that we are free to choose the meaning we make from it.

In writing this, I am sending out a prayer through the roots, trunk, and branches of the Tree of Life that we can each reach for a vision of our collective future that includes but goes further than our fear might usually allow. An inspiring vision is necessary if we are to cross this ocean of the unknown and find new ground.

Shall we?

BUBBLE, BUBBLE, TOIL AND TROUBLE

When I sat down to ask for guidance as to what my offering here should consist of, I was shown an image of how much of our trouble in the present has its roots in the unacknowledged and undigested stories of the past. Trauma is at the root of our predicament. Unhealed trauma creates more trauma, keeping us on adrenalized high alert and minimizing our capacity to be present. Apparently the people of our planet are becoming increasingly traumatized. They carry the wounds of the past and so continue to create more trauma to break our descendants' backs.

If we look back far enough, we will find endless histories of what we have done to one another in the name of all kinds of ideologies. Although it's no excuse for bad behavior, I believe it's true that only hurt people hurt people. And it's clear that if we choose as a species to continue the blame-shame, finger-pointing game, we are guaranteed to keep the wheel of suffering spinning at high speed.

So common sense tells me that as a matter of urgency, we need a whole treasure chest of healing modalities and practices to challenge our status quo and open us to a bigger picture. What we call "reality" is a patchwork of our own experience, the dominant story of our times, and the experience we inherit from our ancestors. From those raw materials, we're all constructing and reconstructing the worlds in which we live. The only question is whether we do that unconsciously and call it "just the way things are," or do we take a giant leap of evolution and discover that wherever we begin, there is a power that we can all develop. And that power is the power of choice.

INSPIRATION FROM THE FOREST

The Achuar are a warrior people. I'm glad that my family and I have many friends among them. They live in some of the most biodiverse rain forest left on the planet, in the Amazon of Ecuador and Peru. They have never been defeated. For as long as they can remember, they have been at war with each other and their neighboring tribes. Then one of their shamans, Raphael Taisch, had a vision that there was a much greater threat coming their way in the form of the modern world's thirst for oil and timber.

They recognized that they needed help and they called it in in the form of a Catholic priest named Padre Bola. He helped them to make peace and organize themselves to defend the forest. His efforts to convert the Achuar to Christianity were tolerated but unsuccessful. In fact, they gave him his Achuar name, Yankuam, and considered him *Achuaringi* (an adopted member of their tribe). He was a much-beloved member of the Achuar community until his death.

The Achuar and their neighbors, such as the disappearing Sápara nation, have kept the forest standing against all odds. Following the powerful dreams and visions of their shamans, living and ancestral, the Sápara have forged powerful partnerships with people in the modern world through Indigenous-led initiatives such as the Pachamama

Alliance. Despite the David versus Goliath nature of the fight, they remain undefeated. Not only that, they have inspired a global network complete with educational programs with the clear intention of changing the dream of the modern world.

TURNING TOWARD OUR FEAR

The Achuar and their neighbors could have ignored the bigger-picture threat they had seen in their dreams and gone on killing each other. But central to their culture is the clear knowledge that dreams point toward everyday reality in very precise ways. Dreams teach their children not to be afraid of fear but to boldly investigate its source. They recognize a greater need than honor and revenge and they turn the full force of their warrior spirits to protecting the forest—not just for themselves, but for us all. Their courage, maturity, and total refusal to countenance defeat is an inspiring story and a microcosm of our global situation.

There are many differences between modern-world humans and the Indigenous peoples of the Earth. In the modern world we are increasingly disembodied and distracted. We are taught that we and our dreams don't matter and that the rational mind's version of reality is reality itself. On top of that, we did our best to kill off our own shamans and wise folk generations ago. But they are returning. And the discoveries of our scientists are beginning to converge with the Indigenous knowledge of the simple reality of interconnection.

THE RELEVANCE OF THE SHAMAN

The shaman holds an important function for the health of the community. Through ritual and initiation, shamans keep people connected to the larger picture in which their lives are taking place. The ancestors, descendants, and the spirits of the natural world are present in their everyday awareness of the present, the past, and the future. They are the original ecologists and systems thinkers, and they know that the health of the whole is dependent on the health and interconnectedness of its constituent parts.

IN THE BEGINNING

I'm Jewish, and through a thirty-year initiatory journey, I accepted the role of shaman as reflected back to me by my Indigenous elders and teachers. Throughout my journey, one after the other, elder shamans from the Amazon, Indonesia, and the Arctic, none of whom previously knew me or had anything to gain, recognized me and asked me to own who I really was. For my own well-being—yes. But also because they saw that our modern world's fascination with material growth at the expense of all else was becoming deadly to everything they held precious. They told me I had a job to do in my own culture. Many of the shamans I met and worked with were clear that they could see the brilliant creativity of modern-world humans. But they could also see how much we were living in our ideas rather than our experience. More than that, most of us are nowhere near our bodies. Why? Well one reason is the unhealed trauma that is appearing through the cracks everywhere!

If you want to know what unhealed trauma creates, look no further than the ongoing tragedies in Israel and Palestine. As always in conflict, it's always the other side's fault. It's crystal clear to me that every individual, and every nation, deserves to feel safe in their body and on their land. My people have every right to a homeland. And so do the Palestinians. If we're going to find out who is to blame, we're going to have to unpack the thousands of stories of who did what to whom since two brothers had an argument that they failed to sort out more than five thousand years ago. There's plenty of lead in this story, and where there's lead, there's gold. This particular tragedy and its mycelium-esque roots, crisscrossing time and space, are at the heart of the vision that gave birth to the work that my wife and I have committed our working lives to.

At the age of five I wanted to know, If God created all this, then what created God? The mystery tickled me into its embrace every night as I fell into a dreamworld that seemed more real than anything in my waking life. Each night, the far reaches of universal time and space enticed me into their mysteries and I never looked back. But each morning, I woke up again in a body. My dreams whispered to me throughout the day as the world and its ways left me cold and with an aching feeling of loss.

In a nutshell, dealing with that challenge has been at the core of my life. And I believe it may be at the core of yours too. How can we build a bridge between the eternal, limitless, and unified reality of spirit and the finite, diverse, and limited reality of physical existence? How do we fully incarnate and unearth the courage to bring that which we dream into form? It takes chutzpah to bring our pristine visions for how life could be all the way down to this messy and dangerously unpredictable physical reality called life in a body on Earth.

My teachers have ranged from a lightning strike in my early twenties to plant medicine initiations in the Amazon. Early in my journey, I was guided most especially by two people. Matthis Penta was a traditional Sami elder who dreamed me in and warmed my heart with reindeer medicine in the frozen Arctic north. Gabrielle Roth was the sassy, streetwise raven in human form who Susannah and I apprenticed to for eighteen years. She often taught that although we can learn many things from the wisdomkeepers of other traditions from other lands, *shamanism is indigenous to its own culture.*

At fifty-seven, I'm just entering the landscape of eldership. My wife and I call it my "manopause." I see my death often and he humorously reminds me every day that my and our time here is precious, and the body impermanent.

WE LOST THE PLOT

The lack of shamans in the modern world is the result of an attempt to kill off the role entirely and replace it with dogma and a new story that the Earth and everything on it was given to us to do with as we please. A people without shamans forget their ancestors. They forget the cycles of life. They lose touch with the powers of nature. And in the case of the modern human, they let their minds run riot. And because the body is missing, the consequences of their brilliant ideas on the world around them has gone largely unnoticed until present times. Why? Because disembodied life quite simply means that we are not here or present.

My teachers were always clear that my wife and I weren't being taught to carry their traditions. We were being initiated in order to re-create the lost traditions of our own land. We were asked to translate the essence of what we were learning into a form that was embodied, made space for the heart, and taught us to use the power of the mind in a more responsible and integrated way. The result of those three decades of practice and research is the contemporary shamanic practice known as Movement Medicine. It's been a ride—wild and terrifying and as sweet as the nectar of connection that thirty-five years in the fire together brings.

SHAMANIC ALCHEMY

My spirits tell me that incarnation is the winning ticket in the universal lottery. I know it often doesn't feel that way. Loss is inevitable. Pain too. But we humans are brilliant when we have to be. And if we are here now, and if as a species we are to come through the initiatory threshold of these times, then many more of us will need to stand up, grow up, and play the role we came here to play. And it would certainly help if more and more of us were able to find the brilliant, shining gold of our own souls. To do that, for our own dignity and for the generations that follow, a little shamanic alchemy is going to be needed.

I find it helps to imagine that everything that has ever happened, and I mean everything, is an invitation for us all to develop and bring our most essential self here. As human beings, we are storytellers. We make meaning and identities from our experiences according to the limits or liberty of our imagination. Part of the gig here on Earth is to assume the authority of choice. It's unlikely that anyone will give that to us. It's a matter of taking the ingredients of our lives, including the echoes of our ancestors' experience, and putting the whole shebang into the alembic of the human body-heart-mind, and alchemizing those ingredients into gold. The more of us who are willing to partake in this everyday ceremony, the better our chances of finding our way through the eye of the needle into the kind of heaven on earth so many of us dream of.

Why lead and gold? Gold, once it becomes gold, stays gold. Freeze it, burn it, chop it into pieces—it will remain gold. Imagine that reality as a basis or ground for our sense of self. Lead represents all that is heavy and poisonous within us. It represents our hurts, our losses, and that which feels broken inside us. There are many days in these times when I experience the amount of pain in our world as heavy and dull as lead. I feel it in my body and soul. Parallel to that, I feel the dawn chorus in my body each day, waking me up to the miracle of life, singing praises and asking me, "Hey guys, life is a miracle! Tell us, what do you dream? What really matters to you?"

In a world where the only guarantee is that at some point we will all breathe our last breath, the risk of answering is clear. Fear of failure is common. But never to discover why we came here or—worse still—to know and to let our fear be greater than our courage, is to take the champagne of life and pour it down the drain.

A TIME OF INITIATION

The Movement Medicine ceremonies that we hold are designed to focus our attention and generously give it back to the body and heart. Our medicine is rhythm, breath, and movement. Gabrielle taught us that the *fastest way to still the mind is to move the body.* When I began this way of working in my early twenties, I hated dancing. But I quickly discovered that it wasn't dancing that I hated. It was the feelings of discomfort and self-consciousness that overwhelmed me because I was stuck in my head. It took twenty minutes for me to discover the creative power of movement inside me that was just waiting for me to let go.

Since then, our Movement Medicine ceremonies have supported

people from all walks of life and from many different cultures and backgrounds and body types in making that leap. Imagine what it might feel like to move past that self-consciousness into embodied consciousness itself and you'll start to get a flavor of Movement Medicine. Once we stop being concerned about what others might think, we can get down to work.

In shamanic cultures worldwide, as individuals or systems evolve from one stage of development to the next, the need for initiation ceremonies to mark the change is obvious. If we want to know what happens to cultures who give up their initiation ceremonies, all we need do is open our eyes. It seems to me that all the traditional markers of such a transition are present. We are at a threshold in our evolution. In the disembodied virtual realm of social media, and in the increasingly polarized conversations about who is right and who is wrong, a fight for our attention is going on.

In any initiation ceremony worth its salt, the known sense of self reaches its limits. What follows is a crisis of identity. And if the initiation is well held, and the initiate is well prepared, participants then begin to understand what the beautifully evocative phrase *crying for a vision* actually means. The dominant story of the times—which basically insists that the more we accumulate, the freer and happier we will be, rather like the unfortunate emperor—has been stripped of its clothes. Revealed as an empty promise, we have collectively arrived at a new threshold. And a new threshold needs a new story. Not only are we crying for a vision, but so are all the strands of the biosphere that are being eroded by our current dream or set of priorities.

BREAKING THE CHAINS

The realms I visited in my journeys, both with and without the aid of plants, became a refuge. At times I ran back into the arms of those spaces to escape the trauma of this world. But alongside the refuge, I have more often than not received a high-voltage kick in the ass to bring the medicine back home. And I have been shown again and again that we must acknowledge, digest, and learn from the past if we are not to repeat it.

In my late twenties I did a full recapitulation of my life up to that point. Recapitulating the past is the nitty-gritty of shamanic work. It's working with the lead or the *prima materia* on both an individual and a collective level.

When we release what doesn't belong to us, and call back or call in anew those aspects of soul that had to hide away or that never landed, we gain the energy needed to develop our personal power. And let's be clear about this. There is no way we're making it through this dark night of our adolescence to the possibility of our maturation as a species by remaining victims of the past. Unhealed victims in the present become persecutors in the future. We've been doing that dance for a long time. And it's time we moved on. Whatever level of empowerment we begin from, developing our personal power and dedicating it to what truly matters to us is the way we exercise choice.

I once ran a weekend workshop in Dublin that was focused on our ancestors. We worked really deeply through movement, focused attention, and embodied imagination to gain a deeper sense of relationship with them. Fury was released and rivers of tears were cried. Just as we were entering the integration stage of our work, I heard the quiet whisper of one of my own ancestors at my back.

She said to me:

"You know Ya'Acov, it's really wonderful that you are doing all this work to create a stronger connection with us. We love being in touch with you. And . . ."

. . . and I took a sharp intake of breath . . .

" . . . you haven't yet asked or answered the most important question."

"What's that?"

"What kind of ancestor will you become? What will you leave behind?"

That question is pure gold, and I invite you to sit with it, dance it, paint it, and while your heart still beats, do your best to answer it.

ALCHEMY ACROSS THE ARC OF TIME

In the end, life becomes the ceremony, and one clear intention that is emergent in these times is to look beyond our fears and beyond our own death, toward the future. I already mentioned crying for a vision. To cry for a vision as I understand it is to pray with everything we've got. I love Andean ceremonialist and healer Arkan Lushwala's description of prayer: *to be in direct relationship with.*

This is not about belief. It's about being present in the body and speaking to the Creator personally and directly from the heart. If we are praying for a vision to be revealed to us, then we must first reveal our own heart to life. Trying to abide by spiritual ideas that we think make us spiritual people gets in the way of discovering the genuine blend of spirit and matter that is actually who we are. I have discovered again and again that only when I open my heart and communicate fully what's in there will the door to vision be opened.

Movement is among the most potent of medicines I have been blessed to meet. It's the one that brings the level of sobriety needed to integrate our visions and risk bringing them into form on this Earth. When we dance so deep that we disappear into the dance, those same doors that open through the ingestion of psychedelics can open just as widely.

Imagine what it might be like to give your whole being to the rhythm, to really give the body over. To let go and to allow the unbroken intelligence of life, which is movement, to take you to the place where the mind has surrendered its control. In this place, all weathers of the heart are acknowledged, and the mind opens like a flower so that new guidance may land. Imagine doing that alone and then imagine the current we create when we do this together. The roots go deeper into the velvet, fecund Earth. The trunk is fluid and strong. And the branches reach out for the golden light of the sun. In this space, visions for a future on Earth that is more just, regenerative, and fulfilling for the whole biosphere become visible and tangible.

Guided by clear intention and the spirit of the dance itself, the dancing shamans awaken. They don't go anywhere. They stay right there at the center of their circle, the past at their backs and the future stretching out beyond their mortal coil. Their body becomes the bridge across the arc of time and the connection is made. The power of that place is elemental. We are earth and fire and water and wind. And in that place, the calm at the center of the storm, the lead of the past becomes the gold of the present and the doors to a new chapter are open wide.

Shalom! Salam! Here's to you and here's to the power of peace!

24

The Ritual Roots of Talking Plants

Michael Stuart Ani

MICHAEL STUART ANI is a healer, filmmaker, and storyteller with over seventeen years of jungle experience. As a boy, the Lakota sage John Lame Deer sent Michael on his quest to find the lost steps of the Ghost Dance. His book entitled *The Ghost Dance: An Untold History of the Americas* is a study of the ritual uses of sacramental plants. Because of his outreach medical work with his organization the Amazonia Foundation, he became a member of the Explorers Club and the presidentially certified Orinoco Wild Bunch. Michael has also remained a longtime part of the remote Mazatecan community of Oaxaca, which is famous for its use of sacred mushrooms. He is currently working on the Healing Garden project (through www.talkingplants.org) to bring seeds of plants that cure introduced diseases to tribal communities throughout the Americas.

◆ ◆ ◆

I CAN FEEL THE STARE of the skeleton of Huehueteotl, the Fire God, from across his ancient tomb, and I turn off my flashlight to avoid his gaze. But even in the darkness, I can feel his foreboding presence as the sounds of the creatures of day fade into the stillness of night. Then the Old Turtle Woman lights a beeswax candle, illuminating the tomb at the exact moment of silence between the time the cloud forest animals of day go to sleep and those of night awaken. And so the *velada* ceremony begins.

Within the silence I can hear the faint sound of a distant wind as it rustles the leaves of faraway trees. The Old Turtle Woman's husband, the Old Turtle, puts a single, sacred mushroom inside a special compartment in the pre-Columbian, golden pendant of the Fire God. When he places the pendant upon the stone altar, the Old Turtle Woman begins to purify the rest of the mushrooms called the "Little Ones" in the copal smoke.

After Old Turtle Woman blesses the Little Ones, we eat them in pairs so they won't be lonely on their journey to the world of the dead. As we finish, the Old Turtle Woman begins to chant. Her melodic inflections and modulated guttural tones unlock the doorway into my vision. Keeping rhythm with Old Turtle Woman's chanting, the Old Turtle breathes deeply seven times through the hollow leg bone of a blue heron. The wind approaches as he slowly lets the last breath out through his fingers. He moves his hands in mudra-like hand gestures that usher in the sound of rapidly beating wings.

Old Turtle's animal guide, a shimmering, purple-headed hummingbird, appears suddenly in the tomb, and when I close my eyes I see the spirit bird in my head. As I follow the flight of the hummingbird through my mind, it leads me past a carnival of lights and morphing geometric patterns. I later learn that these psychedelic "parlor tricks" are meant to mesmerize unprepared initiates and stop them from proceeding further into the mystery of Talking Plants.

Moving past the psychedelic carnival, I follow the Old Turtle's spirit hummingbird through a bluish-white hole in time, hearing the Old Turtle Woman softly whisper the word *Desheto,* as I pass through the hole. On the other side, I watch as the mask opens its eyes to the sound of what can only be described as a slow, percolating, underwater marimba. Ushered in by the distant wind and introduced by his iconic song, the spirit of the Little Ones slips into a corner of the crypt. Breathing heavily, the spirit begins to speak.

"I am Desheto, the Prince of Plants, born from the seed of the

Plumed Serpent, to save his dream of civilization. In Huautla, my sacred song has been sung and the dance has just begun. Now I will heal you."

She places a clear quartz crystal on my stomach, and through it the wound in my body appears as a breach in a luminous basket. The Old Turtle Woman appears to stick her fingers inside me to mend the wound. When she's done, Desheto begins to chant, petitioning the rain god Sequah Nindo, and the rains come pouring down. In this moment my relationship with Talking Plants begins.

The Old Turtle and Old Turtle Woman had warned me that sacred practices must be kept secret until the time arrives that they are meant to be used, and if they aren't used then, they will lose all their power. Following their lead, I have kept what I know about rituals to myself for decades. But based on current events, I believe the time has come to share some of what I have learned.

The use of visionary Talking Plants has spanned human history, and the rituals needed to communicate with them are still practiced today. In the Mazatecan tradition, the rituals become a bridge of communication that allows humans to tap into the subterranean Tree of Life, which is the mycelia internet that plants use to communicate with each other.

Indigenous healers believe without question that Talking Plants and their rituals give initiates a true healing vision. But many Western scientists dismiss the theory of interspecies communication with plants as a placebo effect caused by a hallucination originating in our own minds. After more than half a century speaking with Talking Plants and taking part in their rituals, I've become convinced that Talking Plants not only *can* communicate with us, but are possibly the key to our survival through their ability to heal our relationship with nature.

In this chapter, I hope to shine light on the techniques needed to perform an effective plant sacrament ritual. I'm sharing the sacred knowledge that was passed down to me in the hopes of giving a wider audience the opportunity to benefit from the vast knowledge of the few remaining traditional practitioners who have mastered the art of ritually communicating with plants, as I have.*

There are many different types of plant ceremonies, but most fit into two basic categories: personal and community. Personal ceremonies are most often used to heal one person, and involve the individual and a practitioner, while community ceremonies are used to unite the tribe as one. Tribal cultures from the Amazon to Alaska perform group ceremonies to define their tribal identity. Ayahuasca among the Piaroa of the Amazon and peyote among the Huichol of Mexico are just two examples of plant-based community ceremonies.

BEGINNINGS AND ENDINGS

The ritual begins long before the ceremony takes place. Although the ceremony is the actual performance, the ritual is the entire progression of events surrounding the ceremony. Among the Mazatec, when the ceremony is completed, the initiates are immersed in water to make them whole again. After the ritual, an initiate will also refrain from doing any chores or dangerous activities until the process is finished. This process gives the clay time to harden. Patience is the key to completing a successful ritual.

For rituals to work, they must have a specific agenda to establish the intent needed to manifest the desired goal. Every step of the ritual must be done at exactly the right time and in the correct procession in order to pass through the "hole in time," which is needed to achieve the goal of the ritual. Days before a ceremony, the practitioners start to change their focus from the events of daily life to the contemplation of the purpose of the ritual. During this time the initiates may come to realize that all the events of their life so far have been leading them toward the moment of the ritual.

---

*I use the word *practitioner* as opposed to *shaman* for the reason that shamanism is a belief system of Siberia and Eurasia and not the Americas. To use the word *shaman* implies that the belief system of Native Americans came to the Americas over the Bering Strait, and did not originate in American soil and blossom with its Talking Plants.

SETTING AND TIMING

The terrain that you choose must be inviting to attract the spirits, but also safe and undisturbed so you're not distracted from your purpose. Like all wild things, spirits are most comfortable in a place they know. If you are not in a place they know, make sure there are shadows to hide in because that is their natural domain.

While many spirit workers only begin personal ceremonies after dusk, the Yanomami of the Amazon will begin a ritual at any time of day that a sign appears. I've found that performing a ceremony in daylight makes it much harder to conjure up the intense concentration that is needed to focus on a healing ritual. Those who cure during the day often cover their eyes to block out distractions.

Every accomplished practitioner will develop a uniquely different style, but the basic ceremony remains the same. It is also important to have a caretaker nearby to deal with anything that might happen while you're possessed by the Spirit and unable to deal with logistical issues that can arise.

ALTAR CREATION

The altar is the launchpad and reentry base that gives structure to the ceremony. Your altar is a stable place to take off from and an exact destination to return to if you lose your way. Fire is always the centerpiece of the altar. In a Mazatecan velada ritual a single beeswax candle is lit, but tribes like the Piaroa and the Lakota and many others use a firepit. It is interesting to note that in addition to the Amerindian people, Tibetan Bon tribesmen also believe that the spirits enter and leave this realm through the crest of Grandfather Fire's flame.

Everything on an altar must be "real" and relate directly to the ritual, with no room for any confusion that can be caused by meaningless clutter. Often, the sacred objects used are ancient effigies that tie practitioners to their past or objects they have made themselves specifically to attract a particular spirit.

Many traditional medicine workers also use wildflowers in honor of Precious Flower—Xochiquetzal—the Goddess of Plants. Incenses like copal or sweetgrass are always burned to purify and attract the spirits with their fragrant smell. Everything on the altar is set up to work together toward one purpose: to draw the spirit into the ceremony.

All practitioners have a medicine bundle of herbs, stones, and sacred items—such as the ashes of a deceased practitioner of their same lineage—that can also be placed on the altar. These bundles can be so powerful that if they are lost, the practitioner will go insane. For this reason, medicine bundles are protected and guarded with great care and intention. The same is true of ritual weapons that are used to fend off any demons that may show up to sour the ritual or cause illness.

If you are just starting on this path and don't possess any of these sacred objects, I suggest obtaining a colorless quartz crystal. Tribes of the Amazon basin believe that quartz crystals are shards of hardened semen of the sun's jaguar spirit and possess great power. They are used by tribal healers throughout the Americas to amplify the spirit's connection to the ceremony.

HEALING

When traditional practitioners use a Talking Plant to cure themselves, they ingest the plant and then look through a quartz crystal to locate the ailment inside their body. Viewing the body in this way, illness will appear as a breach in a luminous basket. If the breach can't be mended by hand, medicinal plants can be used to aid the recovery. To learn which combination and what dosage of medicinal plants is needed you must learn to talk to the plants in *their* language, and that takes time.

To speed up the process of learning a new language, it's best to first study the medicinal plants of the region. Once you know them it's much easier for the Talking Plants to communicate their medical qualities to you and bring them together in a comprehensive understanding. Simply, you learn faster because you have something in common to talk about.

In the Americas there are two separate lineages of healing

ceremonies that, over time, have been combined together. The first is the belief that humans by nature are healthy and all disease is caused by malevolent witchcraft that ritually sends disease into the body. Tribes like the Yanomami only cure by exorcizing demons and don't use any herbs to cure except for their epene, an entheogenic snuff that they take to commune with the spirits they call *hekura* and *xapori*. Hekura are the spirits of animals and xapori are the spirits of exalted holy people and healers.

But many other tribal groups of the Americas combine the uses of both exorcism and botanicals. They use herbs to purge the illness from the body and to heal the wound after the patient is cleaned. This is commonly called a *"limpiada"* ceremony. Sometimes an egg is used by rubbing it on the patient to absorb the illness and extract it from the body.

Healing is an art, and like all art it takes years to master the techniques needed to be proficient. When working with Talking Plants, patience is key to learning their language, and the ritual is the means to manifest their knowledge.

DANCE AND RITUAL

The words for dance and ritual are the same in most traditional American cultures, because a ritual is a dance with ancestral spirits. To perform a ritual correctly, you must learn the steps of the dance directly from ancestral spirits who have danced it many times before. The timeless dance of the ancestors is what has kept the relationship with Talking Plants alive so that humans would have a means to survive. The ritual uses of Talking Plants are the means by which communication with the spirits is achieved.

The ancestral spirits teach us that in addition to working on ourselves, we must also work to strengthen our communication with nature. Without healing our tattered relationship with the Mother, there will simply be no "us" to work on. While synthetic psychedelics can heal the mind of ailments created by civilization, the wild Talking

Plants can open the door to the healing possibilities of nature. Curing the mind and body together to heal our bond with nature is our ritual of life.

I hope this experience-based testimonial has cast some valuable light on the importance of the connection between rituals and Talking Plants. This symbiotic relationship may hold the answer to the question of why the human species even exists. We breathe the oxygen that plants release at night, and the breath we exhale helps make their flowers grow. Desheto once told me that life is the ritual that teaches us our purpose in the weave of nature. Maybe that is as simple as helping the flowers to grow.

Metamorphosis
By Martina Hoffmann

25

Growing Cannabis

Submitting to the Wisdom of the Plant

The Dank Duchess

THE DANK DUCHESS is an international hashish consultant, cannabis cultivator, and public speaker. Trained by the late, renowned hashish evangelist Hash Master Frenchy Cannoli, she has dedicated the last seven years to raising awareness—via print, film, and social media—about high-quality cannabis and hashish. Dozens of her hash stories and hash tutorials have appeared in *Weed World UK, Weed World Italia, Cannabis Now, Skunk Magazine,* and in the books of Ed Rosenthal, American horticulturist and cannabis advocate. Duchess has also made several media appearances including seasons 1 and 3 of VICELAND's *Bong Appetit.* Duchess received a Cosmic Sister Women of the Psychedelic Renaissance Grant to write this story. Her website is: http://thedankduchess.com.

◆ ◆ ◆

BEFORE I SLIDE THE ZIPPER down to open the tent, I feel the heat emanating from the garden. My skin turns clammy as I say a silent prayer. Gingerly I pull both the vertical and horizontal zippers and immediately a wave of hot air rolls over my face. I cannot have been prepared for the destruction before me. I stand at the tent opening and look on in quiet despair as the evidence of my neglect stares me in my face.

Without the constant push of cool air through the air conditioner, the temperature in the grow tent had skyrocketed to one 113 degrees in the space of a few hours. All of the cannabis plants, save for one, seem to be holding on by the most tenuous of connections. After months of buildup to this key point in the flowering stage, I may have killed my garden in less than a day. After eighteen years of growing, I am still making mistakes that befit a novice. So, too, as known civilization has spanned thousands of years, it is still subject to the folly of its citizens.

Our societal structure extols quick and unilateral decisions, predatory action, capitalist intentions, and operating in a vacuum. We are left spent, disconnected, spiritually diseased, and unfulfilled. It is uniquely meta that, when we engage in the act of growing cannabis, our thoughts, approaches, and activities comprise the spiritual medicine that heals us as we grow the medicine that will continue to heal us from inside and out.

Cannabis spirit is a gentle guide able to alleviate our substantial pain of existence. It neither leads nor follows as it makes its circular journey from seed to plant and eventually back to seed again. Rather, it stands as an ever-evolving testament to the harmony in which we are free to indulge. Growing cannabis means embarking on a relationship with a patient entity whose development affords many opportunities to stop and take stock of our own skewed foci, maladaptive strategies, and selfish beliefs.

The transformation of a society is a result of the transformation of the individuals within the society. Rather than taking a large-scale, zoomed-out approach to alleviating the stresses and ills of existence, let us zero in on the only change we can reliably execute—a change within our own selves. To that end, I submit my eighteen years of cultivating as a backdrop to my journey to be a better human.

The ubiquitous nature of cannabis gives credit to its nickname "weed" because it can literally grow in any situation. Around the world, cannabis has been cultivated on arid mountaintops and in deep jungle valleys. Cannabis grows on its own, so if left to its own devices, it will grow any which way. When the goal is high quality, unseeded, high yielding, some minding is required.

We humans are not unlike the wild spirit of cannabis. Given the proper nutrients, we can certainly survive with little guidance. But unlike cannabis, which you can practically guarantee will survive and possibly thrive if left to fend in any circumstances, humans are creatures of community. As such, we are bound to run into conflict with each other as our existence goals do not run parallel at all times. Our friction is unavoidable but can be eased by intentional self-control, which acknowledges that we all have our place in the great system, and a properly working system can sustain everyone.

Cannabis grows as freely as possible and yet self-regulates so its needs may be met. Its branches expand outward, carving space for itself until it reaches a boundary. Unlike kudzu or ivy, which overwhelm everything with no regard, cannabis will stop short once it senses the possibility of entanglements that will likely result in overexertion of energy for growth that is likely to be stymied by lack of space and precious light.

Engaging in the conscious cultivation of cannabis requires important decisions that dictate our paths for the following three to six months. We can take the well-worn path, force-feeding the plants nutrients in an effort to "make" them as commercially viable as possible, mimicking nature as best as possible, or coming up with a hybrid version that applies human sensibilities in tandem with more natural processes. Right now, our society is running suboptimally as we pare complex situations into simple binary equations, get drunk on the largess of ego inflation, and ignore the destruction that is consequently wrought. To its eventual detriment, commercial cannabis farming continues to follow this flawed model.

As an alternative, small-scale "organic" farming strips us down to our most humble place. In the quiet of a personal grow, we are able to listen to the plant's needs and act accordingly. In the famous stoner movie *Friday,* Chris Tucker's character, Smokey, declares matter-of-factly, "The weed be letting you know." This simple statement is a running motif for cannabis in every way. Cannabis is not a shy plant. Rather, it provides clues to the breeder, grower, processor, and finally the person ingesting it. Experience. We need only listen.

An open and receiving ear is what I attempt to cultivate every day. As I stare at the forlorn plants in front of me, their erect branches draped with limp and shriveled leaves, I am straining to hear what the plants might be trying to say to me. The plants desperately need water . . . but what is the state of the roots? If I overreact and give them too much water, their dried-out roots will likely drown. If I do not get enough water to them, the phloem and xylem are likely to collapse, and any hope of saving the garden will be lost.

PATIENCE

The dismal state of the garden has lit a fire under my anxiety. I have to make a change, and it must be now. I feel my vision narrowing to a single goal—fix the problem as quickly as possible. I am practically trembling as I begin to search the internet for methods to save the dying plants. In my quest, I am given a few options—fast and forceful or slow and hopeful.

When you're cultivating cannabis there is often an urge to get to the bottom line as fast and as fat as possible. Therefore, the synthetics trade, with its targeted solutions and "set it and forget it" mentality, is always busy. I have used synthetic nutrients in the past, but have since come to realize the enormous benefits of patiently watching organic and sustainable practices take root (no pun intended). It is a no-brainer that I must address this situation using organic inputs, but my mind is fixated on the speed at which I can pivot. I breathe deeply to still my agitated body and rationalize that until the last leaf has floated to the bottom of the tent, I still have a chance. That chance is strengthened or weakened by my attitude toward the plants. I look to them for answers and remember that this dance is like threading a needle. First and foremost, I must not rush. A small amount of water is poured at each base. I mist the plants lightly for foliar absorption. And then I wait.

MINDFULNESS

I wait at the mouth of the tent, quietly pleading for the plants to spring back with turgid leaves that stand up in defiance of the whims of their environment. But fifteen minutes later, nothing has happened. Two hours later, the plants have yet to perk up and my fears begin to creep. At the edges of my mind, all the self-doubt dust bunnies begin to collect themselves, knitting themselves into a blanket of self-disappointment, fear, and shame. My monkey mind becomes rambunctious, imagining all of the detriment to my ego, my career, and my medicine. Breaths come in shallow gasps as I see all of my hopes and dreams tumbling down the mountain, waiting for my Sisyphean attempts before my inevitable return to the depths of the unworthy.

I claim an existence in tune with nature, and yet I have managed to kill everything. My breaths get even more shallow until I feel like I am sipping wisps of air through a straw. Erratic thoughts strangle any attempts at stability. Now is the time for a joint. As I take short puffs, I feel the vise around my chest begin to loosen, and thirty minutes later, I feel some semblance of calm. If this garden must be restarted, it will be an opportunity to take ownership of my mistakes and use my platform to assure many less successful growers that anyone can find themselves at the mercy of poor circumstances. I will have the chance to hold myself in a cocoon of grace as I pick up the pieces and start afresh. If the garden must be redone, I can and will do it better. And with that understanding, I return to the tent to be surprised by all of the plants' top colas standing at attention.

RELEASING OF PAST ATTACHMENTS

Two days later, hundreds of leaves that were once so full of life hang devoid of all energy again. The plants look haggard as their healthy, bright-green foliage has been reduced to brown crisps that sound like screeches on a chalkboard every time I crush one in my hands. It will not do to leave barely surviving leaves dangling off of branches.

I methodically pull yellow and burnt-orange leaves from each branch. As my pile of death grows, so does my fear. Plants acquire their energy through their leaves, and the plants stand bereft of the ability to feed themselves. But the old leaves serve no purpose.

As my heart sinks looking around the garden, I take solace in the fact that fewer leaves mean I will have greater airflow, and I remember that, for some growers, extreme defoliation (a.k.a. schwazzing) occurs at day twenty-one. And I am only one day short.

Perhaps I can be thankful that I don't have to kill healthy leaves in an effort to push my plants to produce more. That has always seemed like bottom-line behavior that is more for the benefit of the grower's pocket than the plant's life experience. But now I am saved from making that hard choice, and I appreciate being forced to release these attachments.

HANDLING PAIN AND SHAME

What will people think? As it stands, I have tens of thousands of fans and followers who cheer my every win and soothe my small losses, but they *do* expect me to shine. Insecurity and self-doubt have taken up semipermanent residence in my head. How could I have been so irresponsible? How can I ever bounce back from this terrible time when the camera—which has so patiently documented my beautiful and blissful garden sites—mocks me, daring me to show the world my weakness and vulnerability?

How do I soothe my own sadness, as what was once my refuge now stands as a testament to the accumulation of my failures? Who exactly can I run to when I want no one to know of my misactions, as they may now see me in a less lofty light? I cry off and on for days on end. And I hide. I hide behind the dazzle of my smile. When the ever-present camera is off, I patiently sit in the tent and listen to the soft whir of the fan. I will the plants to get better. I block out anything outside of the tent. I am in a bubble of healing. I have no one. I have myself. I have the plants. I bask in their healing.

Day by day, as I watch the plants get stronger, the voice of self-recrimination gets weaker.

APPRECIATING THE MUNDANE

Six days have passed and a single cluster of bright-green leaves lifts my spirits. The small, young leaves have sprouted about 75 percent of the way up the branch of a Banana Split OG cross, leaving the smallish colas still relatively bare. The presence of two leaves, each sporting three leaflets, is a sign that the garden is tentatively changing course. So many older leaves, the primary drivers of photosynthesis, have succumbed to thermal beatdown, each wrinkled leaf an indication of the plant's impending death. Now, with little fanfare, two bright spots of hope have appeared. I am as astounded and as cautiously optimistic as when the young seedlings willfully burst through the soil surface, their cotyledons spread as wide as they dare as they determinedly unfurl a lifetime of potential.

These are not the nine-fingered beauties that I would expect at this juncture, thirstily sucking up artificial nourishment from the LEDs hanging high above. Instead, these two small, three-fingered leaves, barely visible, are beacons of light urging the dormant new shoots to spring forth and help the plant survive. I am grateful. I am appreciative of the small bounty reminding me that despite the apparent failure, there is hope, no matter how small. I can hold fast to the notion that the garden may suffer tonight, but there is likely to be relief tomorrow.

RIGHT ACTION

Struggling without leaves, my plants need as much support as they can get. The roots have been damaged, and the soil biology is off-kilter. As the cannabis plants are slowly returning to form, I am overwhelmed to the point of tears. I have professional photographers coming in a month, and my plants are not up to snuff. For a brief moment I contemplate bringing in other plants to maintain my precious image, but I drop that foolish notion. This garden is more than sufficient. If I take the right actions, informed by good practices and buttressed with compassion, my garden will survive.

Starting with basic components, I introduce kelp meal for shock and Biolive for overall nutritional supplementation. I take stock of soil pH and check religiously for any signs of worsening damage. I spend four hours a day in the tent, working only for the benefit of my precious plants. I can feel in my bones that the garden will prevail. I whisper to each plant, remind her of her greatness.

And I wait.

FAITH

Video chatting with another grower, I reveal the garden as it is beginning to rebound. After the significant loss of leaves, the branches stand fairly nude, save for small popcorn clusters that cling to the thin branches. Looking upon the failed potential, the other grower says they will never swell to the size I expect, so I might as well chop the whole garden down. After an extra-long vegetative process of five months and twenty-eight days of flowering, chopping down my efforts is the last thing on my mind. I can see and feel that the plants are coming back. Without a surefire path to full health, my plants are trodding back toward the homeostasis under which they once flourished. I have no guarantee, but I have faith that every action I take to support their continued wellness will be returned. I tend to the plants, treating each branch gingerly as I see the results of my efforts. The plants are stronger and are adding leaves, even though vegetative growth has markedly slowed in the flowering phase.

Still the plants press on. My faith grows stronger.

And time passes on.

PERSEVERANCE

Today I stand at the tent opening and smile. Each plant is laden with heavy buds, and the top colas are worthy of a spread in my favorite cannabis magazine. If yield has been massively affected, I do not notice. Approximately 25 percent of the leaves have been recovered, and necrotic edges on some of the older leaves are the only evidence of hard times. The terpenes are expressing widely, and multiple layers of aroma waft out of the tent. The plants gently sway in the fan's breeze, and the new leaves whisper of heightened possibilities and triumph over unfortunate mistakes. They had been bent and almost broken, but still they persevered. I am proud to have played a small part in their recovery.

I have not saved the environment, nor have I saved the world. I have not even saved myself. But cannabis has given me a better understanding of the principles that make me a better grower and a better person in the process. Before taking the first toke of that sweet sinsemilla, I am being healed of the trauma of a fast existence with easy, straightforward, zero-sum answers. In the face of my greatest garden tragedy, the plants and I still stand and are much wiser for the experience.

We establish our personal ethos based on the mores of our society. We translate our personal beliefs into our everyday routines that inform how we show up to ourselves and others. A broken-down society is an unfortunate role model as we unknowingly incorporate greed, selfishness, and apathy into our dealings. A cannabis garden is infinitely easier to handle than an entire complex society, yet its management and our personal relationship to it is relatable.

Healthy inputs and outlook equate to a healthy output. At the end of the day, that is all we can hope to expect.

Be joyful though you have considered all the facts.
WENDELL BERRY, FROM "MANIFESTO:
THE MAD FARMER LIBERATION FRONT"

26

The Cosmic Punch Line

Adam Strauss

ADAM STRAUSS is a writer and performer based in New York. His monologue *The Mushroom Cure* is the true story of how he treated his debilitating obsessive-compulsive disorder (OCD) with psychedelics. The *New York Times* said it "mines a great deal of laughter from disabling pain." The *Chicago Tribune* called it "arrestingly honest and howlingly funny," and Michael Pollan called it "brilliant, hilarious, and moving." Adam is also the creator of *The Trip Report,* a comedic psychedelic news show streaming now. Adam writes and speaks about OCD and psychedelics in articles, on podcasts, and at conferences. His website is: https://adamstrauss.com.

◆ ◆ ◆

A RECENT STUDY in a highly regarded scientific journal found that over 90 percent of psychedelic users routinely experience laughter during psychedelic trips. Okay, it was a Twitter poll by me, but still, the results warrant discussion, especially when you have a book chapter on the topic due in two days.[1]

Why is laughter so often part of the psychedelic experience? Drunk people laugh, too, but that seems due to simple social disinhibition. With psychedelics, laughter often feels integral to the journey, and not merely a side effect of being high—not just a reaction to, but also a means of deepening wonder, acceptance, humility, and sheer hilarity.

As with the psychedelic experience itself, our understanding of laughter is very limited. While a number of plausible theories have been advanced, science still doesn't know the purpose of this highly specific, largely involuntary behavior that is universally engaged in by people of all ages and cultures (save, perhaps, for a recent U.S. president).

Comedians, though, can tell you exactly why people laugh: surprise. That's the *punch* in *punch line:* you get hit by something you didn't see coming. And the best jokes deliver a classic one-two combo. After the initial wallop of surprise levels you, something else lands: recognition. As unexpected as the punch line is, in hindsight it seems obvious—even, in some sense that may defy logic, fundamentally *true*. Your prior perspective is instantly rendered incomplete, if not entirely wrong.

Being floored by something you didn't see coming but now seems obvious also happens to describe a key concept in contemporary psychedelic research: the full mystical experience. In truth, it's really just a rebranding of something that's probably as old as humanity itself. It's what the famous American philosopher, historian, and psychologist William James called "religious experience." It's what Timothy Leary, Ralph Metzner, and Richard Alpert referred to as "ego loss," and what's now most commonly talked about in the psychedelic community as "ego death." There are numerous facets, but at its core is the realization (or, better put, the felt experience) that the separate self is illusory, and that ultimately, all is One—that we're each not just a part of the whole, but simultaneously—and paradoxically—the *whole* whole.

One of the most remarkable aspects of this experience is that we somehow remain present for it. Though the ego evaporates, some facet of self remains, observing—and, in my experience, not just observing, but *feeling,* and with unequaled intensity. And in those moments, where words are wholly inadequate, there's only one possible response, at least for me: laughter. (Words are inadequate because language, of course, serves precisely to differentiate among all the seemingly discrete things comprising our experience, whereas here one experiences the undifferentiated *every*thing.)

Part of the laughter is sheer awe, but part of it is how hilarious it is that I didn't see this before (or even funnier, I *have* seen it on previous trips, yet somehow forgotten this most basic of facts).

It may feel like a stretch to compare a joke to the revelation of ultimate truth. But no matter how trivial a joke's subject matter may be (the execrable quality of airplane food, say, or the frustrations of LA traffic), it accomplishes something that's not far off from magic: it induces a dramatic change in perspective that's as sudden as it is irrevocable. Once you get the joke, you can't un-get it.

You've changed. And effecting change is what psychedelics do.

It's particularly what mushrooms do, and not just psychedelic ones. Mushrooms decompose—that is, transform things into a more basic, fundamental form. And out of these building blocks, something new can—and inevitably, will—be created.

Most current psychedelic research is focused on this process of de- and re-composition at the level of individual psychology. On the psychedelic journey, conditioned responses, habitual patterns, unquestioned assumptions, and entrenched emotions may be broken down so that new, more useful ways of being and doing can take root and flourish.

And this is especially true for research subjects who've had a full mystical experience. Investigators at Johns Hopkins University have gone so far as to quantify the phenomenon with their Thirty-point Mystical Experience Questionnaire. What they've found is that people who have more complete mystical experiences also realize the greatest relief from depression, addiction, and a host of other ills. But individual healing, as crucial as it is, is not enough. Our collective challenges—environmental destruction, ideological and religious extremism, systemic racism, and staggering economic inequality, to name just a few—seem ever more insurmountable.

To be sure, there are many courageous individuals attempting to address these challenges by reforming government bodies, economic and social systems, religious institutions, and other pillars of society. While

I admire these people and wish them luck, I don't hold my breath. I fear we're past the point of reformation.

We need decomposition.

Decomposition, at least to our eyes, is never pretty. It reeks of death and defeat. And it flies in the face of perhaps our most deeply cherished, and least questioned, belief: steady progress. If we have faith in anything, it's that a better tomorrow is built upon the foundations of today; that progress accretes like the rings of a tree. Yet a rotting tree is also progress, just not as strictly linear. It's a harder type of progress to celebrate, built as it is upon loss.

To truly let go of what's no longer working and grow into something new, we need to accept loss. And here, laughter is a powerful ally. When you laugh, you're open. You can't be simultaneously judging and laughing. (I'm talking about true, uninhibited laughter here; derisive laughter is something else entirely, a strategic weapon rather than an authentic reaction.)

Laughter is letting go.

Comedians know this, too, and the best of them deploy laughter's spoonful of sugar to help the medicine of painful truth go down, where it can (though not necessarily will) be metabolized into seeds of change.

And there's another great benefit of laughter: humility. Precisely because it's a loss of control, we can't take ourselves too seriously when we're laughing. Plus the act itself forces us to drop our carefully constructed masks—literally—as our features contort and we emit odd noises. (This may be why that recent president is incapable of genuine laughter: his utter terror of not being taken seriously, which to many of us, makes him the ultimate fool. Derisive laughter comes easily to him, because it serves the opposite purpose: in denigrating others, it exalts his ego.)

More than any other single factor, it's lack of humility that's gotten us into this mess. The belief that we humans are the center of the universe—a literal, gospel truth (just ask the sixteenth-century

Dominican friar, philosopher Giordano Bruno), as well as a bedrock assumption of economics, science, politics, and philosophy throughout most of human history—has justified our treating the planet and its trillions of life-forms as an all-you-can-eat buffet. We take what we want and toss much of what's on our plate after only a few nibbles since, after all, we can always take more and the tab is on the house. But of course, we *are* the house, and though the larder's running perilously low, rather than tighten our belt, we're stuffing ourselves with ever more frantic abandon.

And humility will be indispensable to get us out of our predicament. "In the beginner's mind there are many possibilities," the late Zen monk Shunryu Suzuki tells us, "but in the expert's there are few." In order to truly change, we must first acknowledge the colossal scale of our collective six-millennia-and-counting fuck up. We thought we knew, we thought we understood, we thought we could control. Key word: *thought*. At a deeper, physical/spiritual level (for where can Spirit reside if not the body? Surely it is a faculty separate from the mind), even children know that the universe is composed of mystery and limned with wonder. We need to connect to the deep truth—maybe the only absolute truth—of not knowing.

To be clear, I'm not saying that humility and acceptance will save us. I'm also not saying psychedelics will save us. Frankly, we may not be savable. Humanity itself may well be decomposed (and by forces we ourselves have unleashed, which is itself quite funny). But it's worth noting that the Hopkins team has found that mystical experience results in sustained increases in empathy and altruism. This should hardly be surprising, for when you experience yourself as everything, you'll naturally care more about others and the world at large. And if we're to have any chance of survival, it's clear that collective concern will be critical.

In the darkest days of World War One, it was said that the Germans declared the situation to be serious but not desperate. The Austrians rejoined that it was in fact desperate—but not serious. In the face of the gravest threats humanity (and many other species) has ever faced, some might wonder if we can afford to laugh.

I don't think we can afford not to.

27

What Really Matters

Bruce Damer, Ph.D.

BRUCE DAMER is an astrobiologist at the University of California at Santa Cruz, and chief scientist at the BIOTA Institute. He is a follower of the evolutionary edge of culture, an occasional wanderer on the path of plant medicines and elixirs, and is the curator of extended archives of figures such as Timothy Leary and Terence McKenna. For a more complete bio, please refer to Damer's much longer chapter 17.

◆ ◆ ◆

THE DAY BEFORE the passing of Terence McKenna, a group of us gathered in a circle at Ancient Oaks Farm in San Fernando, California. Up in San Rafael just north of the San Francisco Bay, Terence lay surrounded by those who would see him across his own, very personal boundary dissolution. He transitioned early in the morning of April 3, 2000.

Rolling the clock forward a dozen years, I was assembling a series of events for the year 2012, which would remember and honor Terence's life and work. Dennis McKenna and I had finally met the previous year and were wrangling with some challenging revealing of his brother's difficult dance with his mushroom teacher and his growing fame as a psychedelic bard. We worked it out and I delivered this new story in the most loving way we could, at a place very dear to Terence, the Esalen Institute perched high on cliffs on the coast of Northern California. But something else turned up in our research, which I saved for the Sunday morning of the workshop in the big yurt. A person very close to him reported that a few days before Terence passed, he came to a moment of clarity in between comatose states and the haze of antiseizure medications. Not being physically present, I can only paraphrase what was reported.

Sitting upright, Terence uttered: "Psychedelics, they're not about ideas, they're not about any of that shit . . . they're about love!" Sometime later as he was again lapsing in and out of consciousness, he looked around to the caring people surrounding him and offered this timeless advice: "Keep breathing people, keep breathing." I have come to call these lines "Terence McKenna's Greatest Rap." I figured it only lasted about nine seconds but was a breathtaking insight that erupted after a lifelong working-out of his worldview and innumerable journeys to strange otherworlds, and the literally mind-altering transformation of his illness, a rare form of brain cancer. Terence described himself as not being "a love bug," and chose to ply the mental waters of medicinal recipes, hermetic history, and philosophy. He brought us some of the wildest, most creative reports from hyperspace yet Englished (or perhaps, Irished). In the end, for Terence, it was not all about ideas but about something else that really matters. The medicines and our other spiritual practices can and should be about love—love erupting from a fully opened heart, love pushing through a beautiful mind like a healing fountain to fill the room and spread out to the world.

At Esalen on that Sunday morning as I came to the telling of this last part of his story, my own heart opened, as did the hearts of all who were present. We instinctively rose and rearranged our chairs in a circle, leaving one empty but for its occupation by a DMT-inspired piece of art. As we sat in silence, we reached out to find Terence, projecting our deep appreciation for him as a human, for all he was and all he had done, and reveled in the grace of his coming to love.

Through our sobs we sensed him arrive, fully embodied, and take his assigned place. Hearts and minds reached out to touch him and to say: "Terence, we know you, we love you, and you belong to us, so welcome back."

And yes, we kept breathing.

In Conclusion

Stephen Gray

Dear Reader,

If you have arrived at this page having read all or much of this book, I want to thank you on behalf of all the contributors who have put so much care into the chapters they wrote for this offering. To dust off a hoary cliché, it really has been a labor of love. And I would also like to think that our beloved, wounded world will be a beneficiary of your attention and care, of your willingness to listen and consider.

You may recall a couple of "pithy" quotes from the introduction to the book. One is about the necessity of having confidence in "the possibility of possibility." If there is any one connecting, narrative thread that stands out from the others in this book, it might be the understanding that individually and collectively we *Homo sapiens sapiens*—for all our stunning ignorance and missteps—are capable of remarkable and perhaps ultimately near-limitless vision and manifestation. And as I suggest in that introduction, a lot of us feel strongly that for everyone capable of doing so, devoting oneself (and not without a sense of humor) to the work of contributing to a Great Transition is far and away the single most important task on this beleaguered planet. I'm sure many who have come to this book hold that view already, with at least some degree of unequivocal commitment.

Whether you are among that congregation or not, I hope that, having read the book, you have found inspiration that has helped clarify and fortify your own resolve. I keep coming back to a term from Tyson Yunkaporta—we are a *custodial species*. (A clarifying thought here about this "call to hearts": I don't believe there's a rule book for *how* that care is manifested. That's between each of us and Spirit, isn't it? This is reflected in NAC roadman Kanucas Littlefish's reminder to "stay behind the medicine/Spirit"—or as some like to say, "Let go and let God." We each have our own natural "watercourse way.")

The embrace of the twenty-five remarkable, caring visionaries and wisdom carriers who have written for this book extends far beyond those of us in corporeal form at this unprecedented nexus point of great danger and great potential. As the saying goes, it's for the "seventh generation." Meanwhile, here in the present, our emphasis on the inner work of healing is because we recognize that the vehicle has to be roadworthy if it's going to take us where we want to go and where we need to go. However, it's certainly *not* about endlessly tinkering with, polishing, and perfecting our vehicle in the garage every day. We know that we must and can take our brokenness with us as we engage in compassionate and creative action.

That is the reason the psychedelic medicines, sacraments, and allies have played such a prominent role in the book. They're by no means the only effective tools available, and certainly are not appropriate for everyone. But if we make optimal use of these potent mind- and soul-manifesting medicines, if we gain from them what they are best suited to and eminently capable of doing for us and with us, we are, one would hope, learning "to die and become." We are learning that we can see into and clear away what holds us back and keeps our vision occluded. We are learning that we can actually lower the barricades and open our hearts to the whole grand and tragic panoply. And then, in gradually dying out of our old, perhaps safe but stale and constraining cocoons, and beginning to settle into unconditional reality, we might come to understand the admonition of the great American novelist, poet, and environmental activist Wendell Berry: "Be joyful, though you have considered all the facts."

Visionaries and wisdom carriers tell us that that joy is founded in the realization that we are all, every one of us, facets of the same eternal, creative, loving cosmos. We really are capable of awakening to the great liberating truth that we *are* home and that we're all ultimately able to feel *at* home here. We each "just" need to discover and learn to trust that. Lord knows it ain't easy. But once so much as glimpsed in brief "aha" moments, we begin to see and trust that it's not a fantasy, a belief, or a position. It's simply what Buddhist teachings call "What is," or what in ancient Chinese philosophy is termed the *Tao*—the way that is in harmony with the natural order.

It's like the anecdote attributed to Gautama the Buddha himself. When someone asked him how he knew he was enlightened, he put the palm of his hand on the ground beside him and said, "This solid Earth is my witness." This is the great, open secret, and the whispering in the breeze telling humanity that now is the time. And that suggests the other "pithy" quote from the introduction, Victor Hugo's insight that "Nothing is more powerful than an idea whose time has come."

An essential point must be stressed in these times of rapid, disorienting, and even frightening upheaval. I hope I can safely speak for the rest of the book's participants, as well as a great many others, in saying that no matter how dark the horizon appears, allowing oneself to sink into cynicism, despair, and hopelessness serves no one and nothing. Of course such thoughts and feelings will inevitably come up, even for the bravest and clearest among us. But maybe that's where our wisdom-warrior qualities kick in. As the great teachings would say, it's just a thought, the voice of what the American spiritual teacher Vernon Howard calls "the false identity." Challenging as it is for almost all of us, we can acknowledge self-sabotaging, energy-draining thoughts without judgment, and allow them to drift away like the vaporous things they are. We can catch ourselves in the falling, and take our seats again in dignified presence. As that wonderful thirteenth-century, mystic poet Jalāl ad-Dīn Rūmī put it, "Come, come, whoever you are. Wanderer, worshipper, lover of leaving. It doesn't matter. Ours is not a caravan of despair. Come, even if you have broken your vow a thousand times. Come, yet again, come, come."[1]

So once again, dear wild, mixed-up, and wonderful sisters and brothers, "Let us take heart." To quote the poet Rainer Maria Rilke, "Everything here seems to need us." As the road gets increasingly bumpy, we're going to have to get stronger. But there is nothing better we can do, and the message from the wise is—we can.

Be well.

Glossary

5-MeO-DMT: An extremely powerful, short-acting psychedelic found in numerous plant species and in the glands of the Sonoran Desert toad. Many people say that the synthesized version of "5" is equally effective and that the endangered toad should be left alone.

ancestor mind: Tyson Yunkaporta's term for the timeless state of deep, calm presence that Jamie Wheal calls the "Deep Now."

Anthropocene: The current geological age, viewed as the period during which human activity has been the dominant influence on climate and the environment.

Atman: The supreme universal self, the spiritual life principle of the universe.

autopoietic: A living organism that is self-maintaining and self-regulating.

ayahuasquero: A ceremonialist and healer who works with the ayahuasca medicine.

Banisteriopsis caapi: A liana, or vine, native to South America, typically brewed with a DMT-containing plant such as chacruna to produce ayahuasca.

BIPOC: Black, indigenous, and people of color. A recent and increasingly popular acronym that is seen by many as a necessary shift away from less "person-first" terms like *marginalized* and *minority*.

Brahman: A member of the highest Hindu class—the priesthood class.

chacruna: A DMT-containing plant commonly brewed with the *Banisteriopsis caapi* vine to produce ayahuasca.

Daime: The name given to ayahuasca in the syncretic church known as Santo Daime; literally translated from Portuguese as "give me."

daimista: Someone who drinks Daime in the context of Santo Daime rituals.

demotic: of or relating to the common people (as used by Tyson Yunkaporta).

Diné: "The People." The Diné are also known as Navajo, a name they neither use nor like.

DMT: *N,N*-Dimethyltryptamine (DMT) is a "substitute tryptamine" occuring in numerous plants, including chacruna (*Psychotria viridis*). DMT is the most common admixture plant accompanying the *Banisteriopsis caapi* vine in the ayahuasca brew.

ecstasis: Rapture, ecstasy, trance (out of or beyond stasis).

entropy/entropic: Lack of order or predictability, gradual decline into disorder.

epistemology: The branch of philosophy dealing with the study of knowledge, with theories and limits of knowledge; as used by Ailton Krenak, the term suggests worldviews and their assumptions.

eukaryotic cell: A cell with a nuclear membrane that surrounds the nucleus.

hekura: The spirit of an animal.

heterarchical: Nonhierarchical system of organization (essential for sustainable futures).

iboga: A visionary/healing perennial shrub native to western equatorial Africa (see chapter 2 for more detail).

ibogaine: The primary psychoactive alkaloid extracted from the root bark of the iboga shrub and often used in addiction treatment programs.

ícaro: A healing song sung by *ayahuasqueros* in ayahuasca ceremonies and healing work; these songs are said to be channeled or received from the medicine spirits.

maloca: In South America, a large communal dwelling often used for ayahuasca ceremonies.

mamos: The sun priests of the Kogi and Arhuaco, Indigenous people of Colombia.

Ñande Rekó: Way of being.

neuroplasticity: Put simply, the ability of neural networks in the brain to change, to reorganize synaptic connections, and to adapt in response to experience.

noosphere: A term coined by influential French philosopher and Jesuit priest Pierre Teilhard de Chardin (1881–1955); it describes (or postulates) the sphere of thought, or consciousness, enveloping the biosphere.

numinous: Having a strong religious or spiritual quality, indicating or suggesting the presence of a divinity.

ololiúqui: The Nahuatl (north and central Mexico) name for the seeds of a species of morning glory that contain an alkaloid similar in structure to LSD.

ontology: The branch of metaphysics that addresses the nature or essential characteristics of being; put most simply, it's the study of being (or as used by Tyson Yunkaporta in chapter 15, the essential "beingness" of an organism).

opy: A maloca or house of religion, a term used by the Krenak Indigenous people of Brazil.

orixás: Ancestor spirits that function as links between the spirit and human worlds.

oxytocin: A hormone produced in the hypothalamus and secreted into the bloodstream by the posterior pituitary gland; it has physical effects and also plays an important role in many human behaviors, including empathy, trust, sexual activity, and more.

pachacuti: The end of a world and the turning over of a new era; in the context of this book, the time we are in now.

petai: Tobacco; often used by South American Indigenous people for healing and spiritual purposes.

pety: Tobacco plant (see *petai* above).

petyngua: Bowl for burning tobacco (petai).

plasticogen: A newly proposed name for medicines that induce neuroplasticity.

progenitor: Ancestor, parent, source.

Prophecy of the Eagle and the Condor: Ancient Incan prophecy indicating that when the Condor of the south flies together with the Eagle of the north, the four directions will be joined and the Indigenous peoples of the world will unite the human family. This and other Indigenous prophecies imply that that time has come.

psycholytic: As in *psycholytic therapy* versus *psychedelic therapy*—low to moderate doses of a psychedelic medicine as opposed to powerful, often ego-dissolving psychedelic doses.

psychonaut: An explorer of altered states of consciousness, especially through the use of psychedelic plants and substances.

Psychotria viridis: Also known as chacruna; a DMT-containing plant commonly used in making ayahuasca.

roadman: The ceremony leader in Native American Church peyote prayer ceremonies.

Salvia divinorum: A psychoactive member of the mint family endemic to the Sierra Mazateca mountainous region of Oaxaca in Mexico.

San Pedro: Also known as Huachuma, a cactus native to the Andes Mountains of South America whose primary psychoactive alkaloid is mescaline.

Schedule 1: A drug with a "high potential for abuse" and "no currently accepted medical use"—the same absurd category in which our largely benign, ancient ally and friend cannabis continues to languish.

semi-synthetic: Drugs that use naturally occurring materials as a starting point. Examples are LSD, MDMA, and heroin.

syncretic: In the context of this book it usually refers to *syncretic religions* that combine different traditions, most commonly Indigenous practices and cosmologies that have blended with Christian influences; examples are Santo Daime, the Native American Church, and the Bwiti religion of Gabon and surroundings.

táádidíín: Corn pollen (Diné/Navajo).

teonanácatl: From the Nahuatl, literally "god mushroom," referring primarily to psilocybe mushrooms.

theosis: Divinization (see chapter 10 "Becoming Divine Beings" for a powerfully inspiring discussion).

totemic: Symbolic or representative of a particular quality or concept.

velada: A ceremony or ritual. For example, in the game-changing 1957 *Life* magazine photo essay feature "Seeking the Magic Mushroom," amateur mycologist Gordon Wasson described how he was invited to a psilocybin mushroom ritual, or *velada,* guided by the Mazatecan curandera Maria Sabina.

virtue signaling: Often used as a slur meant to imply moral grandstanding.

xapori: The spirits of exalted holy people and healers.

yagé: Another name for ayahuasca.

Notes

INTRODUCTION. EMBRACING AN ESSENTIAL VISION

1. Chief Seattle, from goodreads (website) quotes.
2. Prechtel, *Secrets of the Talking Jaguar,* 283.

CHAPTER 1. THE BIRTH OF THE FUTURE HUMAN

1. Grof, *LSD Psychotherapy.*
2. Bache, *LSD and the Mind,* 222–23.
3. Elgin, *Awakening Earth,* 121.
4. Bache, *Dark Night,* 241.
5. Bache, *Dark Night,* 245.
6. Bache, *LSD and the Mind,* 176–83 and 200–206.

CHAPTER 2. THE GREAT MEDICINES

1. Cowan, *Plant Spirit Medicine,* 4.
2. El-Seedi et al., "Prehistoric Peyote Use."
3. Cristancho and Vining, "Culturally Defined Keystone Species."
4. Samorini, "Oldest Representations of Hallucinogenic Mushrooms"; Gartz, *Magic Mushrooms;* McKenna, *Food of the Gods,* 39.
5. Hamilton Morris, "A Brief History of 5-MeO DMT," YouTube video, 2019.
6. Thomas Ray, "Mental Organs and the Breadth and Depth of Consciousness," YouTube video, 2017.
7. Holland, *Ecstasy,* 6.
8. Holland, *Ecstasy,* 2.

CHAPTER 4. OUR STORY IS OUR FUTURE!

1. MacGregor, *In Awe*.
2. Jacques Verduin GRIP materials for prisoners, quoted in *Choosing Earth* (2020), 15.

CHAPTER 5. THE TURNING OF THE SOIL

1. The Church of the Eagle and the Condor website (accessed August 27, 2021).
2. The Urban Dictionary (website), "Innerstand," December 29, 2017.
3. Real People's Media website, "The Inca Prophecy of the Eagle and the Condor," December 5, 2016; Turtle Lodge, "The Prophecy of the Eagle and the Condor at Turtle Lodge," YouTube video, June 3, 2017.
4. Sacred Land Film Project website, "Hopi Prophecy by Thomas Banyacya (1995) Part 1 of 2" video, March 31, 2020.
5. The Church of the Eagle and the Condor website (accessed August 27, 2021).
6. Virginia Tech: College of Liberal Arts and Human Services website, "History Repeating."
7. Carole Hart, "13 Grandmothers: First Gathering Part 1," YouTube video, January 14, 2010.
8. Capelin, *Source of the Sacred*.
9. Reichard, *Navajo Religion*, 37–45.
10. Steve Darden, "Bila Ash Dka, II—The Five Fingered One" lecture handout, Success and Direction Enterprises, 1990.
11. Tarrell, Portman, and Garrett, "Native American Healing Traditions," 462.
12. Tarrell, Portman, and Garrett, "Native American Healing Traditions," 461.
13. Kahn-John and Koithan, "Living in Health, Harmony, and Beauty."
14. Witherspoon, "Central Concepts of the Navajo World View."
15. Grand Valley State University website, "The Monomyth (The Hero's Journey): The Hero's Journey," last updated June 10, 2021.
16. Kathy Ratcliffe, "Innerstanding," *Quantumology* (blog), March 26, 2019.
17. Damien, *Self-Destruction of the West*, 28.
18. Raworth, *Donut Economics*, 187.
19. Lissa Rankin, M.D., "Sacred Reciprocity: The Indigenous Spiritual Principle of Giving & Receiving," LisaRankin.com (blog), December 22, 2019.
20. Agnes Baker Pilgrim, AZ Quotes (website), accessed September 25, 2021.

21. Indigenous Corporate Training Inc. "What is the Seventh Generation Principle?" *Working Effectively with Indigenous Peoples* (blog), May 30, 2020.

22. Stotijn, *Bridge to the 5th Dimension,* 135–36, 205.

CHAPTER 6. THE COSMIC ORPHAN
AND THE WOUND OF THE WORLD

1. Perry, *A Study of Prose Fiction,* 314.

2. Shulgin and Shulgin, *PiHKAL.*

CHAPTER 11. BEYOND MEASURE

1. Chris Letheby, interview by Shayla Love, "Do Psychedelics Just Provide Comforting Delusions?" VICE (website), June 8, 2021.

2. Sanders and Zijlmans, "Moving Past Mysticism."

3. Carhart-Harris et al., "The Entropic Brain."

4. Shayla Love, "Do Psychedelics Just Provide Comforting Delusions?" VICE (website), June 8, 2021.

CHAPTER 26. THE COSMIC PUNCH LINE

1. @atomstrauss, 2:05 p.m., July 30, 2021.

IN CONCLUSION

1. Jelaluddin Rumi, from goodreads (website) quotes.

Selected Bibliography
and Recommended
Reading

Bache, Christopher. *Dark Night, Early Dawn*. Albany: State University of New York Press, 2000.

———. *LSD and the Mind of the Universe*. Rochester, Vt.: Park Street Press, 2019.

Baring, Anne. *The Dream of the Cosmos*. Shaftesbury, U.K.: Archive Publishing, 2013.

Barks, Coleman, with John Moyne. *The Essential Rumi*. New York: HarperCollins, 1995.

Barnard, G. William. *Liquid Light: Ayahuasca Spirituality and the Santo Daime Tradition*. New York: Columbia University Press, 2022.

Berry, Wendell. *The Selected Poems of Wendell Berry*. Berkeley: Counterpoint, 1999.

Bourzat, Françoise, with Kristina Hunter. *Consciousness Medicine: Indigenous Wisdom, Entheogens, and Expanded States of Consciousness for Healing and Growth*. Berkeley: North Atlantic Books, 2019.

Buhner, Stephen Harrod. *Plant Intelligence and the Imaginal Realm*. Rochester, Vt.: Bear & Company, 2014.

Capelin, Emily Fay. *Source of the Sacred: Navajo Corn Pollen; Hááne' Baadahoste' Ígíí (Very Sacred Story)*. Colorado Springs, Colo.: Colorado College, 2009.

Carhart-Harris, Robin L., Robert Leech, Peter J. Hellyer, Murray Shanahan, Amanda Feilding, Enzo Tagliazucchi, Dante R. Chalvo, and Davi

Nutt. "The Entropic Brain: A Theory of Conscious States Informed by Neuroimaging Research with Psychedelic Drugs." *Frontiers in Human Neuroscience* (February 3, 2014).

Cowan, Eliot. *Plant Spirit Medicine*. Boulder, Colo.: Sounds True, 2014.

Cristancho, Sergio, and Joanne Vining. "Culturally Defined Keystone Species." *Human Ecology Review* 11, no. 2 (2004): 153–64.

Damien, François. *The Self-Destruction of the West: Critical Cultural Anthropology*. N.p.: PUBLIBOOK, 2007.

Darling Khan, Ya'Acov. *Jaguar in the Body, Butterfly in the Heart: The Real-life Initiation of an Everyday Shaman*. London: Hay House UK, 2017.

———. *Shaman: Invoking Power, Purpose, and Presence at the Core of Who You Are*. London: Hay House UK, 2020.

Davis, Wade. *Into the Silence*. New York: Alfred A. Knopf, 2011.

———. *Magdalena: River of Dreams*. Toronto: Vintage Canada, 2021.

———. *One River: Explorations and Discoveries in the Amazon Rain Forest*. New York: Simon and Schuster, 1997.

Elgin, Duane. *Awakening Earth*. New York: William Morrow, 1993. (Free PDF available at DuaneElgin.com.)

———. *Choosing Earth: Humanity's Great Transition to a Mature Planetary Civilization*. N.p.: Duane Elgin, 2020.

———. *Choosing Earth: Humanity's Journey of Initiation Through Breakdown and Collapse to Mature Planetary Community*. Revised Edition. N.p. Duane Elgin, 2022.

El-Seedi et al. "Prehistoric Peyote Use: Alkaloid Analysis and Radiocarbon Dating of Archaeological Specimens of Lophophora from Texas." *Journal of Ethnopharmacology* 101 (2005): 238–42.

Gartz, J. *Magic Mushrooms Around the World: A Scientific Journey Across Cultures and Time*. Los Angeles: Lis Publications, 1996.

Gilding, Paul. *The Great Disruption: Why the Climate Crisis Will Bring on the End of Shopping and the Birth of a New World*. New York: Bloomsbury Press, 2011.

Gray, Stephen. *Cannabis and Spirituality: An Explorer's Guide to an Ancient Plant Spirit Ally*. Rochester, Vt.: Park Street Press, 2017.

———. *Returning to Sacred World: A Spiritual Toolkit for the Emerging Reality*. Hants, U.K.: O Books/John Hunt Publishing, 2010.

Grof, Stanislav. *LSD Psychotherapy: The Healing Potential of Psychedelic Medicine*. Pamona, Calif.: Hunter House, 1980.

Harvey, Andrew. *The Hope: A Guide to Sacred Activism*. Carlsbad, Calif.: Hay House, 2009.

Hofmann, Albert. *LSD: My Problem Child: Reflections on Sacred Drugs, Mysticism, and Science*. 4th ed. San Jose, Calif.: Multidisciplinary Association for Psychedelic Studies, 2017.

Holland, Julie. *Ecstasy: The Complete Guide*. Rochester, Vt.: Park Street Press, 2001.

———. *Good Chemistry: The Science of Connection; From Soul to Psychedelics*. New York: HarperCollins, 2020.

Howard, Vernon. *Mystic Path to Cosmic Power*. West Nyack, N.Y.: Parker Publishing Company, 1967.

Hugh-Jones, Stephen. *Amazonian Indians*. New York: Gloucester Press, 1979.

———. *A Closer Look at Amazonian Indians*. London: Hamish Hamilton, 1978.

Johnson, Matthew W. "Consciousness, Religion, and Gurus: Pitfalls of Psychedelic Medicine." *ACS Pharmacology & Translational Science* 4, no. 2 (2021): 578–81.

Kahn-John, Michelle (Diné), and Mary Koithan. "Living in Health, Harmony, and Beauty: The Diné (Navajo) Hózhó Wellness Philosophy." *Global Advances in Health and Medicine* 4, no. 3 (2015): 24–30.

Kilham, Christopher S. *The Ayahuasca Test Pilots Handbook*. Berkeley: North Atlantic Books, 2014.

———. *The Lotus and the Bud: Cannabis, Consciousness, and Yoga Practice*. Rochester, Vt.: Park Street Press, 2021.

Kimmerer, Robin Wall. *Braiding Sweetgrass: Indigenous Wisdom, Scientific Knowledge, and the Teachings of Plants*. Minneapolis, Minn.: Milkweed Editions, 2013.

Krenak, Ailton. *A vida não é útil* [Life is not useful]. N.p.: Companhia das Letras, 2020.

———. *Ideias para adiar o fim do mundo* [Ideas to postpone the end of the world]. N.p.: Companhia das Letras, 2019.

———. *The Life Is Wild*. Rio de Janeiro: Wild Notebooks, Before Publishing Company, 2021.

———. *O amanhã não está à venda* [Tomorrow is not for sale]. N.p.: Companhia das Letras, 2021.

———. "Receiving Dreams." Interview with Alipio Freire and Eugênio Bucci. TEORIAeDEBATE (website). Accessed May 20, 2021.

Krenak, Ailton, and Emanuele Coccia. "Conversa Selvagem" (Wild talk). Streamed live on September 16, 2020. Available on YouTube.

Kurzweil, Ray. *The Singularity Is Near: When Humans Transcend Biology.* New York: Penguin Publishing Group, 2005.

La Barre, Weston. *The Peyote Cult.* Maidstone, U.K.: Crescent Moon Publishing, 2011.

Lash, John Lamb. *Not in His Image: Gnostic Vision, Sacred Ecology, and the Future of Belief.* White River Junction, Vt.: Chelsea Green Publishing, 2006.

Lee, Martin, and Bruce Shlain. *Acid Dreams: The Complete Social History of LSD.* New York: Grove Press, 1985.

LeGuin, Ursula K. *Lao Tzu: Tao Te Ching.* Boulder, Colo.: Shambhala, 2019.

MacGregor, Betsy. *In Awe of Being Human: A Doctor's Stories from the Edge of Life and Death.* Whidbey Island, Wash.: Abiding Nowhere Press, 2013.

McKenna, Terence. *Food of the Gods.* New York: Bantam Books, 1992.

Narby, Jeremy. *Plant Teachers: Ayahuasca, Tobacco, and the Pursuit of Knowledge.* Novato, Calif.: New World Library, 2021.

Perry, Bliss. *A Study of Prose Fiction.* Boston and New York: Houghton, Mifflin, 1902.

Pinchbeck, Daniel. *When Plants Dream: Ayahuasca, Amazonian Shamanism and the Global Psychedelic Renaissance.* London: Watkins Publishing, 2019.

Pollan, Michael. *How to Change Your Mind.* New York: Penguin Press, 2018.

Prechtel, Martín. *Secrets of the Talking Jaguar.* New York: Jeremy P. Tarcher/Putnam, 1998.

———. *The Unlikely Peace at Cuchumaquic.* Berkeley: North Atlantic Books, 2012.

Raworth, Kate. *Donut Economics: Seven Ways to Think Like a 21ˢᵗ-Century Economist.* White River Junction, Vt.: Chelsea Green Publishing, 2017.

Reichard, Gladys A. *Navajo Religion: A Study of Symbolism.* Princeton, N.J.: Princeton University Press, 1977.

Robinson, Kim Stanley. *The Ministry for the Future.* New York: Orbit Books, 2020.

Samorini, G. "The Oldest Representations of Hallucinogenic Mushrooms in the World (Sahara Desert. 9000-7000 B.P.)." *Integration: The Journal for Mind-Moving Plants and Kultur* 2–3 (1992): 69–78.

Sanders, James W., and Josjan Zijlmans. "Moving Past Mysticism in Psychedelic Science." *ACS Pharmacology & Translational Science* 4, no. 3 (2021): 1253–55.

Shulgin, Alexander, and Ann Shulgin. *PiHKAL: A Chemical Love Story.* Berkeley, Calif.: Transform Press, 1991.

Solnit, Rebecca. *A Paradise Built in Hell: The Extraordinary Communities That Arise in Disasters.* New York: Penguin, 2010.

Stamets, Paul, editor and contributor. *Fantastic Fungi: How Mushrooms Can Heal, Shift Consciousness, and Save the Planet.* San Rafael, Calif.: Earth Aware, 2019.

Stotijn, Daniëlle. *Bridge to the 5th Dimension: Master Your Mind, Body & Spirit; The Fast Track to Autonomy, Health and Light.* Breda, Netherlands: Obelisk, 2021.

Stuart Ani, Michael. *The Ghost Dance: An Untold History of the Americas.* N.p.: CreateSpace Independent Publishing Platform. 2016.

Tarrell, A., A. Portman, and Michael T. Garrett, "Native American Healing Traditions," *International Journal of Disability, Development and Education* (2006): 453–69.

Trungpa, Chögyam. *Shambhala: The Sacred Path of the Warrior.* Boston: Shambhala Publications, 1984.

Tutu, Desmond, and Mpho Tutu. *The Book of Forgiving: The Fourfold Path for Healing Ourselves and Our World.* New York: Harper One, 2014.

Weil, Andrew. *The Natural Mind: A Revolutionary Approach to the Drug Problem.* Revised edition. Boston: Mariner Books, 2004.

Wheal, Jamie. *Recapture the Rapture: Rethinking God, Sex, and Death in a World That's Lost Its Mind.* New York: HarperCollins, 2021.

———. *Stealing Fire: How Silicon Valley, the Navy SEALs, and Maverick Scientists Are Revolutionizing the Way We Live and Work.* New York: HarperCollins, 2017.

Williams, Paul S. *Das Energi.* New York: Warner Books, 1973.

Witherspoon, Gary. "The Central Concepts of Navajo World View (I)," *Linguistics* 12, no. 119 (1974): 41–60.

Yunkaporta, Tyson. *Sand Talk: How Indigenous Thinking Can Save the World.* New York: Harper One, 2020.

BOOKS OF RELATED INTEREST

Cannabis and Spirituality
An Explorer's Guide to an Ancient Plant Spirit Ally
Edited by Stephen Gray
Foreword by Julie Holland, M.D.

LSD and the Mind of the Universe
Diamonds from Heaven
by Christopher M. Bache, Ph.D.
Foreword by Ervin Laszlo

The Psychedelic Explorer's Guide
Safe, Therapeutic, and Sacred Journeys
by James Fadiman, Ph.D.

Mindapps
Multistate Theory and Tools for Mind Design
by Thomas B. Roberts, Ph.D.
Foreword by James Fadiman, Ph.D.

Psychedelic Medicine
The Healing Powers of LSD, MDMA, Psilocybin, and Ayahuasca
by Dr. Richard Louis Miller

DMT: The Spirit Molecule
A Doctor's Revolutionary Research into the
Biology of Near-Death and Mystical Experiences
by Rick Strassman, M.D.

Psychedelic Cannabis
Therapeutic Methods and Unique Blends to
Treat Trauma and Transform Consciousness
by Daniel McQueen
Foreword by Stephen Gray

Psychedelics and Psychotherapy
The Healing Potential of Expanded States
Edited by Tim Read and Maria Papaspyrou
Foreword by Gabor Maté, M.D.

INNER TRADITIONS • BEAR & COMPANY
P.O. Box 388
Rochester, VT 05767
1-800-246-8648
www.InnerTraditions.com

Or contact your local bookseller

DO YOU DARE VISIT
MOUNT TERROR?

BY MEGAN QUICK

Enslow
PUBLISHING

Please visit our website, www.enslow.com. For a free color catalog of all our high-quality books, call toll free 1-800-398-2504 or fax 1-877-980-4454.

Cataloging-in-Publication Data

Names: Quick, Megan.
Title: Do you dare visit Mount Terror? / Megan Quick.
Description: New York : Enslow Publishing, 2024. | Series: Scary adventures around the world | Includes glossary and index.
Identifiers: ISBN 9781978535961 (pbk.) | ISBN 9781978535978 (library bound) | ISBN 9781978535985 (ebook)
Subjects: LCSH: Volcanoes–Juvenile literature. | Antarctica–Geography–Juvenile literature. | Ross Island (Ross Sea, Antarctica)–History–Juvenile literature. | Terror, Mount (Antarctica)
Classification: LCC QE523.T47 Q75 2024 | DDC 551.21–dc23

Published in 2024 by
Enslow Publishing
2544 Clinton Street
Buffalo, NY 14224

Portions of this work were originally authored by Maeve Sisk and published as *Mount Terror*. All new material in this edition was authored by Megan Quick.

Designer: Tanya Dellaccio Keeney
Editor: Megan Quick

Photo credits: Series background Le Chernina/Shutterstock.com; cover, p. 1 Cindy Hopkins/Alamy Images; p. 5 joelindsay/iStock.com; p. 7 Rainer Lesniewski/Shutterstock.com; p. 9 https://upload.wikimedia.org/wikipedia/commons/6/60/2020Oct21-Mount-Terror-Repeater-Install-HR.jpg; p. 11 (top) https://upload.wikimedia.org/wikipedia/commons/c/cd/Franklin_Expedition_1845_-_HMS_Terror_-_Erebus.jpg; p. 11 (bottom) https://upload.wikimedia.org/wikipedia/commons/a/a3/James_Clark_Ross.jpg; p. 13 https://upload.wikimedia.org/wikipedia/commons/1/10/The_siege_of_the_South_pole%3B_the_story_of_Antarctic_exploration_BHL48381922.jpg; p. 15 https://upload.wikimedia.org/wikipedia/commons/3/3f/Scott%27s_party_at_the_South_Pole.jpg; p. 17 https://upload.wikimedia.org/wikipedia/commons/d/d0/2020October21-Cape-Bird-HR.jpg; p. 19 https://upload.wikimedia.org/wikipedia/commons/d/db/ErebusTerror.jpg; p. 21 Bernhard_Staehli/iStock.com.

Printed in the United States of America

CPSIA compliance information: Batch #CSENS24: For further information contact Enslow Publishing at 1-800-398-2504.

Find us on

CONTENTS

Words in the glossary appear in **bold** type the first time they are used in the text.

NO ORDINARY MOUNTAIN

It would be hard to find a place that sounds scarier than Mount Terror. But is its name really a good fit? Mount Terror rises about 2 miles (3.2 km) into the sky. It is located on Ross Island in Antarctica, the coldest, iciest place on Earth. That could definitely be scary!

But don't let the name trick you. First, Mount Terror is not just a mountain: it is also a **volcano**. And it did not get its name because it is terrifying. Read on to find out the truth about this icy giant.

Mount Terror is located on the eastern side of Ross Island.

FIND THE FACTS

BELIEVE IT OR NOT, ANTARCTICA IS A DESERT! A DESERT IS A PLACE WITH VERY LITTLE RAINFALL. ANTARCTICA ONLY GETS ABOUT 2 INCHES (5.1 CM) OF RAIN A YEAR.

TERROR'S NEIGHBORS

Mount Terror is a volcano, but it is not active. This means it no longer **erupts**. It probably hasn't erupted in a million years. But there are other volcanoes in the area, and one is quite active.

Mount Erebus sits about 19 miles (30.6 km) from Mount Terror. It is 12,447 feet (3,794 m) tall. At the summit, or top, of Mount Erebus is a lake of **lava**. It spits out "lava bombs"! It's likely Mount Erebus is the most southern active volcano in the world.

This map shows the four volcanoes of Ross Island. Mount Erebus is the only one that is active.

MOUNT BIRD

ROSS ISLAND

MOUNT TERROR

MOUNT EREBUS

MOUNT TERRA NOVA

COLD AND DARK

Most people visit Mount Terror during the summer months. That is a smart choice, because winters in Antarctica are cold! **Temperatures** on Ross Island can get as low as −49°F(−45°C). And winds can blow more than 100 miles (161 km) per hour. This makes it feel even colder at the top of Mount Terror.

Do you need another reason not to head to Antarctica during the winter? It is very dark. In fact, there is barely any sun for several months.

Workers place **equipment** at the summit of Mount Terror in freezing temperatures.

FIRST SIGHT

Mount Terror got its name in 1841. British **explorer** James Clark Ross was on an **expedition** in Antarctica. He led two ships: the HMS *Erebus* and the HMS *Terror*. It was very hard breaking up the Antarctic ice to keep the ships moving.

In late January, Ross spotted an island with a volcano puffing smoke. Next to it was another volcano. He named the two volcanoes after his two ships: Mount Erebus and Mount Terror. The island was later named Ross Island after the explorer.

Here, the HMS *Terror* and *Erebus* set off to explore. The *Terror* was built as a warship used in the War of 1812 against the United States.

FIND THE FACTS

DURING HIS TRAVELS, ROSS MAPPED OUT LARGE PARTS OF ANTARCTICA. THIS WAS A GREAT HELP TO FUTURE EXPLORERS. AFTER HE RETURNED TO ENGLAND, QUEEN VICTORIA NAMED HIM A KNIGHT.

FROZEN SOLID

Ice continued to be a problem for Ross's expedition. The ships were smashed up by the chunks of ice and often needed to be fixed. Ross wanted to keep exploring, but he finally hit ice so solid and thick he knew they couldn't move any farther.

Ross returned to England. He did not go on the next expedition of the *Erebus* and *Terror*, this time to the Arctic. It was a good decision. The ships became trapped in ice. The crew was never seen again.

In this picture, the HMS *Terror* battles ice in Antarctica.

FIND THE FACTS

IN 2014, THE SUNKEN *EREBUS* WAS DISCOVERED. TWO YEARS LATER, THE *TERROR* WAS FOUND ABOUT 62 MILES (100 KM) AWAY. EXPERTS ARE HOPING THE SHIPWRECKS WILL HELP THEM FIGURE OUT WHAT HAPPENED TO THE CREW AND SHIPS.

RACE TO THE POLE

In 1902, Robert Falcon Scott arrived in Antarctica to explore the area that Captain Ross had named 60 years before. He climbed the side of Mount Terror and could see out across the mainland. He began to think he could reach the South Pole, something no one had ever done before.

Scott did not succeed. He tried again in 1912. This time, he reached the South Pole. But he was upset when he learned that he was not first. Roald Amundsen of Norway had beaten him to it by about a month.

This photo shows Robert Scott (standing, center) and his men at the South Pole in 1912. They didn't make it home alive.

FIND THE FACTS

ROBERT SCOTT'S 1912 EXPEDITION ENDED IN TRAGEDY. HE AND THE REST OF HIS GROUP DIED FROM COLD AND HUNGER ON THEIR WAY BACK FROM THE SOUTH POLE.

THE VIEW FROM THE TOP

Robert Scott climbed the side of Mount Terror to get a view of what lay beyond it. Does that sound like something you would like to do? People go to the top of Mount Terror every year, but not many. It is hard to get to, and it is a tough climb.

There are three main paths to the summit. The climb takes several days in all, and should be done in the summer. Rock-climbing skills and tools are important, since some parts are very steep.

The view from the top of Mount Terror, shown here, could make the climb worth it.

HIT THE SLOPES

Once someone reaches the summit of Mount Terror, they usually climb back down. Unless they bring skis! Since it is snowy all year, skiers see it as an ideal place to test their skills. They can expect to ski about 2 miles (3.2 km) downhill.

Most ski mountains have lifts that carry skiers to the top. In Antarctica, skiers have to make their own way to the top and bundle up for the very cold and windy conditions. Could you do it? Many people get terrified just thinking about it!

ANTARCTICA IS NOT EASY TO REACH. PEOPLE USUALLY START BY FLYING TO SOUTH AMERICA OR NEW ZEALAND. FROM THERE, IT'S A TWO- OR THREE-DAY BOAT RIDE TO REACH THE ANTARCTIC PENINSULA. IT MAY BE LONGER IF THE WEATHER IS BAD.

Skiing Mount Terror (far right) and Mount Erebus (far left) is a goal for daring skiers.

19

DO YOU DARE?

Do you dare visit Mount Terror? It can be a dangerous place. But there are also larger dangers facing all of Antarctica. **Climate change** is causing Earth's water to heat up and the ice to melt. Scientists believe that Antarctica is losing about 150 billion tons (136.1 billion mt) of ice every year.

It will take many people working together to slow down climate change and protect Antarctica. It is an area of great natural beauty. If you decide to go, you will experience a place that very few people in the world will ever see.

FOR MORE INFORMATION

Books

Barone, Rebecca E. F. *Race to the Bottom of the Earth: Surviving Antarctica*. New York, NY: Henry Holt, 2021.

Batten, Mary. *Life in a Frozen World: Wildlife of Antarctica*. Atlanta, GA: Peachtree, 2020.

Websites

DK Find Out! Antarctica
www.dkfindout.com/us/earth/continents/antarctica/
Learn more about Antarctica, the surrounding ocean, and some of the animals that live there.

Ducksters: Roald Amundsen
www.ducksters.com/biography/explorers/roald_amundsen.php
Get the facts about the man who was the first to reach the South Pole.

INDEX

GLOSSARY

climate change: Long-term change in Earth's climate, caused mainly by human activities such as burning oil and natural gas.

equipment: Tools, clothing, and other items needed for a job.

erupt: To burst forth.

expedition: A trip made for a certain purpose.

explorer: A person who searches in order to find out new things.

lava: Hot, liquid rock that flows out of a volcano.

peninsula: A narrow piece of land that extends into water from the mainland.

temperature: How hot or cold something is.

tragedy: A terrible accident.

volcano: An opening in Earth's surface through which hot, liquid rock sometimes flows.

A huge chunk of ice falls into the sea as temperatures rise in Antarctica.

FIND THE FACTS

IN MARCH 2022, TEMPERATURES IN ANTARCTICA ROSE MORE THAN 50 DEGREES ABOVE NORMAL. SCIENTISTS BELIEVE THAT CLIMATE CHANGE IS THE CAUSE.